Two Years
in Kingston Town

Two Years
in Kingston Town

A Peace Corps Memoir

Jeff Koob

Writer's Showcase
San Jose New York Lincoln Shanghai

Two Years in Kingston Town
A Peace Corps Memoir

Writer's Showcase
an imprint of iUniverse, Inc.

For information address:
iUniverse, Inc.
5220 S. 16th St., Suite 200
Lincoln, NE 68512
www.iuniverse.com

ISBN: 0-595-21449-5

Printed in the United States of America

To Maria, my partner in the adventure of life.
To all addicts in recovery—"respect due!"

Foreword

I met Maria when I moved from Alabama to Beaufort, South Carolina in 1981. We soon discovered we had a lot in common: both military brats, both divorced and childless in our thirties, and both mental health professionals. Our values and tastes proved to be amazingly similar. It didn't take us long to fall in love.

We each knew we liked living abroad. Maria had lived in Guantanamo with her family as a girl and in Korea with her first husband when he was in the Army. I had lived in Vienna for four years when my father was stationed at the American Embassy and in West Germany for three years as an Army Lieutenant. We'd each seriously thought about serving in the Peace Corps long before we met.

We share a love of the performing arts. In the years I've known her, Maria has studied modern dance and taken piano and saxophone lessons. I'd done some acting and singing in my youth and landed my first leading role in tryouts for a play being staged by the Beaufort Little Theater, shortly after my arrival. Maria took courage from my example and started trying out for, and getting, supporting roles in plays. She proved to be a natural and was soon getting leading roles. During our Beaufort years, we had the pleasure of playing the starring roles together in *Play It Again, Sam* and *The Rainmaker*.

It took almost nine years of courtship for Maria to overcome her wariness of marriage, and the Peace Corps played a role in the timing of our decision. Each of us had an itch to travel, to get out of our routines; and both of us liked the idea of Peace Corps service. But we knew the only way we could serve together would be as a married couple. So we got married in a small ceremony on a floating dock amid the beautiful marshes of St. Helena Island in April, 1990, and shortly thereafter submitted our applications.

Still under the mistaken notion that we were applying for Peace Corps service on her initiative, Maria asked me, "Are you *sure* you want to do this?"

"Sure I'm sure. I've wanted to go somewhere—*anywhere*—in the Peace Corps for years."

"Before Maria?"

"Before Maria. Honest. I love living overseas!"

"In Europe."

"Meaning I don't know what it's like to live on the local economy in a poor country, like you did in Korea? Granted. But, hey, I went to The Citadel. I'm a rock! I'm out to change the world. So, what do *you* expect to get out of it?."

Maria sighed. "I don't know. It's not altruism, I don't think. I don't know if I could really expect to change anything—wherever it is they send us. I think I just need to rattle my cage, to shake things up. I wonder what other people say when they're asked why they volunteered."

"Actually, I don't really have much in the way of illusions about saving even a little piece of the world. I mainly see the Peace Corps as a way to immerse myself in a foreign culture for two years, maybe learn another foreign language to complement my rusty German. And to have an adventure with milady, of course. I think I know what to expect."

"I have no idea what to expect." Maria shrugged. " I guess that's part of the appeal."

"Well, I didn't mean literally 'know what to expect.' I'm saying I know there'll be hardships. It won't be easy. I think I'm prepared for that."

"So you *really* want to go? For yourself?"

"For myself. But *with* you."

It took most of a year before we got an offer. We'd expressed a willingness to go anywhere the Peace Corps might choose to send us, knowing that being choosy can limit your chances of acceptance and that only one-out-of-six applicants gets a chance to serve. We submitted reams of required paperwork and signed releases so they could verify that we weren't fleeing the law or a massive debt burden. They paid for our physicals.

The Peace Corps gets requests from host countries for X number of Volunteers in each of the five service sectors: Education, Health, Agriculture, Small Business, and Community Development. It then has to match the skills of its current applicants with the requests. In this sense, most Volunteers get chosen by their country of service, rather than the other way around.

Peace Corps Headquarters in Washington could easily place Maria, as there has always been a high demand for nurses. But, because she was married to me, they had to find a placement where the host country could also use a Volunteer with a Bachelors in English and a Masters in Psychology. Our recruiter jokingly referred to me as Maria's ball-and-chain.

I didn't know what kind of assignment I'd get. I thought I might end up teaching English, but if they wanted me to learn some improved technology for making mud bricks and then teach brick-making in an isolated village somewhere, I'd do it. I never dreamed that the Peace Corps could use me as a psychologist.

In the Spring of 1991 we received an invitation to serve in Kingston, Jamaica. So much for living in a mud hut in the jungle. We knew that Maria would be teaching psychiatric nursing somewhere, but all I knew about my assignment was that I'd be working in some capacity with drug addicts. We had two weeks in which to accept or decline, but it didn't take us even an hour to decide. We started reading up on Jamaica and putting our lives in order for a two-year sojourn in the Tropics.

We quit our jobs and arranged to store most of our worldly belongings in the massive attic of Maria's father's house on his farm near Bell Buckle, Tennessee. In August, we loaded our household goods in a rental van and made the move. I drove the van and Maria followed in her car—an aging Pontiac Phoenix that she'd bought from her mother for a dollar, years before. Her car dropped out of sight behind me in the middle of Atlanta, leaving me wondering what had happened to her.

I waited for a half hour by the side of Interstate 85, just north of Atlanta, to see if she'd catch up. Then I drove to the nearest pay phone I could find and called Maria's father, Joe. As I'd hoped, she'd already called him. Her car had broken down. The mechanic had told her he'd have it fixed in an hour or two, so I had to drive the rest of way by myself. I got lost near Bell Buckle after dark and had a nightmarish drive, navigating the big van down narrow, winding country roads, trying to get my bearings. I arrived at Joe's house just minutes before Maria pulled up in the driveway.

We felt like gypsies during our last month in the U.S., visiting friends and relatives, with only the few remaining possessions we could carry in our cars. We had a new appreciation for George Carlin's classic monologue on "stuff" we can and can't live without, and the theoretical question, *what ten books would you want with you on a desert island?* suddenly seemed relevant. We could each take only two suitcases totaling eighty pounds when we flew off on our adventure.

As we neared our departure date, we made a last trip to Bell Buckle to say our goodbyes and to drop off Maria's car with her father. Then we drove to Charleston and stayed with my parents for our last week Stateside. Following Peace Corps recommendations, we packed cookware and other essential domestic items, to be mailed to us during training.

One by one we checked-off items on our checklist. We received our airline tickets in the mail. We weighed our provisionally-packed suitcases on a bathroom scale, making the final, hard decisions. We bought new Birkenstocks and I got a fat Swiss Army knife. Having resolved to keep a journal in Jamaica, I bought several blank books to write in. Finally, I sold my car. On September 15 we said our goodbyes and loaded our luggage in my father's car, and he drove us to the airport.

On the way I remembered and recited the limerick he'd written in celebration of our wedding:

On a pier was once coupled a pair
Whose philosophies verged on the rare.
So with laughter and song
Let us speed them along
To—does anyone really know where?

We flew first to Miami, where we first met the other members of our
training group for what the Peace Corps calls a Staging. That's where you
get oriented, introduced to your training group, and innoculated. I
remember an address by the Country Director, Ed Hughes. He said that
since he had started working for the Peace Corps and introducing himself
as an employee of the agency, the two most common responses he had
gotten from people were, "The Peace Corps…is that still around?", and,
"You know, I used to think about joining the Peace Corps, but…" Ed
went on to say that some people referred to *giving up* two years of your life
to serve in the Peace Corps. " If any of you are thinking in those terms, let
me tell you something. Jamaica doesn't need you that badly. What the
Peace Corps needs is people who want to *live* for two years in Jamaica."

Maria and I gave up a familiar lifestyle and some creature comforts. In
return we got a priceless opportunity to live in Jamaica and to learn from
its people. But what has been said of mountain climbing is equally appli-
cable to Peace Corps service: in the process you learn more about yourself
than you do about the mountain.

Part I

Training

The day of our arrival in Jamaica started around seven thirty, high above the Miami streets in our room at the Sheraton. Maria and I had been up until nearly one, repacking our bags. We'd just been told that we wouldn't be reunited with most of our luggage until we moved in with our host family several days hence. After breakfast, we joined our fellow trainees in the lobby, adding our gear to the growing mountain of luggage. I volunteered to be a team leader, shepherding the group onto the buses, collecting and dispensing tips to porters, drivers, and redcaps, and arranging for our expeditious processing through the Miami airport. Then it was hurry-up-and-wait until the plane took off shortly before noon.

Most of the view consisted of clouds over the blue-green sea. Then the pilot announced that we were about to fly over Cuba. Suddenly, as I caught my first glimpse of the island beneath us, the prospect of entering the so-called Third World started to get very real.

We landed in Kingston around two o'clock. As soon as we were off the plane, we began to run sweat in the moist, tropic heat. We all trooped into the terminal and got in line to go through Immigration and Customs. When Maria and I got to the counter, the friendly Customs agent wanted to see Maria's saxophone, but little else. He was surprised to discover some of Maria's underwear in the saxophone case and in the horn itself, where she'd stuffed it to conserve packing space.

The terminal bustled with activity. In the crowd of brown-skinned travelers and airport employees, I suddenly found myself feeling very white.

Once we made it to the street we got many offers to carry our bags and to taxi us into Kingston. We declined, explaining that we were Peace Corps, but nobody seemed to know what that meant.

The airport is on a crescent peninsula across the harbor from Kingston. Behind the distant city loomed green mountains that rose into the clouds. We loaded most of our luggage onto one chartered bus and then boarded another for the half-hour ride to the hotel where we were to stay for our first three nights. I saw right away that in Jamaica you drive in the left lane.

The bus driver drove wildly down a narrow peninsular highway bordered by palm trees and scrub brush—the vast, blue-green Carribean to our right, the harbor to our left. He passed slower moving vehicles near curves, blowing his air-horn as a warning to oncoming traffic. We soon got to the coastal outskirts of Kingston, the mountains now to our right.

My first impressions of the city were of wooden and concrete block buildings, and rundown zinc-roofed shanty towns, many of the structures painted in bright hues. High concrete walls surrounded a lot of residences, some of them with broken shards of glass embedded in a layer of mortar on the top. Potholes pocked the dusty, littered streets. Even in the bus we could smell the stench of burning trashpiles, exhaust fumes, and sewage. The roadsides teemed with black people in brightly colored clothes. On almost every block we saw painted shacks and pushcarts dispensing sodas, snacks and beer. Every second or third block seemed to have either a rum bar or a church—or both.

Just out of school, hundreds of uniformed children trooped down the roadside toward home. Goats roamed free and a cow munched grass on a traffic median, oblivious to the traffic. Trees hung heavy with fruit and varicolored blossoms. I caught glimpses of the network of cobblestone drainage canals that criss-crosses the city—a legacy of the colonial era. As we got deeper into the city, slums sprawled around us in all directions, labyrinths of wood, bamboo and zinc roofing. I had never in my life seen such a juxtaposition of beauty and ugliness.

Shortly after passing the National Stadium, the bus left the busy city streets and drove into a middle-class neighborhood. Before long we arrived at the Sandhurst Hotel, in a suburb of Kingston at the base of the foothills of the surrounding mountains. Probably a classy residence in its day, the Sandhurst was a faded, funky remnant of colonial days. A fenced compound with security guards at the gate, it was run by an aging, expatriate British lady who knew how to pinch a shilling and didn't trust the help. (If you ordered porridge for breakfast, the cook had to go to the office and get the box of porridge from the old lady.) The rooms weren't air conditioned, but had ceiling fans. Here and there, patches of paint curled away from the bare walls and the faint scent of mildew hung in the air. Since the window louvers had to be left open for ventilation and window screens are unknown in Jamaica, small, green lizards came and went as they pleased, crawling the walls. But that was okay, because they were interesting to look at when they puffed out a bright orange membrane on their throats, and they ate mosquitos.

The best feature of the Sandhurst was its spacious veranda, where we sat at round tables and drank our first Red Stripe beers in Jamaica as the sun sank, casting a red-gold glow on a vista of coconut palms and breadfruit trees. I wore shorts and a tank top. Les, one of our group, commented on the small yin/yang tattoo on my shoulder.

"You can't argue with that," he said.

In the twilight some of us walked through the neighborhood to Hope Road, looking for a little local color. From our trip in on the bus, we knew that Hope Road was the nearest commercial thoroughfare to the hotel. We'd been warned not to stay out after dark. We joked about vampires, but we made sure we returned to the hotel before the last sunlight had faded from the sky. Exchanging greetings with some of the people we passed, we soon learned that in Jamaica "good night" is used before bedtime, in the same manner as "good morning" or "good day." It was tolerably warm by then, and the perfume of tropical blossoms filled the air. On our way back through the neighborhood, I looked up just in time to see a white owl—the first I had ever seen—fly past overhead. I later learned that Jamaicans regard a white owl as a portent of impending death, but I took it as a good omen.

It had gotten fully dark by the time supper was served, the veranda lit by strings of colored Christmas lights. We helped ourselves from an eclectic buffet: curried goat, jerk chicken, peppery Jamaican beef stew, rice-and-peas (red beans), greens, salad and bread, with watermelon and papaya for desert. Maria and I ate at a table with two of the non-Peace Corps guests at the hotel, Ibi from Curacao and Rick from Aruba, who were visiting the island for a postal service workshop. They had never heard of the Peace Corps, but asked polite questions. English was a second language for them, their primary lingo being a creole of Spanish, Portuguese, Dutch and Africanisms.

After dinner, two of our group, Tim and his wife Teresa, told us of how they had found time during our stay in Miami to sit in on several hours of the Noriega trial. They related hearing matter-of-fact testimony of murders and massive drug deals, given by a fat cat now in the Witness Protection Program. Like a prosperous farmer paid thousands *not* to plant corn, he was getting paid $100,000 a year *not* to sell drugs!

With the window louvers open and the fan on, our room *almost* felt cool. Outside, the yaps and howls of dogs filled the air. Dogs, we soon learned, are the Jamaicans' primary form of protection against burglars. This was just a typical night of canine cacaphony—the first of many to come. Between the barking and the mosquitos and the excitement of the first night of a foreign sojourn, it took me some time to fall asleep. My last thought as I drifted off was that, somewhere nearby in the tropic night, a white owl hunted.

Although the official language in Jamaica is English, on the streets you mainly hear Jamaican patois, an amalgam of African dialects and English. As is probably the case in most cultures, one's speech reflects one's social class. Some rural and lower-class Jamaicans try hard to speak the Queen's English and resent the notion that they speak patois; but although professionals can all speak English clearly, most who are not overly class-sensitive can freely lapse into different levels of patois, depending on present company and context. It's a continuum: English, patois, deep patois, *very* deep patois. So where a doctor might say to one person, "I don't think so," he may say to another , "Me na t'ink sah."

"Mon" is universal on the street. Even little girls are addressed as "mon", as in " Yeh, mon, me wan summa dat carnbread." "Im" is also universal as to gender and status: "Im tek de mohney from im 'usband befahr im spen' it ahl ahn rum." The plural is "dem", as in "dem na want ta teef (i.e. steal), but dem na av nah mohney." Singular nouns are made plural by adding "dem". Thus "the men" is "de man dem."

"Fi" means "for to" (i.e. in order to), as in archaic English, or as in the lyrics to Polly Wolly Doodle: "I went down South *for to* see my Sal." "Mek" means "let" as well as "make": "Me go to town fi mek de chillun see dem gran'faddah." "Seh" means "that," as in, "Me t'ink seh de soup too hot." In deep patois "chillun" becomes "pickni", "eat" becomes "nyam", and "you" (plural) becomes "unu."

Sometimes it took all of my concentration to follow even the gist of a conversation between speakers conversing in patois, but I soon learned that there's a poetry to the language. Some of the pronunciations have the charm of an Irish lilt or a Charleston dialect.

You hear certain British English terms used commonly in patois: "Im *vex* me when im tahk like dat." Then there are traditional Jamaican terms that you just have to learn. A Jamaican ghost is a "duppy"; and you don't ask for "baggies" in a grocery store, as this is the street term for women's undergarments. ("Mi open im sahxophone case an' fine im baggies in im harn!") There are also modern slang terms to get used to. Semi-transparent plastic shopping bags are called "scahndalbahgs", apparently because everyone can see what you've got in them.

Our first full day in Kingston started early and hot. On a cool winter day you can sometimes walk below the sweat line (that is, without sweating), but not so in September. After we had walked the twenty minutes up Hope Road to Bamboo Pen, the Peace Corps training center, we were drenched in sweat. We'd been told that our blood would thin after a few weeks in the tropic heat, but that only meant that you would sweat a little less. Most of the year, between eight in the morning and midnight, you couldn't even *sit* below the sweat line.

Other than the heat, the walk up Hope Road was pleasant enough, if only for the novelty. "Crush hour" traffic clogged the potholed road, and the floral perfume of the night before was overpowered by exhaust fumes. The sides of the road teemed with people going to work and with school-children in their distinctive uniforms. The girls wore skirts in their school colors and white blouses, and the boys wore khakis and school ties.

Skin shades ranged from cafe au lait to dark chocolate. Caucasians were seldom to be seen in this part of Kingston. Although we stood out, with our white skin and our American clothes—generally drab by Jamaican standards—the people we passed mostly ignored us. Some we made eye contact with smiled back at us and returned our greetings. A few times we "got begged" by children and street people. This, we soon learned, would be a daily occurance. Although we didn't dress like tourists, we were clearly Americans and, therefore, by Jamaican standards, rich. We quickly learned not to give money to anyone who begged us on the streets. It just made you a target for the most persistent beggars. We weren't tourists; we were going to *live* here.

Bamboo Pen is a walled colonial-era compound, once the estate of a beer magnate, and in 1991 both the Peace Corps training site and a recreation center for embassy personnel. Uniformed Jamaican guards manned the iron gate, but our white skin was apparently sufficient ID to gain us entry. Up the driveway stood a white, raised, one-story estate house with porches lining the front and the side visible to us from the entrance. Several outbuildings surrounded the main structure, and as we walked up the drive we spied tennis courts and a pool off to the left. Croton bushes, with their varicolored leaves, hibiscus, lignum vitae, lime trees, almond trees, tamarind trees, mango trees, flame trees, coconut palms, and bamboo thickets dotted the lawn. We saw a few grazing goats tethered to trees, and egrets, which you see all over the island.

The most interesting presentation on that first day of training was one on Jamaican patois, by a professor from the University of the West Indies. He explained the difference between pidgin speech and a patois, or creole. A pidgin isn't actually a language, but a spontaneously-evolved form of oral communication developed by a first generation of people coming in contact with people of another culture who speak a different language. It uses elements of both the native and the foreign language, but is crude and has an imprecise, thrown-together grammatical structure. By the second or third generation, however, a precise grammar develops, incorporating elements of both languages. This patois is a true language, and no true language is demonstrably more rich and precise than another. Language, the professor told us, is a natural function of humankind. Grammar is hard-wired into our brains.

In another class one of the Peace Corps staff—a Jamaican—gave a safety orientation. She was realistic about crime in Jamaica. Because of the widespread poverty, a small percentage of the population made their living as "teefs"—pickpockets and purse snatchers, burglars and strong-arm robbers. We would need to be alert in public and security conscious even in our residences, as teefs could be quite ingenious. Never leave valuables out in the open, she said, even when you're home. With window louvers open, a teef could stick in a pole with a drawstring on the end and easily pick up a wallet or purse from a table or dresser top.

We were told that although we were unlikely to be robbed at weapons-point, all of us would probably get "picked" on the street or on a crowded bus at some point in our two-year tours, so we shouldn't carry any more cash in our pockets than we could afford to lose. Large bills should be kept concealed beneath our clothing. (I carried my ID and most of my cash in an ankle wallet, worn inside my sock. Many of the women stashed large bills in their bras or in body wallets.) Backpacks and purses should be carefully guarded, as some teefs would slash them open with knives or razors.

"You're ahdults," she said, "so we cahn't tell you how you mohst dress or ahct. Bot dressing like tourists will cohmplicate your lives. Most Jamaican women are mohdest, so you women should ahlways wear bras, and a slip if you're wearing a light dress in the daylight. Pay attention. Be yourselves, bot be prudent. Be friendly, bot not *too* friendly."

We were on our own for lunch, having been given "walkaround money"— enough for the meals we had to buy for ourselves and the occasional Red Stripe. It started raining as we set out, but most of us had umbrellas. Just outside the gate, on Hope Road, was a shopping district called Liguanie, with street vendors ("higglers"), grocery stores, and fast food restaurants. Buying lunch promised to be an adventure.

One choice was the box lunches sold by higglers. These consist of a small portion of jerk chicken or pork (jerk being a barbeque sauce made with spicy-hot Scotch Bonnet peppers), or curried goat, rice-and-peas, and the local version of slaw, made without mayonnaisse. Another popular street food is the patty, a folded, semi-circular meat and/or vegetable pie.

We saw fruit vendors everywhere, selling bananas, mangoes, pineapples, papayas, grapefruits, green navel oranges and other tropical treats. A staple thirst-quencher is the "jelly" coconut, an unripe coconut with hardly any meat but a lot of milk. The vendor pulls a chilled jelly from inside his ice-filled cart, neatly cuts off the top with a machete, and you drink the cool milk out of the shell. Then he hacks up the shell and you can scoop out the thin layer of coconut jelly from the husk.

The fast food restaurants are much like those in the U.S., but with a local twist. At the King Burger they sell a deluxe burger called a Whamperer. You can get a hot dog or a cheese sandwich at the Munchwagon, but the menu on the wall also lists curried goat, as well as tripe and bean. (Try asking for *that* at McDonalds.) Should you eat at the tables outside, you have to shoo away the roosters, who think they own the yard.

Many street higglers sell from wheeled, wooden carts with steering wheels mounted on the rear, attached by rope-and-pulley to the front axle. Thus they steer them through crowded streets, sometimes riding them downhill. Some have wooden ice-box superstructures and shelving built onto the cart. Many are brightly-colored and have menus and Rastafarian slogans painted on them: Lion of Judah, Ethiopian Queen, Jah Rules, and the like.

While buying lunch on the street one day during training, I saw my first naked man in public. He didn't pester anyone, he just walked around wearing only an idiot grin. Clothes aren't really necessary in Jamaica's hot climate, except as mosquito protection, and apparently any laws against public nudity weren't enforced as long as you didn't accost people. Going naked seemed to be a declaration of exemption—a social statement, rather than a fashion statement. I saw the naked people as a variant faction of the madmen one saw on the streets. Some madmen carried bizarre accessories—decorated sticks or electronic components—to complement their tattered clothing, their appearance reflecting the disorder of their minds. I wondered aloud to other trainees if they hold an annual convention: The Society of Naked Persons. Easy to join.

Some madpersons on the street muttered or ranted, but they seldom acted violently. Another variant subgroup was the Rasta madmen. Most Rastafarians one saw were neither scruffy "raggamuffins", nor weird in their appearance. They could be identified by their long braids, or dreadlocks, which clearly set them apart from the mainstream. Rasta slogans could be seen everywhere, and images of Bob Marley—the best-known Rasta in the world—were never far away. A popular FM station played Reggae music twenty-four hours a day, and even non-Rastas seemed to appreciate the Afrocentrism and racial pride that Rastafarianism represents. Although a distinct minority in Jamaica, Rastafarians strongly influence the popular culture.

Rasta madmen not only wear dreadlocks, but seldom bathe or change clothes. I recall a Rasta madman in Liguanie that I saw throughout my stay in Kingston. I called him The Watcher, because that's all I ever saw him do. He stood in or near the same sheltered bus stop every day, all day—didn't even take Sundays off—just *watching*. As he didn't bathe and apparently only changed his clothes every few weeks, he always had the bus stop to himself. I never saw him conversing with anyone, so I don't think he sold ganja (marijuana). He was a permanent feature of the urban landscape, like the shelter he inhabited.

I speculated that if he wasn't there to watch, Kingston might fade away—that if he was hit by a runaway minibus, (a distinct possibility for someone who spent as much time on the curb as he) and died, another Rasta madman would emerge from the crowd and take his place. A different costume, maybe one of those Dr. Suess hats that some of the Rastas stuff their dreadlocks into, but the same job description. Hey, *someone's* got to do it.

We spent our first six weeks on the island in a limbo status. Neither tourists nor Peace Corps Volunteers, we were Peace Corps Trainees—the 58th group to be trained for service in Jamaica. Although most of our official training took place within the confines of Bamboo Pen, our real immersion in the pool of culture shock took place outside the walls. Many of our first lessons involved public transportation.

After our first three days in-country, we lived with host families for the duration of training. Most of the homes in which we stayed were in or near Spanish Town, the second largest population center on the southern coastal plain where Kingston is located. Some days the Peace Corps staff provided charter buses for the fifteen mile trip from Spanish Town to Bamboo Pen, but as our training progressed we usually depended on Jamaican buses for the commute. The trip from Spanish Town to Kingston is about ten miles through the verdant countryside at the foot of the Blue Mountains, with another five miles within the city to get to

Bamboo Pen. Coming in mornings, we could either change buses at a terminus called Halfway Tree, next to Nelson Mandela Park, or walk the last mile-or-so up Hope Road. With the slow press of crush hour traffic, you could walk nearly as fast as the buses could move, but it was hard work in the tropic heat. Either way, we arrived at Bamboo Pen for our eight o'clock classes dripping sweat.

We quickly learned some commuting tricks, such as boarding a crowded incoming bus a stop or two before it gets to the route terminus and empties out, giving you a shot at a seat. Personal space is an irrelevant concept on public transportation in Kingston. Think *sardine can.*

Getting a seat is as close as you can come to having your own space; but if you *do* get to sit, you might be given parcels to hold, or even a small child. Standing, you might end up balancing on one foot, hanging onto a seat or an overhead rail for dear life as the bus jerks into motion or to a stop, or rounds corners at breakneck speeds.

You're also much more vulnerable to pickpockets if you're standing. You have to keep a constant vigil to keep from getting picked. The teefs often work in pairs—one to distract you, and one to pick your pockets or slit your knapsack.

I often wore my backpack in front on crowded buses. When I placed it on the floor I kept it firmly clamped between my feet and kept a close eye on it. Even seated, you had to be wary on a packed bus. Despite all of my precautions, I got picked several times.

The intimate press of bodies wasn't usually unpleasant, as people on the buses were generally courteous and clean. Only the drunks and the poorest of the poor dressed in dirty clothes and didn't wash. Over time you got used to close contact with strangers—on a crowded bus, *really* close contact. Only tour buses were air-conditioned, so on public transportation you shared sweat with the warm bodies pressing against your own. At some stops, bootstrap entrepreneurs boarded the buses to hawk frozen plastic bags of fruit-flavored sugarwater called bag drinks, and many passengers sucked away on them as they rode.

In the crush of bodies, accidental intimate contacts occur without comment, although I'm sure that sometimes romantic liaisons must result from spontaneous meetings on a crowded bus. Inevitably, in such crowded conditions, women sometimes get groped by strangers; but when this occurs the victim usually loudly confronts the perpetrator, making sure the whole bus knows what has happened. If a molester were to persist, the 'ductor (conductor) would quickly intervene.

Buses come in all shapes and sizes, including vans, which are known as minibuses. They are licensed by the government but privately owned. Many bus drivers are freelancers who own their buses, and name them—painting the names over the front window: Secret Agent, Superhero, X-Rated, Poochie Looie, Sky Train, Relentless, I Will Survive, Popeye, Not Guilty, High Life, Man of the Heart, One Love, etc. They often drive like maniacs between the morning and evening crush hours, because the more runs they make a day the more money they earn.

Drivers, in turn, hire one or more 'ductors , depending on the size of the bus. 'Ductors collect the fares, keep the peace, and pack the buses full. The driver/owners take their share off the top—a standard amount per trip—and the 'ductors split the rest. Therefore the more people crammed aboard each trip, the more the 'ductors make.

It's elementary Third World supply-and-demand economics. The more commuters waiting at the stops, the more buses run. When the crowds thin out the buses wait at the route terminuses until the 'ductors pack in a nearly full load. "Step up!" they call out, "step in! small-up! You, big mon, step aroun'!"

At the bus stops along the route the 'ductors call out the terminus, "Half Way Tree!", and although you may think that not one more person can fit in, five more pile on. Several new fares stand on the bottom step on one foot, holding on to the open door or anything else within reach, hanging out in the warm breeze as the bus speeds down the potholed streets. Those at the stop who can't manage to insinuate their bodies into the press of flesh wait and hope that the next bus won't be so crowded. Lines are unheard of; you just push your way in.

As the last passenger squeezes aboard, the head 'ductor thumps the side of the bus or calls out "DRIVAH!", and the driver takes off. The 'ductors collect fares and continue to harangue the crowd, "Small-up, de bos nah full! You, faht lady, step aroun'!"

When you want to get off at the next stop you call out "one stop!", tap a coin against a rail or, on the more modern buses, reach over and pull a signal cord over the window. The further you are from a door, the earlier you have to start worming your way through the crowd, chanting "excuse me...pardon me...DRIVAH, ONE STOP!" Unless he's engaged in a race for fares with a rival bus on the same route, the driver always stops, knowing that for every passenger who disembarks at a time of day when the stops are crowded, he can get one new fare. At the least.

If a bus is crammed to full capacity and nobody has signalled for a stop, the driver cruises past the bus stop. Would-be passengers try to wave down approaching buses and if the 'ductor thinks there's room, he calls to the driver to pull over.

Fares are most often collected at the door as you board or exit. On the longer routes the 'ductors push their way through the throng collecting money, fans of vertically-folded bills, sorted by denomination, splayed out between their fingers. Digital calculators, you might say. 'Ductors seem never to forget a face, and every fare gets paid. If a 'ductor doesn't have exact change he says "mi get back to you" and, miraculously, he does. Although it's impossible for them to adequately prevent pickpockets from plying their trade in crowded buses, 'ductors also perform a security function. Most are said to carry knives, but you never see them unless a situation calls for their brandishing.

In my whole sojourn in Jamaica, I was never once cheated by a 'ductor. One of them may well have saved my life one day at the main downtown terminus, but I'll tell that story later.

Weekdays are always more hectic than weekends on the buses, as people commute to their jobs and hordes of uniformed schoolchildren join the throng. Only a few private schools have schoolbuses. On weekends few buses run on most routes, and you might have to wait up to an hour in the oppressive heat to get a ride.

The public transportation system may be chaotic, but it works. If you wait long enough and "think Jamaican" (i.e. "every mon fi 'imself"), you can get anywhere on the island sooner or later. Going from Kingston to other parts of Jamaica, you travel on either regular-sized buses or minibuses, where you often spend hours packed in with strangers, or in privately-owned cars that serve as taxis, similarly crammed.

Unless your destination is on the coastal plains, as soon as you leave Kingston you find yourself on narrow, winding roads snaking up through the mountains that form Jamaica's spine. Despite their name, the Blue Mountains are mostly clad in green jungle, sprinkled with blossoms in an amazing variety of bright colors.

Most city buses had deafening airhorns which were used indiscriminantly, to warn pedestrians; to threaten other drivers who might dare to challenge the bus' right of way; to announce arrivals and departures; to greet other drivers, friends and relatives, and pretty women; and apparently at random intervals, just to express the drivers' joy at being alive. Often the airhorn was applied in lieu of the brakes. One member of my training group told of a white-knuckle ride in an evening rainstorm, in a bus whose lights and windshield wipers didn't function—but the airhorn worked fine. The drivers had their priorities, and the airhorn was a bare-minimum necessity.

Some of us in Group 58 were treated like family in their host family placements; others just got basic room and board. Maria and I lucked-out and got placed in Greendale, a middle-class suburb of Spanish Town, with a widow named Alvira. A great-grandmother, she had been hosting Peace Corps trainees in her home since her husband died in the 1960s. She was known as "Sarge" by the Peace Corps staff, for running a tight ship; but we hit it off with her right away, and she became our Jamaican Mama.

We could understand how she came by her nickname. Although small in stature, with wizened features and gray hair, she wouldn't take any crap from anybody and could have stood up to a drunken seaman. Like many Jamaicans with light brown skin, she would bristle at being referred to as a black person. Although she often wore a stern countenance, once you got to know her you discovered a kind heart and a sense of humor beneath her no-nonsense demeanor. Sometimes she'd gently tease us about our cultural misconceptions and we, in turn, teased her about how she'd earned her nickname.

As soon as we arrived she made sure we knew the house rules. "Don' slom doors. Don' waste helectricity; hit very hexpensive. Lock de gate an' de door behin' you when you com in an' go out. Don' tell people on de street who you stay wit'."

Alvira disparaged her hospitality ("my likkle house...my likkle kitchen...I'm not a good cook"), but her home was clean and neat, and she always prepared tasty meals. She made a point of telling us that she served us just what she ate when she didn't have guests, and she gave us lessons in Jamaican cooking throughout our stay. We had a small bedroom and a bathroom to ourselves, and had the run of the house.

The front porch, like many in Kingston, looked something like a birdcage in that it was enclosed by decorative wrought-iron grillwork, to keep out the teefs. The grillwork was in a spiderweb design, painted in the same white as the house. The porch had several chairs and small tables, and contained many houseplants which Alvira said she talked to. Coconut palms and numerous bushes grew in her small yard. In the back yard near the laundry sinks stood a pidgeon coop, up on cinderblocks, with two or three birds inside.

One afternoon early in our six-week stay, we stopped off at a store on our walk in from the bus stop after training and bought three Red Stripes to take home. We offered Alvira one, and the three of us sat out on the porch and drank them while Maria and I told her about our day. She asked where we had bought the beers, and when we told her she suggested that in the future we buy any "likkle groceries" we might need from Mr. Mirage, an Indian gentleman who had a small shop near the bus stop. I suspect she had a business arrangement with him, but his prices *were* more reasonable than other shops, and thereafter we bought our snacks and beers from him.

The following Sunday before our afternoon dinner, Alvira asked us if we'd like to join her in "a likkle hoppitizer" before we ate. We suspected that she meant an alcoholic drink and took her up on her invitation. I was surprised when she broke out a bottle of Johnnie Walker Black Label. Most Jamaicans drink locally-distilled rum, gin and vodka, as foreign brands are prohibitively expensive. We learned that she, like many other natives with relatives living in the U.S., Canada and England, regularly got barrels of food and luxury items like liquor shipped to her from "a-fahren".

When she told us that her son in England had invited her to visit and offered to pay her way, we urged her to take him up on his offer. She replied with a sly smile, "Maybe sohmday ahfter I get old."

On weekdays we got lunch on our own, and Alvira fed us breakfast and supper. For breakfast we mostly had fruits and cereal. Other times she would serve us an egg and fried banana or plantain, with toast or bread-fruit, or local specialties like ackee and saltfish. Ackee is a staple food in Jamaica. Ackees grow on trees and have a reddish skin and yellow meat. Alvira warned us that you never pick or cook an unripe ackee, as they are quite poisonous until they ripen and split open on the tree, revealing large, black seeds. Cooked ackee looks and tastes somewhat like scrambled eggs, and absorbs the flavor of whatever it's cooked with. Saltfish is codfish, which used to be a staple but is now too expensive for everyday use, because it's imported.

Suppers consisted of a modest portion of meat (chicken, fish, beef, or goat), some variety of yam, frequently rice-and-peas, vegetables, and fruit or bread pudding for desert. The vegetable course was often a salad or boiled calaloo, which is similar to spinach. Sometimes we had a soup or stew, and salad. Alvira taught Maria how to make authentic rice-and-peas, with coconut milk, and how to roast a breadfruit, which really does taste like a sweet bread.

She also introduced Maria to what became her favorite fruit drink, soursop juice. The soursop is a large green, asymmetrical fruit, covered with bumps. I dubbed it the uglyfruit, but agreed that it makes a delicious beverage. Other fruits we ate frequently in Jamaica were mangos, pineapples, grapefruit, oranges, avocados, papayas, melons, and bananas. I never found any crunchy native fruits, however, and really missed apples and pears. They were available in some supermarkets, but were so expensive on our Peace Corps stipend that we rarely bought them.

Nights in Greendale were just as noisy as they had been at the Sandhurst, and by the time we moved into our own place we had learned that there is no such thing as a quiet night in the city. Not only did we have to put up with the barking dogs, but Jamaicans like to party late into the night, and monster sound systems set up in the streets or in neighborhood gardens and nightclubs and blare "dancehall" or "deejay" reggae at megadecibel levels until the wee hours of the morning. Dancehall music isn't traditional reggae, with its distinctive beat and usually-upbeat lyrics. It's Carribean hip-hop, with rapid-fire rap lyrics shouted to a staccato beat, interrupted by the gutteral groans and shouts of the deejays who emcee the sound systems. Raunchy sexual lyrics comprise much of the content, along with references to guns and violence. Dancehall performers affect names like Shabba Ranks, Ninja Man, Lieutenant Stitchie, and Tiger, and there's fierce competition for Number One status.

The commercial mobile sound systems, with names like Stone Love, House of Leo, and African Star vie for the best gigs, and have become a fixture of modern Jamaican culture. Getting known via the sound systems is the unknown Dancehall performer's alternative to a recording contract with a major studio. If the sound system deejays like an aspiring rapper's demos, they play them. Again and again and again. Loud. A newcomer seldom gets his recordings played on the radio until he's well-known on the streets.

It's my understanding that many elements of hip-hop, such as scratching (where the deejay moves the record on the turntable with his finger) and sampling (where the deejay intersperses the rapping with brief "samples" of other artists' recordings, on his multiple turntables) began on the streets of Kingston. With many of its native sons and daughters emigrating to other countries, Jamaican culture—like Irish culture—has had an impact on the world disproportionate to the size of the island.

The daily bus rides from Greendale to Bamboo Pen and back became routine. We were getting used to the jostling and the crowding on the buses, the goats on the roadside, the wall of green mountains to the north, the giant cottonwood trees in the fields on the country portion of the trip, and the mazes of zinc-roofed shantytowns we passed on the outskirts of Kingston. We gradually got acclimatized and acculturated, but daily surprises still awaited us.

One morning when we got to the bus stop, Maria and I noticed that it was unusually crowded, mostly with "schoolers." We quickly learned why: there were hardly any buses running. There had been rumors of a possible protest by bus riders, as the government-regulated busfare was being raised. We would have stuck out the wait in the morning heat, but a distinguished-looking gentleman in a suit came up to us and identified himself as a member of the "security forces." He told us that buses were being mobbed and that roadblocks of burning tires had been set up on the highway between Spanish Town and Kingston. Even if we were to catch a bus, it might not make it to Halfway Tree. "The mobs aren't targeting foreigners," he clarified, " but you wouldn't want to find yourselves stranded in the middle of nowhere."

I found a pay phone and called the Peace Corps office. By this time others from our training group had arrived at the bus stop. We were told to stay put for the day. Later, while walking through Spanish Town, I saw a truckload of Jamaica Defense Force soldiers in full riot gear; but other than that I saw no signs of turmoil in the streets. The next day things had gone back to normal, other than the busfares being higher.

We had come to Jamaica at a time of economic crisis. The International Monetary Fund had put pressure on the government to enact austerity measures, the Jamaican dollar was losing value relative to "hard" foreign currency, and the inflation rate was around sixty percent. When we arrived the official exchange rate was one U.S. dollar to thirteen Jamaican dollars; by the time we were sworn in as Volunteers the rate had dropped to eighteen Jamaican dollars and was still falling. Not long after our arrival a ten percent General Consumption Tax went into effect. As our Peace Corps living allowances were paid in Jamaican dollars, we felt the effects along with the Jamaican people.

As in many developing countries where a lot of people in the countryside lead a hand-to-mouth existence, the cities of Jamaica are seen as fountains of prosperity. The north coast has the lure of the tourist industry, but the primary magnet for poor men and women looking for a way out of poverty is the bustling capital, Kingston. Homeless people and squatters living in shantytowns make up at least a quarter of the city's population. Because the dream always exceeds the reality, an army of the unemployed try to eke out a living on the streets. Some turn to street hustles, others become small-time higglers, and many a young man seeks membership in a gang.

Newspapers are filled with stories of gang rivalries and turf wars in downtown Kingston. Although the private ownership of guns is illegal without a police permit, violations of the gun laws are so common that there is a special Gun Court to try cases involving the use of firearms.

Every neighborhood in downtown Kingston is said to have its Don, or crimelord, with links to one of the two major political parties. The Dons reputedly distribute guns among their allies.

The arrival of crack cocaine on the island in the 1980s apparently had a major impact on gangs and crime. Jamaica not only became a base for trans-shipment of the drug from South America to the U.S., but Jamaicans began to get addicted as well. Gang violence went from bad to worse as rival "posses" fought for turf.

At the time we arrived, Peace Corps projects still operated in "dung-tung" (i.e. downtown) Kingston, because if the local Don put out the word that the Volunteers were to be left alone, they *were* left alone and could walk the meanest streets in relative safety. During our stay, however, Volunteers were pulled out of most dungtung projects, due to an increase in safety-related incidents. But that didn't mean we couldn't go there. Indeed, the central bus terminus for the city and the island was a down-town square known as Parade, surrounding a park.

Part of our training involved taking trips around the city on public trans-portation. As I would later be assigned to work one day a week at a Salvation Army shelter located just off of Parade, I was one of the first of our group to visit the Saturday dungtung Coronation Market during training.

The square and the adjoining streets teemed with buyers and sellers, from little old ladies in housedresses to youths in Rasta Bart Simpson tee-shirts. The streets and sidewalks had become one immense market filled with fixed kiosks, movable stalls, tables, and spread blankets overflowing with merchandise. Higglers sold arts and crafts, straw hats, tee-shirts, shoes, sunglasses, and watches. Fruits and vegetables were laid out on ply-wood tables in flimsy wooden stalls shielded from the sun by blue plastic awnings. The air smelled of over-ripe fruit, fish, and excrement.

Higglers with steerable pushcarts hawked snacks and drinks to the chattering throng. Some higglers had only one item for sale—melons per-haps, or eggs, or charcoal. Blankets and tarps spread on sidewalks over-flowed with produce: akees, squash, four or five varieties of yams, onions, plantains, oranges, pineapples, carrots, turnips, sugarcane, and mangos. Every foot of available space against walls was filled with kiosks and tables dispensing leather goods, newspapers and magazines, new and used books, donuts, towels, bolts of cloth, earrings and other cheap jewelry, cosmetics, brooms—you name it.

City dwellers got supplied by their country cousins with fresh produce to sell, and farmers flocked to the Saturday market to sell what they had grown, or simply picked from the trees near their homes. Hawkers and shills filled the air with offers of the best deals, the freshest fruits.

"You deah, white mon, you nah wearin' a hot ta keep de sun off you head. Com buy a hot from me!"

"Got tree kin' mahngo dem. Got julie, bombay an' block mahngo fi sell you, good price."

"Ya mon, de chain an' de ring dem, dey real silver!"

"Ice-col' box drink, bog drink, Red Stripe, Shandy!" (Shandy is a mixture of beer and ginger beer.)

"De fish dem, dey cotch fresh dis marnin'!"

Kingston doesn't get very many tourists compared to the north coast, and most white Jamaicans do their shopping in neighborhood markets and supermarkets, so there wasn't another white person in sight. But other than occasionally being hailed as "white mon", and a few attempts to "beg me", people treated me like everyone else. After that first time on my own in the dungtung market, I could begin to feel at home in Kingston.

Training went on at Bamboo Pen, the classes sometimes interesting, sometimes boring. We were all anxious for the six weeks to end, eager to be sworn-in as Volunteers and to begin our actual service. For our fifth week, Community Orientation Week (C.O.W), we would go to the communities in which we would serve, meet the people with whom we'd be working, and look for places to live. Since Maria and I would be working at the University Hospital, in a suburb of Kingston called Mona, we didn't have to leave the city—somewhat to our disappointment.

So while others in our training group prepared to be driven in agency vehicles to places with names like May Pen, Mandeville, Falmouth, Port Antonio and Montego Bay, we prepared for a week at the Sandhurst and a ten minute daily bus ride to our job sites. However, we had a free weekend before C.O.W., and several of us made arrangements for our first trip outside of Kingston. We were going to climb to the top of Blue Mountain Peak—at over 7,000 feet, the highest point on the island.

Ten of us, a mix of Peace Corps Volunteers and Group 58 trainees, met at 8:00 in the morning and rode up to a village named Mavis Pen in jeeps driven by Carroo, the Training Director, and Froggy, an agency driver. We'd made reservations at a hostel near the trailhead, Whitfield Hall, and had arranged to be picked up in Land Rovers for the rest of the trip there. Carroo and Froggy dropped us off in the village and drove back.

Blue Mountain, which dominates the mountain range of the same name, is within ten or fifteen miles of Kingston as the crow flies; but as you leave the city, the narrow road begins a twisty-turny ascent through a jungle of palms and other tropical trees, and the trip to the trailhead takes two to three hours by car or bus. As you rise up into the mountains, glimpses of the coastal plain below are rare, due to the dense foliage. I saw blossoms in hues of blue, purple, yellow and red that I'd never before seen. The ride itself seemed an adventure.

When you ask somebody in Jamaica how long it will be before something arrives or gets done, the answer is almost always "soon com." You quickly learn that this means, "it will happen when it happens." Awaiting the arrival of the Land Rovers, "soon com" turned out to be about two hours; so we had time to buy sodas and snacks at one of the little roadside snack shacks and to look around. Some of the villagers checked us out and chatted with us, and the word soon got out among the children that we couldn't be begged.

You can drive through Mavis Pen in thirty seconds at twenty miles per hour if you don't have to stop for a donkey or a herd of goats. The village is perched on a mountainside, so to go anywhere other than the main road you had to travel uphill or downhill. We saw everything there was to see and still had plenty of time on our hands.

A woman with a basket perched on top of her head engaged Maria and me in conversation, introducing herself as the local librarian. (I couldn't imagine a library in such a small village, but Jamaica *does* have a high literacy rate for a developing country.) As we spoke, she put down her basket. Although it was early October, we somehow got to talking about Christmas.

"You know 'Silen' Night' in German?", she asked. I speak some German and told her that, in fact, I did.

"You know 'Silen' Night' in Spahnish?" Maria speaks some Spanish and told her that, in fact, she did.

"You sing me 'Silen' Night' in German an' Spahnish?"

I proceded to sing "*Stille Nacht,*" followed by Maria's rendition of "*Noche de Paz,*" much to everyone's amusement. The librarian asked if we could possibly come back at Christmas and sing "Silent Night" to the village schoolers. Being (almost) PCVs and eager for cultural exchange, we said that we might be able to. She produced a pad and pencil and wrote down our names, and we gave her the address of the Peace Corps office. She thanked us, put her basket back on her head, and walked off.

We never heard from her.

The Land Rovers arrived at about eleven and we piled aboard, eager to hit the trail to Blue Mountain Peak as early as we could. We travelled up and up on winding, dusty dirt roads that seemed as much potholes as roadbed. Now truly in "da bush", we saw no more villages or power lines, only isolated shacks perched on steep, green hillsides, and occasional clusters of shacks. We passed goats; men astride donkeys; people with boxes, baskets and jugs perched on their heads; and curious children gawking back at all the rubbernecking "whities" in the jouncing all-terrain vehicles. I saw a forlorn-looking little girl wearing only an adult-sized tee shirt that came down below her knees, with "give me head until I'm dead" printed on the front.

Carroo had warned us that we'd be in ganja-growing country and should stay on public roads or on the Blue Mountain trail, and respect "No Trespassing" signs. Although it is used by Rastafarians and a sizable minority of other Jamaicans, and is smoked openly at reggae festivals and in other public places, ganja is still illegal. A staple cash crop, it's cultivated in secret all over the island, but especially in the Blue Mountains. Ganja farmers don't like strangers trespassing in areas where the so-called "wisdom weed" is grown and have been known to use machetes and guns to protect their crops. We couldn't see any ganja patches from the road, but we took Carroo at his word.

We arrived at Whitfield Hall sometime before one and stashed all but our hiking gear inside. A rustic converted plantation house owned by an English Jamaican, the hostel had several dormitory rooms and a communal kitchen. As there was no electricity at that elevation, you cooked on gas stoves, and Coleman lanterns hung at intervals from hooks on the roof beams.

We ate a hasty lunch of bread, cheese, and fruit, then set off for the nearby trailhead. Most of us carried light day packs with extra clothing, snacks, and water. The air was warm, a refreshing change from the coastal heat; but we knew that it would get cool later in the afternoon, at a higher altitude. Most of us had done a lot of hiking in the States and we all considered ourselves to be in good shape. We set out, confident we could make it the six miles or so to the peak and back down before dark.

The trail wound up through dense jungle at a fairly gradual incline at first, seldom getting very steep. Before long we came to a break in the foliage beside the trail, where we could see Blue Mountain, majestic in the near distance. The forest growth still consisted of palms, and blossom-laden tropical trees and bushes. The air smelled pure and sweet as we ascended into the clouds.

We came to a ridge, which the cloud mist poured over like liquid, turning the forest mysterious and magical. Flies and mosquitos buzzed around us but, as long as we walked, they didn't bother us much. We set a good pace and kept it up, our spirits high.

Around three o'clock we came to a spring in a clearing, which we'd been told was the only reliable source of water on the trail, and was past halfway to the top. Four of our party of ten had surged ahead—Bill, Mary Ellen, Erin and Tim. When the rest of us took a break at the spring, we began to have doubts that we'd all make it to the peak in time to get back down before dark. One of our number, Shannon, was having problems with her knees. Maria and others had slowed their pace to stay with her.

Determined to make it to the top, I asked Maria if she'd mind if I forged on at a faster pace. She didn't object, so I set out alone, hoping to meet the others before they started down from the peak. We'd estimated that we should start back by four thirty at the latest—a poor estimate, as it turned out.

The trail had become a series of steep switchbacks. Now only the exertion of the climb kept me warm and the mist seemed to go right through me. Much to my surprise, at a certain elevation the jungle abruptly changed to coniferous forest. Tiring from the unending ascent, I kept thinking, *it can't be much farther;* but each turn in the trail revealed still more forest ahead of and above me.

Just as I was starting to have serious doubts about making it to the top, I emerged from the forest and found myself within sight of the trail's end. Panting and exhausted, I climbed the last few hundred meters to Blue Mountain Peak.

I looked around but couldn't see the four from our party who'd preceded me. A single, small cabin on the mountaintop overflowed with partying Jamaicans who planned to spend the night. One of them saw me looking and pointed to the elevation marker that stands at the highest point on the peak. There I joined my four companions, who had arrived about fifteen minutes ahead of me and were resting and snacking. They hailed me as they saw me approach.

I took off my pack and chugged from my canteen. I shared some tropical trail mix with the others and they shared chocolate and fruit, as we all took in the magnificent view. We were in luck. Most days, from what we'd heard, the cloud cover obscures the view of the north coast. Today, however, we could not only see the south coast, but could also catch glimpses of the north coast through the drifting clouds. Beyond the coastline, the turquoise Carribean stretched to the horizon. Although disappointed that Maria wasn't there to share the experience, I thrilled to the beauty that surrounded me, tired but exhilarated.

Erin, already a PCV, had been to the peak before and said she thought it was time to start down. It was already four thirty, but we thought we could reach the trailhead before it got pitch dark. Since none of the others had made it to the top, we assumed that they would make it down by sunset easily. We turned out to be wrong on both counts.

I noticed some soreness in my calf muscles, but felt rested and ready for the descent. We donned our packs and started down the mountain. For the first hour or so I hiked in the almost meditative state that one can easily enter when tired and doing serious walking. We still felt confident that we'd make it down in time, but sunset comes early on eastern mountain slopes, and fingers of shadow began to darken the trail even before we got back to the spring where we'd rested earlier in the afternoon.

This time we paused only long enough to fill our canteens and water bottles. A quick inventory revealed that we only had two small flashlights. Sweaty but chilled, I put on my windbreaker. The air smelled of earth and clouds.

We walked as quickly as we could safely move in the growing gloom. The thick jungle took on a stygian aspect around us, the only light a faint glow from above. On the occasional stretches of trail where the foliage on the downslope from us thinned, we could see a sliver of moon above the mountains. Stars appeared as the last traces of the sunset faded from the sky.

At times we needed to use the flashlights in order to keep to the trail. One of them quickly faded, flickered, and went out. I remembered that we were in ganja country and thought of the importance of keeping to the trail. I soon learned that my companions shared my concern.

We had to increasingly rely on the remaining flashlight, but before long it, too, began to weaken. I'd been walking with one eye closed, to preserve my night vision in at least one eye. By nine the second flashlight had given out and I could open both eyes. We talked as we walked, and all agreed that we couldn't have too much further to go. The slope became more gradual and the jungle had thinned-out some. We recalled from earlier in the day that the trail hadn't always been very distinct near the trailhead, and tried to take comfort in this recollection.

"Are you pretty sure we're still on the trail?"

"I *think* so."

"Anyone seen a trail marker lately?"

Silence.

"Um. I don't think we're on the trail anymore. I think we've gotten on one of those paths that intersected the lower part of the trail when we were going up."

"I think you're right."

And then we emerged from the jungle. The moonlight revealed a slope covered with scrub bush, descending into a mountain valley. Light shone from the window of a distant hillside shack, and I thought I could make out the dim outline of a dirt road below us. We continued warily down the path.

By this time we knew that we'd strayed from the trail and were on some path used by farmers. It took us down to the valley floor, where it intersected with the road I'd seen from above. We made our best guess as to which direction would get us to Whitfield Hall, and set off down the road. When we saw a sign from the back, I knew before we got to it what it was going to say: "Private Property. No Trespassing." The warning left us all feeling spooked.

It was bad enough being in this uncertain situation in the first place, but the fact that two of our number were women made it even trickier. Neither came across as panicky, and women who join the Peace Corps tend to be strong, independent types; but I always tend to feel protective of women in situations of potential jeopardy—part of being raised to be a Southern Gentleman, I suppose.

Not far down the road we came to a concrete block house whose windows flickered with lanternlight. I spotted a pickup truck parked beside the house. We were all nervous at the prospect of meeting *anyone* at this point, but we needed directions. As we came within hailing distance, we saw that the cab of the truck was occupied. Both doors opened and two Jamaican men got out. One of them, the driver, addressed us. He didn't sound happy.

"You know you ahn private propahty? You trespahssin' yahso." ("Yahso" means "here", "deahso" means "there.")

We all mumbled apologies and one of us spoke up, assuring the men that we would happily get off their property if they would only point the way toward Whitfield Hall.

The men muttered to each other in unintelligible, rapid-fire patois. Then, apparently satisfied that we weren't teefs or DEA agents, the driver pointed down the road in the direction we'd been headed. "It jos' down de road. Com, get in de trock. Me tek you deahso."

Somewhat relieved, but still wondering what we'd gotten ourselves into, the five of us piled into the back of the pickup. The Jamaicans got back into the cab without another word. The driver started the engine and we set off down the road. Bouncing around in the back as the truck travelled down the rocky, potholed road, we watched what was going on in the cab. The driver pulled a fat joint of ganja from behind his ear and lit it. He smoked some and passed it to his companion in the cab. The smoke drifted out through the open windows, pungent and unmistakable. I don't recall any of us in the back saying anything at the time, but I think we all grinned at one another in the moonlight. I thought, *now I know beyond a doubt I'm in Jamaica.*

We'd assumed that the other five people in our party had long since returned to Whitfield Hall, but as we pulled up to the hostel in the truck we found them just straggling in. We climbed out of the truck bed and thanked the driver, who gave the usual Jamaican response in such situations, "No problem, mon," and drove away.

We joined our exhausted friends and swapped stories. It seems that Shannon's knees had given out at some point, and the others had taken turns helping to support her weight all the way down the mountain. This had slowed their progress considerably and they had found themselves in the same situation as the five of us who made it to the peak, stumbling blindly down the jungle trail. Unlike us, they'd managed to stay on the trail; but the trip had turned into an adventure for all ten of us.

Reunited with our overnight supplies inside the hostel, Maria and I polished-off a flask of gin and lime juice, and fixed a simple supper of macaroni and tuna by lanternlight. The communal kitchen/dining area had long tables with benches. Sitting there, we met some British tourists, a few Jamaicans, and a German couple, all of whom were going to tackle the mountain the next day. We were tired and went to bed soon after supper. Fieldmice frolicked in the rafters, but that didn't keep me awake for long.

The next day we got off to a leisurely start, waiting in the front yard of Whitfield Hall for the Land Rovers to take us back to Kingston. Maria and I breakfasted on bread, cheese and bananas. She played cribbage with a friend while I wrote in my journal. Others sat at tables and chatted or wrote letters.

An enterprising young man who lived nearby asked us if we'd like some real Blue Mountain coffee—which by law can only be so designated if it's grown above a certain altitude. While we'd tasted coffee brewed from the world-renouned Blue Mountain beans in Kingston, we couldn't afford it very often. This man offered a fresh-brewed cup for five Jamaican dollars (less than a Red Stripe from a street vendor), and quickly found he had a lot of customers. This was one home-grown Jamaican drug that even PCVs can use.

He set about boiling water on a camp stove and grinding the beans, which he said he had grown and roasted himself. As the coffee brewed, the air around us filled with its rich aroma. We lined up with our money and our cups, which the young man filled with evident and justified pride. I have never had a more delicious cup of coffee in my life. Unfortunately, the Range Rovers arrived before the man had time to brew a second batch for us.

More than one Jamaican had told me that Jamaica has more churches per square mile than any other country in the world, and that for every church there is a rum bar. *If the stretch between Mavis Pen and Kingston is like the rest of the country*, I thought on the trip down, *that may very well be true.*

C.O.W. was designed to prepare us to "parachute in" to our various assignments around the island. Maria and I had already met some of the people we'd be working with and thought we had some idea of what we'd be doing at our work sites, so our biggest task was to find a place to live within commuting distance of the University Hospital.

I remember several of our training sessions as being especially enlightening in regard to the work we'd be doing for the next two years. A Jamaican presenter told us that there were five distinct stages to Peace Corps service in Jamaica:

"First you will be seen ahs white people. (There was only one black person in our training group and, despite vigorous recruiting efforts, relatively few black people served as PCVs in those days.) Second, you will be seen ahs tourists. Then, ahs people realize thaht you're not jost here for a vacation, they will regard you ahs do-gooders. As a developing contry, Jamaica has seen many do-gooders cohm and go. Eventually people in your community will cohm to see you ahs volunteers—working people who live on the local economy, like themselves. Finally—and noht ahll of you will make it to this stage—sohm people will get to know you as the individuals you are, perhahps even as friends."

Another presenter, a man from the Netherlands with a long career in development work, said one of the most helpful things I heard in training. He said that for the first six months on the job we should keep our mouths shut, our ears, eyes and minds open. The last thing we should say is something like, "here's the way to do it" or, "this is the way we did it in the States." He said that our first goal should be to establish relationships and earn credibility with our co-workers. Even if we thought we had solutions, or better alternatives, we should bite our tongues and wait until we'd become team members with our local national co-workers.

The Peace Corps has a different approach than other development agencies. PCVs aren't advisors or consultants like employees of U.S.A.I.D. and other foreign service workers. They aren't sent to advance any regional goals of the State Department, but are assigned in response to specified requests by the host countries. Ideally, Volunteers do not simply provide services to agencies and organizations in their country of service, but are matched with local national counterparts. The goal is a reciprocal transfer of skills. The Volunteer's project should be able to carry on with greater autonomy after his or her departure. It's called sustainable development.

"Systems," we were told in training, "often do noht fonction ahs they're supposed to. But sohmtimes individual people cahn close the gahps and make things work. It may take sohm time, but most Vohlunteers eventually find their niche and get sohm degree of satisfaction frohm their efforts. Results aren't ahlways tahngible, at least noht in the short term. Sohm prohjects are relatively successful and ohthers fizzle out ahs soon ahs the Vohlunteer leaves the country. Sohm of you will leave knowing that you hahve at least helped individuals, if noht an agency or a village.

"Noht everybody ends op working in their original assignment, for a variety of reasons. The Peace Corps is flexible. Volunteers are encouraged to be the same—ahs well as patient and persistent. If you hahve any spare time, you may want to develop secondary projects on your own initiative. Sohmtimes, when the initial assignment doesn't work out, these projects becohm the Volunteer's primary prohject."

Maria and I were both in the Health sector, like most of Group 58. We'd been placed at the University Hospital of the West Indies, on the outskirts of Kingston. Maria was assigned to work on the faculty of the School of

Nursing, teaching psychiatric nursing. My assignment entailed working with the ward staff on the Detox/Rehab Ward, with the title of Ward Psychologist. The only such program in Jamaica, the ward had been established only months before our arrival, primarily in response to the growing crack cocaine problem on the island.

On Monday morning of C.O.W., Maria and I set out from the Sandhurst and walked to Hope Road together to catch a bus to the University Hospital. Hope Road is a major artery in Kingston. It climbs at a very gradual grade from Halfway Tree up through Liguanie (where Old Hope Road branches away toward dungtung Kingston and the harbor), and onward to a bus terminus and market in Papine, at the base of the Blue Mountains. The University of the West Indies and the University Hospital are an easy walk from Papine.

We boarded a crowded bus in Liguanie and got off ten minutes later at the outdoor terminus, already drenched with sweat. We'd previously toured the hospital, and had our bearings. Papine looked similar to many village squares in Jamaica, with a small park in the center, ringed with parked buses and higglers. We walked through the market, which already bustled with activity. The sun beat down on us and the air smelled of sewage, exhaust fumes and fresh pineapples. Other than the occasional beggar, nobody paid us any special attention.

On the way down the street to the University Hospital entrance, we noticed a sign that we'd seen here and there in the city, this one on the wall of a small shop: "Nah Piss Yahso." A high wall surrounds the hospital, and we crossed the road to take advantage of its shade. A flowering vine with bright pink blossoms, known colloquially as "rice-and-peas", covered portions of the wall. Across from the hospital grounds stood one of the myriad shanty towns we'd become accustomed to seeing all over Kingston, built from scrap wood, bamboo and zinc roofing. Beyond the squatters' settlement, the mountains climbed toward the sky. We soon came to the hospital gate.

The hospital stands adjacent to the University grounds, separated by a chain-link fence. On the wall side of the ring road curving around the low buildings that comprise the hospital are the School of Nursing and a series of four-story dormitories that house nurses and nursing students.

Once inside the gate, Maria went her way and I went mine, both of us a little anxious at the prospect of meeting the people we'd be working with for the next two years.

I knew that the Detox Ward occupied the floor above the Emergency Room, just across the street from the entrance; but I had some time before my appointment to meet the ward staff, and decided to familiarize myself with the layout. Passing the ER waiting room, one side of which was open to the covered walkway I came in on, I heard a chorus of voices raised in song. One of the patients stood in front of the rows of chairs and led the other waiting patients in singing hymns! Most of them seemed to be participating in making a joyful noise. While not a daily occurrence, I found that such spontaneous Christian celebrations weren't uncommon in this place of healing. Occasionally they would even happen on buses.

The hospital is a complex of long one- and two-story painted cinderblock buildings linked by covered walkways. Benches line the hallways in some of the larger buildings, outside the various medical departments. Only a few of the buildings have air conditioning, so the walls contain long rows of louvered windows which are almost always open, for ventilation. Orderlies constantly mop and scrub, and the air smells of disinfectant. Many inpatients wear their own nightgowns, pajamas and bathrobes from home on the wards and in the halls. Doctors and medical students can be easily identified by their white lab coats and stethoscopes; and Sisters (nurses) usually wear the traditional starched white uniforms and caps, with colored belts to identify their rank and station. Student nurses wear a uniform of white aprons over red and white candystripe dresses.

Just before nine o'clock I took the stairs up from the ER area to the Detox Ward. An eight-bed locked ward, it contained a central hallway, a kitchen (although meals were brought from the central kitchen by orderlies), bathrooms and showers, two four-bed wardrooms, two consultation rooms, a dayroom/dining room, and a nurses' station. A Sister let me in the locked door and took me to the nurses station to meet the staff, who were all very cordial, if a bit reserved at first. Only the Ward Sister (or head nurse, whom I'll call Sister M) wore the starched white uniform. By special dispensation the other ward nurses—due to the special nature of drug abuse treatment—wore street clothes. These duty nurses were my local national counterparts, the staff with which I'd be working daily. We quickly agreed to call one another by our first names, although I continued to address Sister M by her formal title in the presence of other staff.

I also met Dr. W, a young, energetic doctor who had just returned from a residency at Johns Hopkins. The first of several physicians who would "rotate through" as ward resident at six-month intervals, he had some perspective on Peace Corps service and would give me valuable advice during the following months. When he spoke, he easily lapsed back and forth between The Queen's English (Jamaican-style) and patois.

By the end of C.O.W. Maria and I each had some idea of the potential opportunities, as well as the frustrations and challenges, that lay ahead. On one hand, we both appeared to be well-qualified for our jobs; on the other hand, everything seemed to be done a little differently here. A Jamaican psychologist that I'd met on the Psychiatric Ward had told me that the profession was practically unknown in Jamaica and said jokingly that the few psychology books in the university library were filed "somewhere between astrology and necromancy."

I wasn't at all sure just what role I'd be playing on the Detox Ward or how my services would be received. The duty nurses weren't formally trained in clinical counseling, and their idea of counseling appeared to be primarily advice-giving. Maria had learned that there were severe shortages of nursing textbooks and practically everything else in the School of Nursing, and that she would have to get licensed as a nurse in Jamaica before she could start to teach—a process that might take several months.

Although Maria had an office in the School of Nursing, ...
work would involve supervising student nurses on Ward 21, the
Psychiatric Ward. Most of my work would be done on the Detox Ward,
but someone had decided that I should also work for half a day a week at
Peter's Lane, a Salvation Army shelter for addicts in the heart of dungtung
Kingston.

So on Thursday morning of C.O.W., I got together with with a
Volunteer named Tom, a social worker assigned to Peter's Lane. We met
for coffee at a fast food restaurant near Halfway Tree prior to going dungtung and he filled me in on what to expect. He wasn't pleased with his
assignment and planned to ask for another if things didn't improve. (A few
months later he "ET'd"—Peace Corps slang for Early Termination of
Service.) He painted a pretty dismal picture.

Peter's Lane, he told me, had been set up basically to house male addicts
who hadn't been accepted for treatment on the Detox Ward. His boss, a
Salvation Army officer from Central America known to all simply as The
Major, considered himself a qualified counselor but knew next to nothing
about either counseling or addiction. His idea of counseling was to preach
the Gospel and to berate and threaten the addicts in his care. He frequently lost his temper and sometimes shoved or cuffed the shelter residents. Tom did his best to provide counseling, but the noise level made
that nearly impossible on the premises. He'd usually take the men down to
a small park by the harbor for group counseling. With drugs widely available in dungtung Kingston, ganja and crack were routinely smuggled into
the shelter.

We took a bus down to Parade and walked through the park to the harbor side of the large, busy square. The park was like an oasis, relatively
serene compared to the surrounding sights, sounds, and smells of street
commerce. Statues stood at intervals along the paved walkways that criss-
crossed the park. Most were of Jamaica's National Heroes, but Queen
Victoria also stood among them, another reminder of the colonial era.

The Peter's Lane shelter was named for the squalid alley off Parade where it's located. The alley smelled of sewage and rotten produce. A guard let us in the locked gate and Tom gave me a tour. The residential area looked more like a prison than a treatment facility, with a courtyard ringed by spartan rooms resembling cells. Tom greeted some of the men and introduced me to a few.

Then he took me to the dingy office area and introduced me to The Major. A big, bluff man in a Salvation Army uniform, he gripped my hand and pumped it vigorously. He laughed and joked a lot, revealing a contemptuous attitude toward addicts in general and his charges in particular. He told me how much I was needed and praised Tom's work. Much to my relief, Tom mentioned an appointment elsewhere and we left shortly afterward. My first impression of The Major bore out Tom's description. I could easily understand why Tom felt inadequate to meeting the treatment needs of the program's residents. I wondered if I could make a worthwhile contribution, given what I was up against.

Looking for a place to live proved to be the most frustrating task of the week, but after several false starts and fruitless leads we finally found a place. Some Volunteers lived in cramped apartments and others rented rooms in Jamaican households; but we found a small house we liked immediately. Located in a nice middle-class neighborhood, within easy commuting distance of the University Hospital, it exceeded our expectations and we hoped we could afford it on our combined living allowances.

It would have been within walking distance of our work sites, save for the immense, green wall called Long Mountain that cuts into suburban Kingston between the two locations. We could walk to the bus stop in ten minutes, and from there a single fifteen-minute bus ride would get us to Papine.

Pushpa, an Indian nurse who would be working with Maria, knew the couple who had just vacated the house and drove us out to look at it. Built of pale yellow-painted concrete blocks with mahogany-colored wooden trim and a blue aluminum roof, the house occupied a walled enclosure along with another small house. Pushpa had keys to the gate and the doors. The front yard had a paved patio and an untended, overgrown garden plot. Two trees grew in the yard—a small banana tree and a ten-foot tree that we later learned yielded an annual crop of gunga peas, tasty beans that grow in pods. An aluminum overhang sheltered the low porch in front of the doorway. Pushpa unlocked the door and we all went inside.

The house had linoleum tile floors, high ceilings, and plenty of louvered windows for ventilation. Sparsely furnished, it consisted of two bedrooms separated by a bathroom, a spacious living room/dining room area, and a small kitchen. Off of the kitchen was a second small bathroom with a shower stall.

After we'd finished our tour of the inside, Pushpa let us out the back door. Against the wall outside the kitchen door, there were twin concrete sinks for doing laundry. Boughs from a lime tree in a neighbor's yard overhung the back fence, and crotons and hibiscus grew in profusion along it.

As soon as we could get to a telephone, we contacted the landlord, a Maylaysian immigrant of Chinese ancestry, married to a Jamaican. We made arrangements to pay the deposit. Dr. Lui seemed very cordial over the phone and said that he didn't like to rent to Jamaicans.

We soon learned that he was a man of many interests. The only licensed acupuncturist in Jamaica at the time, his hobbies included birdwatching, ham radio, photography, and astronomy. He proved to be a friend as well as a fair landlord, and a resource in our later explorations of the island.

Friday afternoon, C.O.W. behind us and lodging secured, we wanted to celebrate. So, after moving back in with Alvira, we went to the Survival Pub, a rum bar that had become the preferred hangout in Greendale for Group 58. Rick and Jennifer—one of the four married couples in the group—and Bill greeted us from their seats at the bar. The pub was crowded with Jamaicans and fellow Trainees, and we had to talk loudly to be heard over the din of loud reggae music and conversation. A typical rum bar, the Survival's walls were plastered with pin-up pictures and reggae posters, and lined with electronic slot machines. Betty, the bartender, busily dispensed Red Stripes, Dragon Stouts, Steel Bottoms (white rum and beer), and the favorite of Jamaican alcoholics, a nasty mixture of 120-proof ("overproof") white rum and Suppligen, a creamy dietary supplement.

With customers lined up two-deep behind the bar stools, Rick called in our Red Stripe order and took our money to give to Betty. By the time he got our beers, we'd managed to crowd our way in to the bar. Bill asked if we were planning to go to Ocho Rios, on the north coast, for the White River Reggae Show the next night. Several people from Group 58 planned to take a taxi from Spanish Town in the morning, and we quickly agreed to join them. We had a three-day weekend ahead of us, Monday being National Heroes Day. It would be a strain on our budget, but we both love reggae and we couldn't resist the lure of our first opportunity to attend a big concert.

At seven o'clock the next morning, we met Rick, Jennifer, Bill and (another) Jeff near the Spanish Town bus terminus, at a point where taxis to the north coast cluster. Most of the taxis were small sedans owned by the drivers. The more people they could squeeze in, the lower the per-person fare. Explaining to a driver that we were workers paid in Jamaican dollars, not tourists, we managed to negotiate the fare down to $J 35 apiece, and crammed aboard. Although it's only forty-something miles from Spanish Town to Ocho Rios, as the crow flies, it took about an hour-and-a-half on the narrow, winding, roads over Jamaica's mountain spine. Maria sat on my lap the whole way, but it was *not* romantic.

We quickly learned firsthand why these taxis were known as "suicide taxis." The more trips drivers can make in a day, the more money they make; so they drive like maniacs, tailgating, passing slow-moving trucks on curves, and speeding every chance they get. They know every twist, turn and pothole in the road intimately, but it's a white-knuckle trip for the passengers.

We alternately sped and crawled up the highway that snaked into the John Crow Mountains above Spanish Town, passing isolated shacks, hamlets, countless rum bars and churches, roadside fruit vendors in bamboo shelters, and breathtaking vistas of jungle-clad mountainside. Pressed together—two in the front passenger seat and four in the back—we jerked and swayed from side to side on the fast stretches, re-discovering Newton's Laws of Motion in a most painful and intimate fashion, as the driver dodged potholes and passed trucks.

At the top of the mountain range, the jungle gave way to hilly pastureland, surprisingly reminiscent of the English countryside. Flocks of sheep and herds of goats roamed the open fields. Then the road began its winding descent back into the tropical forests. About ten miles out of Ocho Rios we passed through an especially lush rainforest known as Fern Gully, named for the giant ferns that created walls of green on both sides of the highway. Past this point every available space at intervals on the roadside was occupied by bamboo shelters, where arts and crafts were sold. We'd entered tourist country.

Finally the road became more level and we left the jungle behind us, finding ourselves suddenly in the outskirts of "Ochi", as it's known to Jamaicans. The driver let us out in the town square, which we immediately noticed was much cleaner than most any neighborhood in Kingston.

My back hurt and my legs prickled as the blood began to circulate again. Maria had a crick in her neck from having to bend over the whole trip. Groaning and flexing our aching limbs, we paid the driver and limped in the direction of the shore. We couldn't see the ocean yet, but the fresh smell of the salty seabreeze beckoned.

We walked toward the row of high-rise hotels that line the beaches of Ochi and soon saw a huge cruise ship docked in the harbor. The second thing we noticed about the north coast, besides the relative cleanliness, was the number of hustlers plying their trade on the streets. Some offered to show us around, some offered us ganja, and others offered a favorable exchange rate for our American dollars. We quickly tired of explaining that we didn't have any.

Arriving at the waterfront, we located the hotel where Rick and Jennifer had made reservations. We'd hoped to all share one room, but the desk clerk looked at us like we were crazy. When Maria and I realized we weren't going to get cheap lodging, I reluctantly cashed one of my few "emergency" traveler's checks and we got a room for ourselves. The spacious room overlooked the placid, blue-green ocean, the water gently lapping at a low sea wall two floors down from us. Waves broke on a coral reef several hundred meters out from the shore. We had air conditioning—a luxury we hadn't enjoyed since Miami. We were in heaven!

The concert, like most in Jamaica, didn't start until after ten and was an all-nighter. We put on our bathing suits and took our first dip in the Caribbean, then returned to the room to rest. To save money, I went out in the early evening and bought some patties and fruit on the street for supper. As the time for the show drew near, we met some of the rest of our party in the lobby. Others from Group 58 had arrived from Kingston.

To my surprise, most of the group had reconsidered going to White River. They'd spent more than they'd intended for lodging and the show cost $J100—only about $5, but a lot on our limited incomes. Besides, the hotel had satellite TV, and some of them wanted to watch football! Disappointed, we returned to our room to get ready. We were older than most of the others by almost twenty years but, apparently, we were the biggest reggae fans in the bunch.

Or so we thought. Just as we were about to go, we heard a knock on the door. All of our friends from Group 58 stood in the hallway, grinning and excited. The lure of reggae had won out over sports. We all set out together.

A twenty minute walk got us to the concert venue on the White River. The grounds outside the music park bustled with patrons and entrepreneurs. Time and again young men offered us ganja. My replies became a litany. "No thanks, man." "I don't use that stuff." "I'm here to get high on the music."

The outdoor arena teemed with happy music lovers, and a cloud of ganja and tobacco smoke hung in the air. The first group played traditional "roots" reggae and hundreds of fans had already crowded up near the stage, bobbing and swaying to the hypnotic rhythms. Maria and I quickly joined the dancing, multiracial mob, and in no time were transported by the music. I never felt a "contact high" from the roiling, pungent smoke overhead, but the hours of dancing and the sight of happily-entranced people flowing with the music induced its own ecstasy. This could be nowhere else but Jamaica, mon.

The music alternated between roots reggae and dancehall. We got to see the latest deejay sensation, Lieutenant Stitchie, up close. He wore the white uniform of a navy lieutenant, but pranced around the stage in a most unmilitary manner. We heard him sing the big hit we'd been hearing over and over in Greendale and Kingston, "Night and Day." The dancehall beat was frenetic compared to the swaying beat of Bob Marley-style reggae, but equally danceable. We weren't familiar with many of the performers, but before the night was over we'd danced to the music of some of the biggest names in contemporary reggae, including Bigga, Mikel Rose, Carlene Davis and Freddy McGregor.

We danced to the point of exhaustion, then caught a second wind and danced some more. From time to time we withdrew from the swaying mob to get a Red Stripe and to rest. The loud music drowned out any attempts at conversation near the stage, but between sets we'd meet up with our friends and talk. "Two more years of this, mon!", Rick exclaimed, beaming.

Maria and I didn't make it through the night, but parted from our younger companions around four o'clock. Our third wind had died out by then, so we walked back to our hotel, happily exhausted. By the time we collapsed into bed, the first, pink light of dawn had begun to brighten the dark sea outside our window.

The next day, we checked out of the hotel and found a less expensive room in a Jamaican neighborhood. Then we set out to explore Ochi. We decided not to go to the famous Dunn's River Falls or to other popular tourist attractions, but just walked around town. We found that everything is more expensive on the north coast and that almost everyone is out to make a buck from the tourists.

While many Jamaicans are genuinely friendly to foreigners, in the tourist centers there are untold dozens of young men who will instantly become your friend and offer to show you around, for tips. The pitch usually starts with a smile and a question, leading to the suggestion that you have *something* in common.

"Wheah you from, mon?"

"The United States."

"Oh! I hahv lots of fahmily in de United States! Sohmday I am going, too. How you like Jamaica?"

"It's a beautiful island."

"Ya mon. My name is Berington. Look, why don' I show you aroun'. You wan' go to Donn's River Fahlls? Tek a rahft ride on de White River?"

No mention is made of a tip, but if you keep the man's company for any length of time or ask any questions, you can be sure that he will ask for one. It's sad that so much of what at first seems like spontaneous friendliness and hospitality is actually profit-motivated; but you can't blame poor people for trying to get money from people they see as rich.

We met Nancy—an attractive young woman from Group 58—in town around lunchtime. She told us about a nearby "jerk center" that had great jerk pork. We were all hungry, so we went there together. The pork lived up to its reputation, so spicy hot the first bites brought tears to my eyes. A young man struck up a conversation with us at the outdoor table we occupied, and we thought at first that he worked there. He told us about a nearby spice mill where we could learn all about jerk seasonings.

After we ate we decided to check out the mill and set out in the direction he'd indicated. As we turned off the main road onto a byway that led uphill into a forested area, there he was ahead of us, beckoning. We joined him and he introduced himself as Clarence. When we came to a mimosa tree, he showed us the seeds, used for beads in craftwork, and crushed a leaf so we could smell the aroma. He pointed to a house up the road and suggested that it had some association with Bob Marley. (To listen to some of these informal tour guides, there was no place in Jamaica that *didn't* have some association with Bob Marley.) We came to a path that led into the forest and Clarence announced that it led to the spice mill.

Nancy seemed ready to follow, but I was in the company of two pretty women and didn't like the idea of following a stranger into the woods. I think Maria and I both got wary simultaneously. Although tourists are generally safe in Jamaica if they don't take foolish chances, and Clarence was probably just a harmless street hustler, we'd been taught in training to err on the side of caution.

I caught Nancy's eye and said I thought it was time to go back to town. She immediately agreed. We thanked Clarence, who tried again to persuade us to go on with him to see the mill. Seeing that we weren't going to follow him anymore, he asked for a tip. When we declined, he acted like we'd cheated him and walked away, angry.

I remarked to Maria and Nancy that sometimes simple eye contact was taken as an invitation for a pitch here. Nancy sadly agreed, saying that she was used to making eye contact but had learned to limit it on the streets in Jamaica, in order to avoid the hassles it often led to.

The sour taste of our disappointment in north coast street hospitality was sweetened that evening by a glass of beetroot juice. Maria saw it featured on the menu at the restaurant where we ate supper and, always eager for new culinary experiences, ordered it. She asked the waitress what a beetroot looked like and said that she'd never seen or tasted it before. The waitress not only brought her a free taste to see if she liked it, but showed her a beetroot and told her how the juice was prepared. Maria liked the taste and ordered a full glass. The experience reminded us that most Jamaicans are genuinely friendly and hospitable to strangers.

We returned to Kingston and our final week in training. The members of Group 58 eagerly anticipated the prospect of being sworn-in as Volunteers on Friday—all but one, anyway. Tuesday morning the training staff informed us that one of our number, a nurse, had ET'd. She hadn't wanted the rest of us to know and had just been driven out to the airport. Others in the group would subsequently leave before completing their service, but this was our first casualty of culture shock.

During the final week of training, we were treated to some experiential lessons in Jamaican culture. A locally-famous performer came to Bamboo Pen to to teach us about Jamaican music and dance. Her delightful presentation covered folk music, gospel, and the evolution of the island's contemporary music from its roots in African rhythms, through rocksteady and ska, to reggae and dancehall. She sang, played tape-recorded music, and danced to illustrate her lecture material.

We not only had a presentation on Jamaica's most popular sport, cricket, by a professional player; we actually got out on the field and played the game. The rules were much too complicated for me to attempt to explain anything about the sport (and, frankly, some elements of the game still have me mystified); but at least I learned the difference between a wicket and a googly, a bowler and a batsman.

Finally, we went dungtung in a chartered bus to see the National Gallery of the Jamaican Art Institute. We saw many styles of painting and works in other media, including a collection of sculptures by Jamaica's most famous artist, Edna Manley. I learned that the work of artists with no formal training isn't called "primitive art" in Jamaica, but rather "intuitive art." The tour provided an impressive conclusion to our six weeks of cultural orientation.

Training is the final stage of the Peace Corps' selection process. Trainees deemed unsuitable for service are culled-out prior to graduation. Happily, all of the remaining members of Group 58 had been found suitable for swearing-in. The evening of the day we found this out most of us met at the Survival pub after training to celebrate. There was a bittersweet quality to the occasion, though. We'd been through a lot together and had grown close as a group. After the swearing-in, we would disperse to locations all over the island. Although all PCVs had to come to Kingston at least four times a year for gamma globulin shots ("G.G.s"), we wouldn't be seeing some of our new-found friends for weeks or months. So we hoisted a few to the Corps and to each other.

We'd already met many of the ninety-or-so Volunteers serving on the island. Some of our number would join graduates of prior training groups in the towns or villages in which they lived. Some would work in already-established projects and others would start new ones. Once you completed training, you got limited staff supervision, but you were basically on your own in your community. We'd been briefed on emergency evacuation procedures. Staff drivers took you and your meager belongings to your new home. You were issued a first aid kit, a 15-gallon water barrel (to keep an emergency supply on hand), and a hurricane lantern. Some Volunteers got mountain bikes and a few stationed deep in "da bush" got motorcycles. You couldn't buy a car, even if you had enough of your own money to get one. Although some older Volunteers drew pensions—a second income—the Peace Corps encouraged us to live off of our monthly living allowances.

Part of the "Peace Corps philosophy" is that you are supposed to live at the local standard. We received a decent middle-class professional wage, by Jamaican standards, but Maria and I had to budget carefully in order to get by on our combined living allowances. Those of us in Kingston and Montego Bay were at a disadvantage compared to those stationed in the country, as rent was more expensive in cities. Some of us thought that the living allowances should be "indexed" to the sixty percent inflation rate, but this wasn't done. We would get occasional increases in our pay, but each one had to be justified to PC headquarters in Washington. Periodic increases couldn't be taken for granted.

When you serve in the Peace Corps you live at ground level, unlike embassy employees and most other American professionals working in developing countries. That means you share the economic hardships faced by the citizens of your country of service.

The long-awaited day of our swearing-in ceremony finally arrived. Other than my first six weeks as a plebe at The Citadel, the training cycle had been the longest six weeks of my life. As I wrote in my journal, " Finally a Volunteer, not a non-person Trainee. The weeks of training have been like a parenthesis in time, existing apart from the normal timestream. Now real time has started again, as our two year term of service begins."

Friday, November 1st, the staff released us from training at noon and we took buses back to Greendale to get ready. Our host families were invited to the swearing-in, and we'd all be transported to Bamboo Pen in chartered buses. Although we'd be spending the night at Alvira's house, we started packing. Then we napped. When we got up, Alvira announced that we weren't having food, only rocks and gravel. In fact, she had made a delicious soup to tide us all over until the dinner after the ceremony. As we ate, I told her the folk tale about stone soup.

In the story a drifter shows up at a hobo encampment by a river. He has no food and the others aren't about to give him any. He produces a big cooking pot from his bag and announces that he'll just make a pot of stone soup. He walks down to the river to get water and goes around carefully collecting just the right stones, which he places in the pot. He builds a fire and starts cooking the stones.

The water is soon bubbling away and the hobo smacks his lips in anticipation. "Nothing I like better than a bowl of stone soup," he says to the other hobos who have gathered around to watch. "Of course, it would be a whole lot better if I had me a carrot or two."

"I got a few carrots," says one of the onlookers. "You can have some if you give me a taste."

The carrots get cut up into the pot. "It would taste even better if I had me a few little potatoes to go with the stones."

"I got three big spuds you can have, if you'll share some of that soup with me," says another hobo.

The cook cuts up the spuds and they go in the pot. "Sure wish I had me some salt," he says.

This goes on until the pot contains carrots, potatoes, tomatoes, two quail, onions, wild celery, salt, and pepper. The cook announces that the stone soup is done to perfection. He fishes out the stones, throws them aside, and feeds the whole camp.

"So how you like my rocks and gravel?" Alvira asked with a subtle smile.

After the meal we all dressed in our "Sunday clothes" and walked down to the place where the chartered buses waited. Once everyone had arrived, we set off for Bamboo Pen.

The ceremony was no small occasion. Jamaican dignitaries had been invited and music was provided by the Jamaican Constabulary Band. Embassy officials and representatives of the agencies, organizations, and institutions in which PCVs served attended. As the band began to play, a gorgeous sunset faded into night and a full moon rose over the trees. Guests took their seats in folding chairs that had been set out on the well-lit lawn. The seats faced a stage that had been erected beneath the veranda of the estate house. Over the stage hung a large banner that read, "Peace Corps Jamaica Group 58."

Maria and I joined our groupmates, who were seating themselves in a rectangle of chairs facing in from one side of the ceremonial area. We had to sit apart from one another, as we have different last names and the seating was alphabetical; so we hugged and kissed before taking our seats.

The band, which had gone silent as the last people seated themselves, struck up the Jamaican National Anthem. Everyone stood. We'd learned the words in training and sang along. Then the band played our own National Anthem and we sang that, too. Everyone took their seats. An Anglican bishop delivered an invocation.

Carroo, the Training Director, spoke first. After welcoming all of the official guests, he went on to praise Group 58 as a truly exceptional "batch" of Peace Corps Trainees. Turning to us, he challenged us to help Peace Corps Jamaica grow and change. He wished us well in our assignments, then introduced the guest speaker, Dr. Errol Miller—scholar, author, and Dean of Teacher Education at the University of the West Indies.

Dr. Miller gave an inspiring talk about the ideals on which the United States had been founded, Jamaica's place in the world culture, and the ties between the two nations. He reminded the audience that the following year would mark the 30<u>th</u> anniversary of Peace Corps service in Jamaica. He spoke of the American emphasis on individuality and how that relates to Peace Corps service. He urged us to both work for Jamaica's development and to learn from the people we met. As I listened, I felt both inspired and elated. I thought again about the story I'd told Alvira earlier, suddenly realizing that it might have something to say about my role as a development worker.

Maybe I was in Jamaica to make stone soup.

After the keynote address, Carroo introduced the Charge D'Affaires from the embassy, who was to swear us in, the Ambassador being in Washington. After a short speech addressed to the Trainees, he asked us to stand and raise our right hands. I felt a slight sense of irony, in that Peace Corps Volunteers take the same oath ("...to defend the Constitution of the United States against all enemies, foreign and domestic...") as I had taken when I was commissioned as an officer in the Army, twenty-one years earlier. But I have never felt more proud to be a citizen of the United States than I was at that moment. I was proud, not only of myself and Maria, but of all the members of Group 58.

After the administration of the oath, each of us in turn walked up onto the stage to shake various hands and to be given certificates proclaiming our new status. Back in the seating area, there were hugs, kisses, handshakes and back-slapping. We'd made it—we were Peace Corps Volunteers!

Part II

November '91–May '92

We had to move out of Alvira's the day after our swearing-in, even though our house had to be painted before we could move in. That left us on our own for lodging, with most of our belongings stashed at Bamboo Pen. Volunteers stationed all over the island were usually very accomodating about letting other Volunteers stay with them while on vacation or in times of need, so we took a room at the Sandhurst on Saturday and asked around. Tom, the social worker who'd taken me to Peter's Lane, said he thought we could stay in the room of one of the two women Volunteers with whom he shared an apartment near the University. She was going to be out of town for several days. We'd already paid for the room at the hotel, but he invited us to come over for supper.

At the apartment we met his other housemate, Sherri, and her Jamaican boyfriend. Jimmy—one of the few white Jamaicans we ever got to know—turned out to be a real character and quite the raconteur. Comprising only about two percent of the population, most whites are holdovers from the colonial era and tend to be quite well-off by Jamaican standards. Jimmy had spent six years getting his college degree in Germany and traveling around The Continent. Despite his distinctive accent, because of his white skin, nobody had believed he was Jamaican.

Throughout the evening he regaled us with funny stories. He described his student days as lean times. He lived in a rooming house with several other foreign students, one of whom (he said) was a son of the chieftain of an African tribe that still practiced cannibalism. Ogun had his teeth filed to sharp points and had never seen money before coming to Europe. Jimmy told of a midnight raid on a pond in a public park, to steal ducks so that he, Ogun, and their Turkish and Chinese roommates could eat.

They nabbed two ducks, which the Chinese student, a chef, cooked for them. Ogun said afterward that it had been a very good meal, then asked while picking his filed teeth, "but do you know what is the *best* meat of all?", and grinned wickedly.

Jimmy swore that the Turk's name was Honda Honda and that, although small in stature, he liked to get drunk and start fights with people in uniforms. He bought a used Volkswagen, with only the driver's seat in place, so that they could all go touring. During his initial inspection of the car, he kicked the tires hard, explaining that that was how you checked out a camel for purchase. You kicked the legs and if it fell over you didn't buy it.

While driving drunkenly through the Spanish countryside, they got pulled over by a policeman, whom Honda Honda attacked. When they were all arrested and taken to the stationhouse for booking, he started a brawl with the officers. This resulted in their being beaten up, fined, and escorted to the border, where their passports were stamped "persona non grata."

Jimmy mostly told stories about Jamaica, however. He told of a retired British Lieutenant General who'd won two Victoria Crosses in World War II and had come to Jamaica to teach at the boys' academy Jimmy had attended. He said to the boys that he'd won one of the VCs for capturing a German general while the man was "on the crapper." The British general said he'd quit the exclusive Liguanie Club in Kingston because they wouldn't let him bring in a sergeant for a drink at the bar, declaring "I'll bloody-well have a drink with him at the Officers' Mess. I can do that because I'm a General. That's the whole point of *being* a bloody General, don't you know."

Jimmy told of a dotty old retired British Army officer who'd been a demolitions expert. He'd kept goats on his estate grounds because he'd heard that goat milk is good for you, but teefs kept stealing his goats. So he'd booby-trapped his gate with explosives. After several teefs got maimed trying to break in, he'd had no more trouble with goats being stolen.

Jimmy said that the officer was reputed to have a lot of money in his house, and that late one night when he was a guest in the man's home he came across a teef who'd broken in. "I told him that if I couldn't find any of the money during the daytime, he certainly wasn't going to find any at night, and he left."

Jimmy said that Jamaicans generally go to great lengths to stay out of the rain, as they believe that getting rained on will make you sick. He said that when Queen Elizabeth and Prince Phillip visited Jamaica and reviewed the troops at a Jamaica Defense Force parade, rain clouds came over the mountains and everyone became skittish. When the rain started to fall, the troops broke ranks and ran for the barracks.

He also told of the Independence celebration at the newly-built National Stadium, on the day that Great Britain ceded direct governance of the island to the Jamaican people. He said that after the Union Jack was lowered for the last time, the Jamaicans replaced it with the wrong flag. He considered this an omen of things to come.

We didn't know how much of what Jimmy said was true, but he kept us in stitches all through supper. When it was time for Maria and me to return to the Sandhurst, Jimmy wouldn't hear of us taking the bus. He and Sherri had a party to attend, and somehow the four of us managed to cram ourselves into his tiny MG convertable for the short ride back.

On Monday we arranged to have our meager belongings transported to our new home, where we met Dr. Lui and exchanged our deposit and the first month's rent for the keys. A short, enthusiastic man, he apologized that the house hadn't been properly cleaned, due to our haste to move in. He intoduced us to Vasanth and Shiv, two young Indian brothers who lived in the other house. Like all the Indians we met in Jamaica, they both spoke English fluently. From the outset they proved to be friendly, helpful neighbors.

After Dr. Lui left we began to unpack and inspect. The stove had no gas cylinder attached and the old refrigerator in the dining area rattled—but it worked. The place was pretty bare-looking and dirty but, after two months of living with other people and in hotels, we delighted in finally having a place to ourselves. We changed into work clothes and started sweeping and mopping.

My parents had mailed our package of household items to the Peace Corps office during training. Our "care package to ourselves" even contained mosquito netting, which proved to be large enough to cover the double bed in the main bedroom. We'd bought a mop and a broom locally as well as—thank heaven—two oscillating fans, which we managed to get just before the new 10 per cent value-added tax went into effect.

Even with the fans going, we sweated profusely as we mopped and scrubbed. Mosquitos attacked us whenever we held still long enough for them to land. Our little radio was set to the reggae station, on maximum volume. The house smelled of fresh paint, bleach, and pine disinfectant. The water in the icetrays had actually started to freeze in the refrigerator's tiny freezing compartment. By late afternoon, with our familiar "stuff" spread out on tables, shelves and dresser tops, the house had already started to look like home.

We walked together to a neighborhood grocery store to buy food and some well-deserved, cold Red Stripes. We also bought some of the mosquito coils we'd gotten accustomed to at Alvira's. Green spirals that perched on little tin holders, you lit the outer tip and they burned like incense, giving off pungently-scented smoke. The brand we bought was "FISH Mosquito Destroyer," manufactured by the Blood Protection Company, Ltd., in Hong Kong. The box they came in proclaimed that the smoke made mosquitos "swirl, swoop, swoon and perish," although I think it merely annoyed the little buggers. Still, without them, the mosquitoes were intolerable.

We walked back in the twilight drinking our beers, my knapsack bulging with supplies. We noticed that a few houses had satellite dishes in the yard. As we went through the neighborhood, we called out "good night" to passers-by and to people sitting out on their porches, behind the inevitable fences and walls. We felt a lot of eyes on us, white people being a rare sight in Vinyardtown. Dogs barked at us from behind the fences as we passed, but the people all seemed friendly enough.

Back at the house we unpacked our bread, milk, packaged food, and produce, putting things on shelves in the kitchen or in the fridge. We were both tired from our day of cleaning. I broke out some gin and made a drink with a lime from the tree in the back.

Maria wasn't ready for a break yet. We'd checked out the double bed in the back bedroom and had found that it sagged in the middle. Maria had noticed some plywood scraps of different sizes leaning against the side of the house, so she set about cleaning them off and placing them between the bedsprings and the mattress. When she was finished arranging the boards, she called me back to lie beside her and test the results. We both pronounced the bed satisfactory.

We decided that she'd get the dresser in the master bedroom and I'd use the one across from the small bed in the guest bedroom. Both bedrooms also had wardrobes for hanging clothes. Besides that, the furniture consisted of a small sofa, several chairs, and a desk in the living room, and a formica-topped kitchen table and four more chairs in the part of the room adjacent to the kitchen, where the fridge stood in the corner. A slab pillar in the middle of the room, between the desk and the table, separated the living room from the dining area.

While Maria resumed unpacking and arranging, I started supper. Since we had no gas for the stove, I was thankful that our parcel from the States had included a plug-in "hot pot." I made macaroni and cheese with tunafish, and a big salad. We listened to the evening news on the radio as we ate. I remember hearing that Tennessee Ernie Ford had just died and being surprised that he'd been well-enough known in Jamaica for his death to make the news.

After supper we both felt tired, but I wasn't about to share my bed with any mosquitos. So I went back to the bedroom and strung up the mosquito netting over the bed. It had an elastic strip attached to the bottom of the netting that fit snugly around the mattress, so you couldn't just hop in and hop out of bed. It took a little getting used to, waking up in the middle of the night to go to the bathroom and squeezing out from under the netting; but it took a pretty crafty bug to slip in when one of us was getting into or out of bed. And if one did make it past the barrier, it sure wasn't going to make it out alive.

Few Jamaican homes had hot running water. Although the sinks and showers in our house all had hot and cold faucets, we only got cold water. We faced two years of hot weather, cold showers, hungry mosquitos, and doing the laundry by hand. We hadn't known exactly what to expect when we'd volunteered, but we'd known we'd have to give up some of the comforts most of us take for granted in the U.S.

"It could be worse," I said to Maria. "We could be in a mud hut in the Mauritanian desert, where it's 120 degrees in the shade."

We took our cold showers and got ready for bed. By the time we settled in under the gauzy tent of mosquito netting, which rippled in the passing breeze of the oscillating fan, our bodies were already sticky with sweat again. The staccato beat of dancehall music blared in the near distance and the neighborhood dogs barked and bayed by the light of a waning moon. We kissed and I turned out the reading light we'd rigged to the headboard.

As we lay snuggled together in the dark I said, "Nighttime on the plains of Kilamanjaro. Me Gregory Peck. You Ava Gardner."

"You full of bull," Maria replied wearily.

The next day Maria had a meeting to attend, but I didn't have to report to the Detox Ward until Monday. My first priority was to get a cylinder of cooking gas for the stove. I looked in the yellow pages of the phone book that the previous tenants had left and located the nearest distributor, on the main road just inland from the harbor shoreline. We'd already opened a checking account at a bank, so I put a check in my ankle wallet, locked up, and set out.

The nearest bus stop for the major bus routes was out on the highway that runs parallel to Long Mountain. When you're facing the mountain and take the highway to the left, it climbs uphill at a slight grade, passing the National Stadium. Past the stadium, it curves around the end of the mountain and intersects with Old Hope Road, which takes you up into Liguanie. To the right, the highway leads down to the harbor and out of town in the direction of the airport and the east coast. At some intersections on my walk out to the bus stop, I could see all the way down to the harbor. We later learned that we lived closer to dungtung Kingston than any other PCVs—right on the borderline of the part of Kingston that the Peace Corps staff considered safe for housing.

A number of places in Kingston have names in common with similar places in America.

Most of Long Mountain is jungle-clad wilderness, but the posh neighborhood on the slopes of the tip of the mountain is called Beverly Hills. The national psychiatric hospital, down by the harbor, is named Belleview—the same name as the psychiatric hospital in New York City. One way to tell someone, "you're crazy" in Jamaica is to say, "Mon, you belahng in Belleview."

Out at the bus stop I again noticed signs of the unfortunate proliferation of U.S. pop culture in Jamaica. Boomboxes on the street more often played the music of Mariah Carey, Natalie Cole, Michael Jackson, and The Beastie Boys than the sweet sounds of reggae. I'd heard Whitney Houston's "I-I-I Will Always Love You" on other peoples' radios so much I'd grown sick of it. At the bus stop I saw people wearing tee shirts with pictures of The Flintstones, Mickey Mouse, The Simpsons, and Garfield. A slang term for "gang" was "posse," borrowed from the Westerns that had been popular on the island in the Fifties and Sixties. Among the gang graffiti I saw painted on walls near the bus stop were "Bugs Bunny Krew" and "Trenchtown Posse."

Many people stood waiting at the bus stop, which is located in front of a large school complex called Olympia School. Street vendors sold sweets to the uniformed schoolchildren entering and exiting the grounds. I waited in the sweltering heat, in the merciless glare of the morning sun. The knot of commuters crowded in the shade of the bus stop shelter dissolved as a bus approached. The bus came to a halt and disgorged passengers. I joined the throng of would-be riders and managed to insinuate my body through the door. The 'ductor called out, "Drivah!", and the bus lurched into motion. I wasn't able to reach a handrail and had to fight to keep my balance when the driver swerved to avoid potholes, even though I couldn't possibly have fallen down. The crowd in the bus pitched and heaved like a heavy tide.

The ride down to the waterfront only took ten minutes, but by the time I got off the bus my shirt was plastered to my sweaty back. I checked buildings for street numbers and got my bearings. I soon found the address I was looking for and went inside the building.

The only person in the office was an old man, who sat on a chair against the wall beside the big, barred window. He appeared to just be passing the time, sitting in the breeze of a floor fan. "Miss Hardware," he called out, " s'mahdy here fi see you!"

Miss Hardware emerged from the door behind the counter. "Wha' I can do fi you?"

I told her I needed a cylinder of cooking gas and she asked if I had an empty cylinder at the house. When I told her I didn't, she said that I'd have to pay a deposit on a cylinder. The empty cylinder would thereafter be exchanged for a full one the next time I ordered gas. She filled out an order form and told me the total cost. I wrote a check. She inspected it, then told me that I could expect Mr. Shakespeare to come by and deliver the gas that afternoon.

My business accomplished, I walked back the way I'd come and found the bus stop nearest the highway I'd ridden down on. I caught the first bus to come along and got off at the stop opposite the one at which I'd caught the bus down to the harbor. I crossed the highway and headed back to the house.

At home I read for awhile, then fixed a peanut butter and banana sandwich for lunch. I feared that "soon com" regarding the delivery of the cooking gas might mean two or three days, but Miss Hardware was as good as her word. Around three, Mr. Shakespeare arrived in a truck filled with gas cylinders. As I'd expected, he more resembled Othello than the Bard of Avon. His crew manhandled a full cylinder through the house to the kitchen, where he hooked up the gas line to the stove, opened the valve, and showed me how to light the pilot light.

I spent most of the rest of the week reading about addiction and drug rehabilitation from the small library I'd assembled before we'd left the States, and organizing for work. A good friend, Pam Flowers, who's a clinician and specializes in drug abuse treatment, had put together some material on recovery and relapse prevention which later proved to be very helpful.

On Friday Maria and I went down by the harbor for a tour of Belleview Hospital. A Sister who worked in the administration building took us across the yard to what she said were some typical wards. As we walked among coconut palms and croton hedges, she told us of problems similar to those faced by state mental institutions in the U.S.: stigma, family abandonment, understaffing, and the smuggling of contraband drugs onto the hospital grounds. She admitted to chronic shortages of medications and medical supplies, but it wasn't until later that we learned just how severe the shortages were.

Although clearly not on a par with modern hospitals in industrial nations, what we saw that day wasn't nearly as bad as what we'd been led to expect. The Sister took us through clean, orderly wards whose patients seemed to be getting adequate care. Wherever we went, however, patients tried to beg us. We didn't tour any back wards, with floridly psychotic and regressed patients.

As we were about to leave one ward to visit another, a white-coated orderly approached us and told the Sister that she was needed in the administration building. She excused herself and turned us over to Lionel, a friendly patient in his fifties who'd been following us around. She encouraged us to continue our tour. Lionel had already told me, in a confidential tone, that he was the Prime Minister.

Emboldened by his new status as our guide, he took on an air of authority. As he showed us around he told us about himself. "Me nah really a patien' yahso. Me nah like dese odders... you know." He tapped the side of his head and rolled his eyes. "In ahctual fahct me de King ob de Worl'. Me inherit de mahntle ob Emperor Haile Sallassie when 'im die."

Haile Salassie, erstwhile Emperor of Ethiopia, is believed by Rastafarians to have been of the linage of the House of David, and the modern incarnation of the Son of God—whom they call Jah. He is given a series of honorific titles such as Lion of Judah, King of Kings, Jehovah Rastafari, Elect of Himself, and Protector of the Universe. I'd heard that true Rastas believe he never died, so I knew that Lionel wasn't a Rastamon. He was obviously, however, Elect of Himself.

Although he seemed delusional, Lionel didn't exhibit any other telltale symptoms of a severe thought disorder, such as impaired concentration or social skills deficits. Indeed, he was sharp enough to shoo away the patients who tried to beg us, saying " Dem Peace Cahr Bolunteer. Dem nah get paid."

When we'd seen enough we excused ourselves and thanked Lionel for showing us around. Not surprisingly, he asked for a tip.

"No, mon," I said. "You don't need money. You're the Prime Minister!"

He grinned and winked. "An' King ob de Worl'."

While I never had occasion to return, Maria would later teach student nurses at Bellview. She got to see parts of the hospital that we hadn't been shown and came home with horror stories about the conditions patients lived under and the treatment they received at the hands of some nurses and orderlies.

On Friday evening those of us from Group 58 who lived in Kingston gave a party at Bamboo Pen to welcome "Group 58 +", which consisted of five PCVs who had been evacuated from Haiti during a coup d'etat, just after their swearing-in. They'd just arrived on the island. They were to get a few weeks training in patois and then go to work. Caroo prepared the main dish, curried goat. The rest of us brought pot luck side dishes, and bought the beer and soft drinks.

The newcomers said they felt overwhelmed by all that they'd experienced over the past month or two. They told of their sudden evacuation by helicopter from their villages in Haiti to the Dominican Republic, in the midst of the military coup. They'd had to leave most of their belongings behind. They'd been sent to Washington to recover, re-provision themselves, and await new assignments. We tried our best to make them feel welcome as "adopted" members of our training group. Maria and I quickly bonded with Paul and Jackie, a married couple in their forties, like ourselves. Jackie would be teaching at the School of Nursing with Maria.

Ever since we got married, Maria and I have shared the household responsibilities. We each prepare supper on alternate nights and we each do the laundry on alternate weeks. On Saturday morning, Maria got up around seven. She ate breakfast and then started washing clothes, to get the chore out of the way before it got too hot. When I got out of bed and joined her out at the laundry sinks, to study her methods, she already had an audience—a big, gray-striped tomcat. At first he regarded me from a distance, like I was encroaching on his territory; but he soon came over and sniffed me, and before long he allowed me to pet him. He proved to be a very affection-loving "puss"—as Jamaicans call cats.

Maria washed the clothes in one sink, rubbing by hand and scrubbing dirty spots with a brush, and rinsed in the other. Then she rinsed the clothes a second time under running water until all traces of the soap were gone and hung the laundry on the clotheslines opposite the sinks. She had to repeat the process with two more loads. The third load was towels and sheets, which she hung on a long clothesline strung in the space between the two houses.

After watching her doing the first load and getting acquainted with the puss, I'd gone inside to eat breakfast and read the newspaper. (We'd subscribed to *The Daily Gleaner*, at that time Kingston's only daily paper.) By the time Maria had finished and joined me inside, I was merely sticky with sweat, while she was as wet as the wash.

Besides the cat, we'd already seen a mongoose in the yard. They're a common sight on the island, having been imported by the British during colonial times to keep down the snake population. There are no poisonous snakes indigenous to Jamaica and, due to the mongooses, snakes of any kind are seldom to be seen. However, the same kind of lizards we'd first seen at the Sandhurst often came in the windows and crawled the walls of our home.

The birds we saw most often were egrets and johncrows—black carrion birds, ugly as buzzards up close, but as beautiful as hawks when viewed in flight, soaring the thermal currents up in the mountains. Of the several species of hummingbirds, the most unusual was the doctor bird— Jamaica's "national bird"—recognizable by its long, curling tailfeathers.

As for the insect population, Jamaica has scorpions, as well as large centipedes that have a nasty bite. Among the several species of cockroaches, the worst are huge, flying roaches that are armored like tanks.

On Saturday afternoon we decided to take the bus to New Kingston, the modern "uptown" business district in the center of Kingston. A hotel just down the street from the Peace Corps office, the Courtley, allowed PCVs to use their swimming pool. Most sunny Saturday and Sunday afternoons you could expect to find other Volunteers there. The poolside and the PC office were major links in the grapevine. Volunteers stationed in other parts of the island almost always visited the office when they came to

Kingston, to check for mail and pick up packages, or to leave notes for other Volunteers on the message board.

Noticing a weekend flea market that had been set up within a walled compound near New Kingston, we got off the bus several stops early to check it out, thinking we might find some inexpensive things for the house. But this market wasn't like its U.S. counterparts, with second-hand items being sold cheaply. Instead, Jamaicans who rent booths at flea markets import U.S. and other foreign goods in bulk (food, small appliances, fabrics, paper products, etc.), and sell them for what the market will bear—slightly less than store prices. The atmosphere was commercial, not down-home. When we saw that there were no cheap, used items or distinctively Jamaican artifacts for sale, we left and walked the rest of the way to the pool.

Once at the Courtley, we greeted several other Volunteers who sat at tables or lay sunning themselves on deckchairs at poolside, and went into the dressing rooms to change into our swimsuits. We spent two or three hours chatting, reading, and swimming. Then we changed back into our streetclothes, checked for mail at the PC office, did some food shopping at Wong's supermarket, and caught a bus back home.

Over the next two years I spent many a Saturday afternoon in similar fashion, sometimes with Maria, sometimes by myself. She's never enjoyed lounging around in the sun the way I do, and was having a harder time adjusting to the tropical heat.

A psychiatric nurse, Maria had never had to wear a nurses' uniform, let alone a starched white cap. However, at her job she'd have to wear the faculty uniform, and she'd had two of them made for her by a seamstress in Papine. In the relative cool of the late afternoon, she modeled her new outfit for me—a strange shade somewhere between pink and tan, unflatteringly cut. Maria hated it.

I took one look and told her she looked like an Iranian stewardess. I teased her into putting on her "cute little nurses cap" and we both got to chuckling; so, leaving her cap on, she changed into her bathing suit and I took pictures of her in pin-up poses. For posterity.

Sunday, after I'd fixed a breakfast of corned beef hash and eggs and we'd both read *The Sunday Gleaner*, we planned to take a long walk around the neighborhood. But just as we were about to leave, dark clouds filled the sky and a hard rain began to fall. The rain lasted throughout the afternoon. We'd become accustomed to almost-daily rain—sometimes just fleeting showers or thunderstorms, sometimes hours of drizzle. I always carried a collapsable umbrella in my rucksack and Maria kept one in her shoulder bag.

This rainstorm was our first gullywasher. At times during the afternoon we had to shout to hear one another over the roar of the rain on our aluminum roof. We went out and stood under the front overhang to watch the torrent, awed by its power.

Monday dawned bright and hot—our first workday at our new jobs. Maria wore her uniform and carried her starched-and-ironed nursing cap in her shoulder bag. I wore khaki pants and a short-sleeved dress shirt—no tie. Sister Burton, a senior member of the faculty at the School of Nursing, had arranged to pick us up in her car on a corner just short of the Olympia School bus stop. As it turned out, she drove us in most workdays, sparing us the hassle of competing for space on buses during the worst of the morning commuter crush. Since we boarded at the Papine terminus for the ride home, the afternoon commute wasn't nearly as bad as what we faced on the occasional mornings that we didn't get a ride to work.

Although Maria continued to address her formally on the job, in the car Sister Burton preferred that we call her Dorothy. A thin, dark-skinned woman in her sixties, she quickly showed herself to be a warm and witty soul. Always willing to answer our questions, she also often made spontaneous, wry observations about her country and her people—especially their politics and their driving habits.

While the buses had to take the long route around the tip of the mountain, Dorothy knew a shortcut that took us up on winding roads past the ritzy estates of Beverly Hills, where satellite dishes were the rule and not the exception. The rich people who lived there, she told us, were characterized as "stoshuss" by the common folk—snooty, putting on airs. "They say, 'Dem t'ink seh dem live inna Hollywood,' " she told us.

Maria experienced much frustration during the first months at her work-site. Due to delays in obtaining Jamaican nursing licenses, the five Peace Corps nurses assigned to the faculty languished in an "extended orientation phase." Maria did her best to use her time meaningfully, spending much of it on Ward 21, the Psychiatric Ward. She got to know the nursing staff and the ward routine, and played dominoes—a popular game in Jamaica—with the patients. She also attended "grand rounds", where some of Jamaica's premiere psychiatrists interviewed patients behind a one-way mirror, then reviewed their symptoms and treatment with attending psychiatric residents.

I, on the other hand, got to jump right into the deep end of the pool. I couldn't tell who was officially in charge of the day-to-day operations on the Detox Ward, and it soon became obvious to me that there was no clearly-defined treatment model to guide ward operations. The treatment of the eight men on the ward consisted of a morning devotional; several weekly ward "community" meetings; individual counseling sessions with the nursing staff, on an as-needed basis; periodic medical assessments by the ward resident; and a few weekly Twelve Step meetings conducted by members of local chapters of Alcoholics Anonymous and Narcotics Anonymous. Nobody seemed to know just what I had to contribute, except perhaps Dr. W, the Ward Resident. He encouraged me to just do what I felt comfortable doing.

Hesitant to comment on the absence of a treatment model, I took Dr. W's encouragement as an invitation to demonstrate my competencies. Having had no structure imposed upon me, I leapt into the breach, hoping to establish credibility as a member of the ward staff. At the first "ward rounds" (weekly treatment staffing) I attended, I asked if it would be appropriate for me to conduct group therapy three times a week. Everybody seemed to think that would be just fine. I asked if anyone had any ideas or recommendations for what else I could do. When nobody did, I asked if they'd like me to do individual clinical assessments on each of the patients on the ward. This also seemed to meet with everyone's approval.

The staff was friendly and polite, but nobody volunteered much of anything to me. In the absence of explicit guidance, I had to either figure things out for myself or ask specific questions. Dr. W spent little time on the ward and Sister M appeared to be more an administrator than a clinical supervisor to the nursing staff—none of whom was designated as the head nurse on the ward. I decided that the first obvious task was to establish good working relationships with the ward nurses. I'd deal with the ambiguities later.

During the first week I mostly watched and listened, learning the ward routines. The current batch of patients were in the second of their four weeks of treatment. I started doing individual clinical assessments, knowing that this would be helpful to me when I started my group work the following week. I wrote down my findings in the patients' medical records.

I declined invitations to join the morning devotionals, as I keep my clinical practice secular. Knowing that most Jamaicans are Christian, I hoped this wouldn't bother any of the nursing staff. They seemed to accept my rationale that some patients wouldn't be Christians and might appreciate having someone on the staff whose treatment wasn't religiously-oriented. I let them know that I personally believe spirituality plays an important role in recovery from drug abuse, and that I recognize the value of Twelve Step programs for many addicts.

The community meetings I witnessed during my first week usually quickly deteriorated into gripe sessions. I saw that the staff nurses either reacted defensively to complaints about treatment, or responded by giving simple advice such as, "you just hahve to be more patient." I recognized the aggressive griping as a tactic being used by some addicts in the program to divert the focus from themselves and the personal problems related to their addictions. Normally I would have called attention to the tactic and brought the focus back where it belonged, but I kept my mouth shut. The nurses didn't appear to be formally trained as clinical counselors or to know much about group dynamics, but I knew this wasn't the time for me to step in. The best thing I could do, I decided, was to get the nurses to co-lead groups with me, and to model counseling techniques and group intervention strategies.

Besides the lack of structured treatment in the program, other problems included ward security and the prohibition against cigarette smoking in the unit. The staff had caught patients surreptitiously smoking. If cigarettes got smuggled in, other contraband could get in. Drug dealers sold their wares right on the hospital grounds.

The unit was a locked ward, but the staff didn't have the means to adequately enforce security measures. When patients left the ward on a pass, to go to the X-ray Department and to other places in the hospital, they went unaccompanied. Visitors came onto the ward without being searched. Meals were delivered to the ward by underpaid orderlies, some of whom could be bribed to drop off contraband along with the food. Many addicts constantly test any limits placed upon them and some can be very charming, persistent, and persuasive when they want something. With three shifts working on the unit, some staff members could be coaxed into relaxing the rules.

"Nurse. You mos' ohnderstahn. Me *wan'* give op crock cocaine. Me *mos'* give op crock, or me fi *dead* frohm it! Me life depen' ahn dis prograhm. But Nurse... me nah wan' give op cigarette-dem. Cigarette nah mek me relopse. Cigarette calm me nerve-dem, help me fight the craving fi crock. *Please*, nurse! When me sistah com visit me tonight, she bring me *wan* pock cigarette-dem. You cahn keep it in de nurse station an' jos give me *wan* likkle cigarette ahfter each meal. Five minute-dem to smohke it out-side. Mek me hahv sahmting to look fahrward to. *Please!"*

In order to be admitted to the program, patients had to sign a treat-ment agreement that included adherence to the hospital's no-smoking policy; but many smokers had no personal motivation to give up ciga-rettes. Some addicts entered treatment to avoid problems on the streets and weren't truly motivated to give up their drug-of-choice, either. Others believed they could give up crack cocaine and substitute alcohol and ganja. Getting contraband substances on the ward became the favorite game of some patients.

The problems with ward security and contraband continued through-out my two years in the program.

One of the biggest challenges I faced in doing group therapy on the ward was overcoming the language barrier. Some patients had received a good education and could communicate clearly in the Queen's English; others understood English perfectly well, but spoke only in patois. When Jamaicans converse with one another, their delivery tends to be rapid-fire. In addition, crack cocaine was the drug-of-choice for most of the patients admitted to the ward. Cocaine addicts tend not to be mellow, laid-back types. Even talking to patients individually, I sometimes had to ask them to slow down or to repeat themselves.

In talking to them, I picked up on some of the drug slang. To "lick on" or "tek a lick" means to take a "hit" of crack or ganja. Crack is often referred to as "rock." Ganja also goes by the name "herbs" on the street. A joint, or marijuana cigarette, is known as a "spliff." Ganja users also smoke it in pipes called "chillum pipes."

Group therapy with cocaine addicts in the early stages of recovery can be very intense, especially in that some of them experience strong cravings and/or have no personal motivation to participate in treatment groups. Some of the addicts on the ward entered treatment thinking that they'd be given medication that would eliminate their cravings. Jamaican men have a reputation for machismo, and men raised with the macho ethic don't want to bare their souls to anyone, let alone strangers.

Conducting group therapy requires that leaders not only carefully attend to the words being spoken by group members, but to the subtle nuances of speech. The group leader also has to observe the body language and behavior of group members, to keep in touch with the emerging dynamics. Every group is unique. I'm sure that I missed a lot during my first few months on the job. It took all of my concentration to keep up with what was being said, while also paying attention to the non-verbal behaviors of the group members.

To be an effective group leader, you need to not only have a thorough knowlege of group dynamics, you have to apply that knowledge strategically in interventions. A professor in my psychology graduate program taught me that all therapies involve overt or covert power struggles. Clients, he said, may genuinely want to change; but that doesn't mean they're malleable or easily amenable to making the changes that will improve their lives. Giving up old habits, cherished self-delusions, and familiar (if maladaptive) defenses is a scary process, even if you're beginning to view them with new insight. Most clients in therapy both seek and resist change, as Freud pointed out.

Dealing with resistance can be a complex process even in individual therapy. In group therapy the complexity increases geometrically, two important variables being the size of the group and the motivation of the group members to engage in the group process. Resistance comes either in the form of one-on-one power struggles within the group, or in "triangulations."

For instance, "Tom" might try to take over the group, engaging in a linear power struggle with the group leader; or he might engage in a one-on-one power struggle with "Dick", trying to curry favor within the group. Triangulations occur when Tom and Dick form an alliance to challenge the leadership of the group leader, or to vilify "Harry" in the eyes of the group. Alternately, Harry may try to form an alliance with the group leader, against Tom. Sometimes there are multiple, simultaneous triangulations going on within the group.

Good leaders have to be aware of the power struggles within the group and to do their best to defuse them. If they can't stay in control of the group process, it becomes therapeutically useless, or even destructive. Happily, some aspects of group process tend to work in the leader's favor.

One of the most effective techniques a leader can use in group therapy is simply to label or describe the tactics he or she observes. ("Tom, you seem to be trying pretty hard to convince us that Harry isn't serious about recovery.") Even if Tom isn't ready to admit to the tactic, at least some of the group members will recognize Tom's behavior as a tactic, and may even let him know that they know. Group members can learn from one anothers' behaviors, especially when group leaders or other members make on-target observations. As they come to realize that the leader isn't judging them for being who they are and won't tolerate destructive criticism within the group, trust begins to grow. Positive alliances form and the group process starts promoting self-disclosure and healing.

The following Monday I held my first group meeting on the ward. I hadn't been able to persuade any of the nurses to co-lead with me and I felt nervous. Would I, a white man from a different culture, have credibility with the men in the group? How would Jamaicans be different from Americans in a group therapy session? I told myself, *expect the unexpected.*

At ten o'clock I set about rounding up the six patients remaining in the program. One man, Alfred, had just been dismissed from the ward, having been caught smoking crack during the weekend. He packed his things to leave as I told the others we needed to get started. Another patient, Trevor, commiserated with him. Before I could start the session, I had to persuade Trevor to join the other five men, whom I'd already coaxed into the dayroom. Two of them had tried to get me to excuse them from group, claiming they felt bad. I'd finally overcome their resistance, but Trevor still held out.

"Me nah wan' com to group, mon. Me too hupset 'bout Ahlfred. Im mek wan likkle mistake, an' you kick im out de prograhm. *Every* mon desarve a secon' chahnce!"

"Trevor, I know you're upset. Alfred, I'm really sorry about what happened, but this is one rule we can't bend. Trevor, if we let Alfred stay it would undermine the whole program. We'd be saying to all of you that you can use, once, and stay. Now come on and let's start group."

"Me tell you, me nah feel like com to group today. Me com nex' time."

"Trevor, if I let you avoid group because you don't feel like attending, that would tell the others that they only have to attend if they feel like it. You signed a treatment agreement that included participating in the program. Group is part of the program. Besides, group is a place you can talk about your feelings. Come on now. You're keeping everybody waiting."

By the time Trevor relented, two of the others had left the group room and had to be rounded up again. When we'd all finally assembled, the resistance was almost tangible.

I started by introducing myself. I talked briefly about my background, what brought me to Jamaica, and my experience with addictions treatment. I seemed to have the attention of four group members. Trevor and another man inclined their bodies away from me and stared at the walls, letting everyone know that only their bodies were in the room with the rest of us.

"My priority today," I went on, " is for us all to tell each other something about ourselves and why we're here, and to discuss group rules. But it's clear to me that at least some of you have other priorities. What's on your minds, gentlemen?"

Nobody spoke. Trevor pointedly avoided looking at me.

"Trevor, everybody here knows you're upset about Alfred leaving the program. Why don't you tell us—"

"Im nah *leave*," Trevor exploded, finally looking at me, "im kick out de prograhm! It nah fair! True, im nah s'pose to use ahn de wahrd. Bot im only tek wan, two lick ah rock. Im *serious* 'bout recohvery. Im jos give in to a craving de wan time. Im desarve a secon' chance! You people got heart-dem ah stohne."

He tried to stir up support within the group. The other patient who'd pointedly ignored me at the start of group allied himself with Trevor in the group's first triangulation, trying to undermine my role as leader. The rest of the group members either gave lukewarm support to Trevor and the other man, or kept their silence. I encouraged each of them to speak his piece. After the momentum slowed and everyone who had something to say had spoken, I responded. As I talked I made eye contact with each man in turn.

"I'm a plain-spoken man and I'm going to tell you exactly what I think. I'm sorry Alfred chose to use and I'm sorry he's not here with us anymore. I wish him well, and if he's serious about recovery he'll attend NA meetings and work his own program. But if we'd made an exception for him, we'd have to make an exception for the next person in this program who uses. If we'd let him stay, we'd have been telling all of you that we don't really mean what we say, and that this program is bullshit."

"Bot Jeff," Trevor interrupted, leaning forward in his chair, "it nah fair—"

"No, wait, let me finish. You've had your say, Trevor; let me have mine. Then you'll all have a chance to speak again."

Trevor sat back, glaring at me.

"Thank you. Here's what I think. I think that every day, every hour, every minute, every second that one of you stays on this ward while you're using, or planning to use, is bullshit. If you can't stay clean on the detox ward, just how do you think you're going to stay clean when you're back on the street? Gentlemen, if we'd let Alfred stay, we would *not* have been doing him a favor. We would have been enabling him. Any of you know what I mean by enabling?"

Most of the men shook their heads and nobody spoke. Trevor seemed to know where I was going, but kept his sullen silence.

"We'll be talking a *lot* about enabling over the next two weeks. Enabling is anything a person does for an addict that helps him to stay addicted. It's rescuing the addict from the natural consequences of his addiction—financial consequences, legal consequences, social conse- *death* quences, whatever. Most enablers do it because they think they're helping. They do it out of love, or kindness, because they don't understand addiction. Like your friend who lends you money only after you swear to him you won't spend it on cocaine, and ten minutes later you're lickin' on your crack pipe. Or your mother, who bails you out of jail for the third time, and you head straight for the crack house. You know what I'm talking about. Guys, one thing I guarantee we will *not* do in this program is to help you stay addicted. Now…what have you got to say?"

Trevor tried again, but with less wind behind his sails. Then someone spoke out in support of the staff's decision to dismiss Alfred, saying that allowing him to stay would have undermined his own chances of benefitting from the program. The consensus slowly tilted away from Trevor. To make sure that he hadn't lost face, I praised him for his good intentions and for caring enough to stand up for Alfred.

The initial conflict apparently settled, we went on to do personal introductions. Some of the men had to be coaxed into telling us more than just their names and where they were from, but others spoke freely about themselves and their use of drugs. The session ended on a positive note. At Trevor's suggestion, we all joined hands in a circle and recited the Serenity Prayer. I felt good about the way I'd handled the first of what would be many power struggles, within my first group in Jamaica.

A natural leader, Trevor hadn't finished challenging my control of the group. When we met that Wednesday, he took me on again. This time, he verbally attacked a man who'd been admitted halfway into the four week treatment cycle, suggesting that he didn't "belahng."

"Shot op, Clarence! You nah know ahll we been tru in de programh. You nah been here frohm the stahrt."

I responded with a technique I call "psych judo." In judo, you defend yourself from attack by, first, sensing how the force of the attack is coming at you. You grab hold of your assailant, joining his momentum. Then you redirect the force and throw him to the ground. My brand of psych judo often involves the strategic use of humor.

"You're right, Trevor," I said with a straight face. " In fact, I think we should brand an "O" on Clarence's forehead."

Shocked silence.

"For 'outsider.' That way we won't forget and treat him like he's one of us insiders."

They got the point and I got my first laugh from the group. Trevor backed off from his attack. He was learning that good strategy almost always defeats mere tactics, and starting to sense that I could be his ally instead of his adversary. As we developed a relationship based on trust and mutual respect, he began to employ his natural leadership abilities in more positive ways during our sessions.

I started the discussion of group rules by laying-out the universal rules of group therapy: confidentiality, no violence, no threats, and no walking out just because you might not like what was being said. I told the men that they didn't have to ask for permission to leave briefly, if they urgently had to go to the bathroom, but asked that they all try to take care of such physical needs before group.

Everyone, I told them, had to attend every session, unless excused by the medical staff. Then I went on to suggest other guidelines and rules that were open for discussion, although not necessarily negotiable once the group had reached a consensus. Any breach of group rules would be confronted.

I said that the display of any emotion, including anger, was allowed, because we can't always choose our feelings. Group members could criticize and confront other members, including me, as long as they made the criticisms in a constructive manner. There would be no reading, eating, or other distracting activities. Everybody had the right to express his beliefs and opinions, but nobody had the right to monopolize discussions. I reserved the right to change the topic if the talk became trivial, or irrelevant to recovery and personal growth. Having already used the word "bullshit", myself, I said that the use of profanity was okay by me, unless some group members had strong objections. Gratuitous overuse of profanity, however, would be addressed as a distraction from the group process.

By this time I had learned quite a bit of Jamaican profanity, on the street. Most of it was scatalogical or sexual in nature, as is probably the case in most cultures. Of course, English being the official language, the common Anglo-Saxon obscenities were often heard.

One of the most frequently-heard native epithets, "Ras!", means arse, as do the terms "bohmba" and "bahtty." Jamaica is a very homophobic society, and gay men are often contemptuously referred to as "bahtty mon." Common obscenities include "rasclaht" and "bohmbaclaht" (arse cloth, or toilet paper), as well as "blohdclaht (blood cloth, or menstrual cloth). Some men, when called one of these last three terms, consider them fighting words; so I asked the group to refrain from using them.

Of course, *all* of the group rules got violated at one time or another. The most serious infractions, such as death threats, could lead to immediate expulsion from the program. Repeated violations of some of the minor rules became grist for the mill in group discussions. Enforcing group rules remained a challenge in all the groups I conducted in Jamaica.

The ward staff seemed to be pleased with the role I'd assumed, and as time went on I felt more and more accepted as a member of the treatment team. In addition to my duties on the ward, I'd been appointed to serve on the Drug Abuse Rehabilitation Team (DART), a planning board made up of representatives from the Drug Abuse Secretariat, the University Hospital, and three other Kingston drug treatment programs. The Major represented the Peter's Lane program. Patricia House was a residential therapeutic community for recovering addicts. Addiction Alert served as an outpatient treatment program, based on the Twelve Step model.

From time to time I would also be asked to do public speaking, give talks on drug abuse at schools, present workshops, and speak on panels. Dr. W had asked me if I would give presentations on peer counseling and counseling techniques for youth workers in the inland town of Linstead, and I said I would.

Due to the limited office space on the ward and the fact that I had nothing to do on the ward when the patients were engaged in other treatment activities than my own, I'd been given a tiny office in a practically abandoned wing of Ward 21. Bare save for a desk, two chairs and a fan, the office served as my retreat from the often stressful environment of the Detox Ward. There, I could prepare presentations, work on my relapse prevention curriculum, and eat lunch.

The empty wing had been a childrens' clinic, as evidenced by the fanciful artwork on the walls of some of the bare offices. In other rooms, dusty books were heaped in mounds waist-high at their centers, or stood in rows of even higher stacks. Discarded library books, a gift from Canada, they included just about kind of book you'd expect to find in a library: textbooks, reference books, biographies, juvenile and adult fiction, how-to books, travelogues, and so on.

They'd simply been dumped, unsorted, and nobody had bothered to do anything to get them distributed. I could see that sorting them would be dirty, tedious work—a task for a true bibliophile. Like me.

I scrounged cleaning supplies and cleaned out my office and a restroom. I had my own key to the wing, and the door stayed locked most of the time. In my spare time, dustrag in hand, I started converting the mound of books into stacks, sorting as I went.

I also started exploring the the adjacent campus of the University of the West Indies. Built on the site of a massive sugar cane plantation, the grounds are criss-crossed by the crumbling remains of a network of aquaducts. Most of the main campus is enclosed within a ring road. A mural depicting aspects of Jamaican life covers the entire wall on one side of a large building at the center of the campus. I discovered the campus branch of our bank near the university bookstore, and soon realized that it was more convenient to use than the branch in Liguanie. On days of good weather when I hadn't packed a lunch, I'd walk over to the university for a sandwich and a "box drink" of fruit juice, and eat lunch at one of the many outdoor tables on the campus.

A chain link fence in the rear of the hospital grounds marked the boundary between the University Hospital and UWI. From my office it took about ten minutes to walk through a sports field, past a row of dormitories and the university library, to the campus center—a trip I'd make at least once a week.

One day I found the gates between the hospital and the university blocked, the barricades manned by students protesting a tuition hike. I showed them my hospital ID, but they said they would only allow people with student IDs to pass. The barricade boss relented somewhat and said that I could go through if I made some gesture of solidarity with the student protesters. I told him that as a PCV I couldn't take sides in local political disputes. He shrugged, and I gave up and turned around. The next day everything had returned to normal.

An Indian pharmacist at the hospital—a United Nations Volunteer— invited me to serve on a panel at a drug abuse treatment symposium. The Pharmaceutical Society and the Lions Club co-sponsored the event. I took a bus the Courtley Hotel on a weeknight and soon found myself in distinguished company. The panel was made up of some of Jamaica's leading experts in drug abuse treatment. Dr. G, author of the Drug Abuse Counsel's master plan, the Integrated Demand Reduction Program ("IDER"), chaired the panel. The audience kept us answering questions until after ten o'clock. I suddenly felt like a relatively big fish in a relatively small pond.

Attending my first DART meeting, I again found myself in the presence of some of the same experts. It looked like I might even have some say in the development of drug treatment policy. However, I also ran into what would prove to be an ethical dilemma. Dr. S, who supervised the resident doctors on the Detox Ward, wanted us to do research in the program. To that end, he wanted me to give the MMPI, a standardized American personality inventory, to every patient admitted to the ward. I'd given the MMPI to many people over the years, but didn't consider it an appropriate instrument to use with Jamaicans.

You interpret MMPI scores by comparing them with statistical profiles developed from years of research. The most you can really say, diagnostically, about an individual's pattern of responses to hundreds of True/False questions is, "this person's pattern of responses is similar to the response patterns of persons who've been given a diagnosis of so-and-so." The research literature on the MMPI is based on the population of North America; its statistical "norms" are American. Given that Jamaica has its own distinctive culture, it's not appropriate to interpret the MMPI results of Jamaican subjects, without first doing research and developing Jamaican norms.

Dr. S. seemed sure that such local norms had been developed but, in many hours spent at both the UWI library and the UHWI medical library, I was never able to verify this. My refusal to give the MMPI on the ward didn't win me any points with Dr. S.

As the time for my presentations in Linstead drew near, I spoke to Dr. W about the travel arrangements. The workshop had been scheduled for the Saturday following Thanksgiving, when the embassy had its annual Bamboo Pen turkey feast for any Americans who could attend. I worried that after I finished my presentations at noon, I might not get back to Kingston in time. Dr. W assured me that he'd make the necessary arrangements. He went on to philosophize about the need to be flexible when you live in the West Indies.

"To survive in the Tropics you have to ahlways hahve to be prepared to adahpt to the situation at hahnd and change plahns at the lahst minute, if necessary. The audience of senior citizens you were tohld to expect may turn out to be school children. If they tell you a hurricahne is cohming tomorrow, you'd best ahlso prepahre for an earthquake."

His words proved prophetic, as regards the Linstead trip. A sedan from the Ministry of Youth fetched Maria and me at our house at six-thirty. I remember that as we left Spanish Town and began the ascent into the jungle-clad hills, the car radio blared the English version of a German drinking song: "In heaven there is no beer/ That's why we drink it here!" The driver turned up the volume. When we arrived in Linstead, around eight, we found that the audience consisted, not of youth workers, but of high schoolers.

Maria had accompanied me, prepared to co-lead the counseling workshops. Our experiences that morning reminded me of how well we perform as a team. She had no lesson plan, but supplemented my prepared presentations on peer counseling and counseling techniques, and helped me to field questions from the students. We finished on time and didn't have long to wait before the sedan arrived to take us back to Kingston.

The driver delivered us at Bamboo Pen in plenty of time to enjoy a traditional Thanksgiving feast. Many Volunteers had come to Kingston from around the island. In addition, lots of embassy personnel and most of the contingent of Marine embassy guards attended. A Navy band on shore leave provided the music, mostly jazz and swing. We gorged ourselves on turkey and even got to take some home with us.

In early December I got to attend a workshop sponsored by the Drug Abuse Secretariat, held at an all-inclusive resort in the seaside town of Runaway Bay. Unfortunately, Maria didn't get to accompany me. For three days I lived in the lap of luxury, but spent most of my time in training sessions. I didn't get to go snorkeling or to take advantage of the many other recreational activities available to guests.

Sister M allocated four hours for the ninety minute trip to the north coast. We arrived several hours before the start of the workshop, so I had a little time to enjoy the tourist amenities. I checked into my air-conditioned suite, took a hot shower just because I could, and tuned-in Headline News on the TV. Hostage Terry Anderson had just been released from Lebanon and, in Miami, William Kennedy Smith was on trial for rape. My suite-mate proved to be most compatable. A retired educator named Val, he frequently called me "my brother."

The Secretariat had hired an excellent Canadian trainer, Dr. Don Meeks, who'd worked all over the world as a consultant for the United Nations and the World Health Organization. The faculty also included several Caribbean drug treatment experts and Dr. Michael Beaubrun, Professor Emeritus in Psychiatry at UHWI and, apparently, the Dean of Caribbean Psychiatry.

In the afternoon we met only long enough for a brief orientation session. After a delicious buffet dinner on a verandah overlooking the sea, I retired to my suite to write in my journal, then went down to the beach bar to indulge in the luxury of a "free" Scotch before bedtime. There I found Dr. S, Dr. G, Dr. Meeks, Professor Beaubrun, and the owner of the resort gathered around the bar, telling dirty jokes. I joined them.

Before long, all but Dr. G. and the resort owner, who introduced himself as "Freddie", excused themselves. Those of us remaining at the bar were joined by Howard, a young dancer from Guyana who worked on the ward as a "movement therapist." We learned that Dr. G. and Freddie had been schoolmates at the time of a major turning point in Jamaican education.

Apparently, prior to their "form", or class, only those who could afford to pay for higher education got a shot at it. Their form was the first to take a national examination that, if passed with a high enough score, opened new doors to boys from lower-class backgrounds. They, and some of their friends, had been beneficiaries of the policy.

As the free liquor continued to flow at the bar, they waxed loquacious about the "brilliant" ones from their form, some of whom had gone on to to be influential "seekers of truth" in the private and public sectors. Some of them, due to their lower-class origins and their independence from the Old Boy network, could get away with telling cabinet ministers where to get off.

They told anecdotes about their personal dealings with both Prime Minister Michael Manley and opposition party leader Edward Seaga. (Manley's People's National Party and Seaga's Jamaican Labour Party are roughly equivalent to England's Conservative and Labour parties.) Manley, they agreed, surrounded himself with sycophants; whereas Seaga could take the truth, even if he didn't like it.

Howard and I listened, fascinated by the insider stories and personal recollections of these two former classmates. I remember Freddie making the observation that nobody would trade his own problems for those of another. He drew an analogy with with baggage conveyor belts in airports. "You'd grahb for the old, fahmiliar cahnvas bahg, with the Air Jamaica tahg, rahther thahn the fahncy Sahmsonite suitcase with Swissair tahgs, because at least you'd know what you were in for when you opened it."

Just before we went our separate ways, he told us that he'd almost died earlier in the day, when his car had spun out on him at 60 mph. Steering wheel in one hand and car phone in the other, he'd barely regained control in time and had almost driven off a cliff. As a result of his brush with death, he said, life had a special savor for him that night.

The next day started with a sumptuous outdoor breakfast, followed by a full day of listening to presenters, doing exercises designed to sharpen our clinical skills, and role-playing. We even worked through lunch, munching sandwiches and fruit delivered to the conference rooms by waiters in immaculate uniforms. By the time the final session ended, the sun hung low in the sky.

I lucked out at dinner and got a seat at a table with Dr.s Meeks and Beaubrun, and an attractive young social worker, Dr.Sonya Davison. At first I felt out of my league as a world traveler, as they compared notes on such places as Moscow, Serbo-Croatia and Kenya. Once the conversation had gotten around to me and I mentioned having been born in Tokyo and having lived in Europe for seven years, I felt more included in the circle.

A tall, distinguished-looking gentleman, Dr. Beaubrun proved to be a delightful conversationalist, witty and astute. We got into a conversation about psychology, and he described himself as "a (spiritual) grandson of Adolph Meyer," one of the founders of the science. Over the years he'd worked with some of the big names in the field: Wolpe, Selye, and Eysinck (a tennis partner as well as a colleague), among others. I'd met only one of those he mentioned, Humphrey Osmond. Dr. Beaubrun laughed and agreed with my characterization of Dr. Osmond as "an odd old duck."

Dr.s Meeks and Davison also turned out to be very engaging dinner partners. If Dr. Meeks hadn't "been there" when it came to establishing drug treatment programs in developing countries, it hadn't happened there yet. He'd already demonstrated his worth as a trainer earlier in the day, combining didactic sessions with experiential exercises. He'd shown himself to be especially adept at maintaining the group's focus—no mean feat with a West Indian audience. Some participants kept up a running commentary with the persons around them, and getting small groups to end their diffuse discussions after an exercise was something akin to putting out multiple brush fires.

On our third and final night at the resort, we had a party and sing-along in the piano bar. It started out with a round of Jamaican folksongs and calypso numbers. Then the lights went up and people took turn telling dirty jokes. Dr. S, a true raconteur, served as emcee. He kept referring to a folksong called "Dig a Hole" that everyone but me seemed familiar with. When the jokes ran out, the song finally got sung: "Dig a hole, dig a hole, and put the devil in it."

The next afternoon, the final role playing exercise went on past the scheduled closing time, three-thirty. Sunita, the primary therapist at Addiction Alert, acted as group leader in what Dr. Meeks called "the group from Hell." The group members received instructions to roleplay various types of difficult clients: the Dominator, the Aggressive Blocker, the Avoider, the Attention Getter, and so forth. They got into their roles and tested Sunita's clinical skills to their limits, but we all agreed afterwards that she'd acquitted herself admirably.

Although many of us wanted to hit the road for Kingston, Dr. Meeks wanted to get some closure on the workshop, and things dragged on until past four thirty. Various people praised and thanked the presenters at length, then Dr. G. asked the Major for a benediction. This turned out to be a speech, followed by a reprise of "Dig a Hole," then "This Little Light," "Amen," and the Jamaican National Anthem—both verses. Finally, the Major gave the benediction and we went to pick up our luggage in the lobby.

Sister M. hated driving at night, and the sun had already set by the time we got on the road. She nervously tailgated other vehicles all the way back to Kingston. I didn't get dropped off at home until almost eight, exhausted by my three days at the resort.

Things had started to settle into a routine at home. After I broke up the soil in the garden plot, Maria planted calaloo, cucumbers and parsley. I began harvesting gunga peas from the tree in our front yard. Now that we had a working stove, we'd started to develop a repertoire of dishes and meals.

For starches, we had a wide variety of yams to choose from, as well as rice, beans, and pasta. Although you could buy beef, mutton, pork, and goat in supermarkets, the staple meats for most Jamaicans were chicken, fish, and canned corned beef. With chicken relatively inexpensive on our income, we would often buy a whole bird and bake it. The leftovers went into a chicken soup, flavored with a dried "cock soup" mix and fortified with rice, callaloo, and gunga peas.

One day a young, dreadlocked Rastamon bicycled up to our gate, introducing himself as Willard. He asked if we had any gardening work for him to do. We hired him, as much of the garden was still overgrown. He went to work with his machete, which he called a "cotlass." Thereafter, he dropped by at regular intervals, often bringing coconuts or mangoes as gifts. We, in turn, gave him iced water, fed him peanut butter sandwiches, and paid him a decent wage. More than once I saw him smoking a spliff in the yard, but I just ignored it.

We couldn't have asked for better next-door neighbors than Vasanth and his brother, Shiv. Vasanth proved to be the more outgoing of the two. A student of hotel/restaurant management at the College of Arts, Science, and Technology (CAST), he hoped to emigrate to the U.S. someday and was as interested in America as Maria and I are in India. Many evenings we'd sit out on the patio and discuss topics ranging from national identity and popular culture to politics.

Vasanth loved Clint Eastwood movies and had no sympathy for law-breakers. He liked the way Dirty Harry dealt with them. One day we got to discussing violent crime in Jamaica. Vasanth said that he was less worried about injury at the hands of thugs on the street than at the prospect of treatment for his injuries in a Jamaican hospital.

From time to time Vasanth and Shiv entertained Indian friends in their house—mostly male-only gatherings, at first. The parties lasted late into the night, and often their guests stayed over until the next day. We'd hear laughter and loud, animated conversation in Indian dialects, with Indian or American pop music in the background. As time went on, Maria and I met many of their friends and got invited to some of the parties that included wives and girlfriends. Vasanth didn't date, knowing that his parents, in India, would soon arrange his marriage.

On a hot Saturday morning in December, we met Rick and Jennifer and some other friends from Group 58 at the Parade bus terminus, for a day out on Lime Key. The expedition would require two boat trips. Our packs loaded with snorkeling gear, food, and drinks, we walked together through the spectacle of Coronation Market. Surrounded by milling crowds and thousands of street entrepreneurs, hustlers, and beggars, we made our way to the ferry terminal.

The Kingston-to-Port Royal ferry was the best deal in town. For one Jamaican dollar you could ride from the smelly chaos of dungtung Kingston to the relative serenity of Port Royal, on the tip of the crescent peninsula that shelters the harbor.

Once the pirate capital of the Caribbean, the village is a ghost of its former, infamous incarnation. Most of what was once a thriving port now lies beneath the waves, having sunk during a catastrophic earthquake, in 1692. Some said that God had sent the disaster to lay waste to what had been called "the richest and wickedest city in the world."

Our merry band boarded the ferry and in about a half hour disembarked in Port Royal. It had the look of a sleepy little fishing village, with streets conspicuously cleaner than those of the city across the harbor. One of our number had already been to Lime Key and knew what to do. Several young men hanging around the main dock had power boats which served as water taxis. We hired one of them to take us out to the small island, located a mile or two out on the Caribbean side of the peninsula. To insure that he'd come out at four o'clock and pick us up, he wouldn't be paid until the return trip. We bought a small block of ice from an ice vendor and put it in the group's cooler.

Filled with a sense of adventure, the seven of us loaded our gear in the launch. Our driver untied the lines from the dock and jumped aboard. We made the trip at full throttle, the sun's merciless heat allayed by the breeze and the salt spray as we sped across the calm sea. Our grins, laid end to end, might have spanned the boat's width.

As the hills of Kingston receded in the distance, a speck in the water ahead of us grew into a flat, tree-clad island. Our driver slowed as we approached its shore, and we could see the coral reefs beneath us. A few small boats bobbed at anchor in the gentle swells around the circumference of the island, but it looked like we pretty much had it to ourselves. Golden beaches beckoned us.

The driver cut the engine and coasted into waist-high waters. We'd worn our bathing suits under our clothes, so we stripped off the outer layers and stuffed our street clothes into our packs. We jumped into the cool water and waded ashore, careful to keep our gear high and dry.

Lime Key had no buildings, no residents. Designated a public beach, its only man-made structures were a few sheltered picnic tables, just landward of the beach. Low, twisty-branched trees dominated thick brush that made the center of the island impenetrable. We saw a few lizards during the day, but no warm-blooded critters. However, we could see two other small groups of people up the beach from us. As we claimed one of the shaded tables and began to unpack, Jennifer looked around and said, in her best Valley Girl accent, " And I'm like, where's Gilligan and the Skipper?"

We couldn't see Kingston from the island. Clouds wreathed the distant green mountains on the mainland, but our sky was cloudless. Pelicans swooped and dove into the ocean, and flocks of smaller seabirds flew with synchronized precision. Between the sea and the sky, I saw more shades of blue than I could possibly describe. We quickly covered the table surface with food and beverages, sunscreen, towels, and snorkelling equipment. It took only minutes to prepare a lunch of sandwiches and fruit.

After we'd eaten, Maria and I explored. Although beaches comprised much of the shoreline, we came across stretches where the high brush that covered the center of the island reached all the way to the water; and we had to walk gingerly over submerged rocks in our bare feet to get to the next beach. The only wildlife we encountered on the way was a young woman, sunbathing topless.

We completed our circuit of the island in less than a half hour. When we returned to the table, we found that most of our party had moved down to the beach. We could see Rick and Bill out in the water, snorkeling amid the reefs we'd seen coming in. We grabbed our borrowed snorkels and diving masks and ran across the hot sand to the water's edge.

Stepping into the cool, blue-green sea, we entered a whole new world. When we were chest-deep, we paused to adjust our masks and snorkels, then swam out to join Rick and Bill. Looking down into the water, I first saw only sand, rocks, and seaweed. Then, up ahead, I saw the coral beds, at a depth of fifteen or twenty feet.

Rick and Bill greeted us with waves and broad smiles, gasping out words like "awesome" and "beautiful." I lay flat in the water, floating effortlessly above the reef, the slow rhythm of my breathing loud in my ears. The coral formations teemed with brightly colored fish, some in schools, others darting to and fro singly. They came in many different shapes, sizes, and colors, striped and spotted with irridescent blues and yellows. The colors of the coral formations and the sea plants seemed muted by comparison. After breathing deeply several times, I held my breath and dove down.

Fish swam all around me, darting away only when I came within inches of them. A moving cloud of small, silver fish came at me, breaking formation around the bulk of my body as they passed. A high, narrow fish with black and yellow tiger stripes flicked its tail with lazy grace and disappeared behind an outcropping of coral. I stroked my way back to the surface, blew the water from my snorkel, and gulped air, the taste of brine on my tongue. Again I floated and surveyed the foreign world beneath me, kicking to propel myself slowly forward.

After several cycles of floating and diving, I swam over to Maria. We dog-paddled and conferred, panting from exertion. Bill joined us, telling us of a particularly beautiful spot nearby. For awhile Maria and I swam side by side, exploring and pointing things out to one another.

"Did you see that huge school of tiny white fish back there?"

"I think that one with yellow and blue markings is called a parrotfish."

We stayed out after Rick and Bill had swum back to shore, paddling, floating, and plunging into the azure depths. Each dive revealed new sights to my eyes—a world of muted sounds and bright, shimmering colors. I had no sense of intruding. Only the insistant hunger for air reminded me that I didn't truly belong.

Before long, we tired and swam slowly back to the beach. We emerged from the sea to the familiar tug of gravity, panting. We lay on towels in the hot sun, and I dozed off briefly to the sound of waves lapping gently on the shore. When I woke up, my swimming trunks had almost dried, but my body ran with sweat. Maria had already retreated to the shelter. I joined her, only to find that the group had started to drink rum punch. After rehydrating myself with water, I chipped some ice from the dwindling block in the cooler, put it in a plastic cup, and filled it with the potent brew. We all toasted to having found heaven, without having had to die first.

For the rest of the afternoon we drank punch, snacked, talked, and sunned ourselves on the beach, taking occasional dips to cool off. I thought about snorkeling again, but decided my limbs were too weak. By the time the launch returned for us, I'd put on my shirt to shield my pink back from the sun's rays, and I felt pleasantly fatigued from the rum, the heat, and my exertions.

Lifting our gear to keep it dry, we waded out to the boat and piled on board. The sea was choppy on the trip back, and the launch bounced over the waves, drenching us with spray. We soon arrived, wet and weary, at the Port Royal dock. We paid our driver, bought sodas and Red Stripes, and awaited the arrival of the ferry.

Back in Kingston, we trudged through the dwindling ragamuffin crowds in the street market to the bus terminus in the twilight. Once at the Parade square, we said our goodbyes and went our separate ways to catch buses to our respective homes.

Over time, Maria and I would visit all the major public beaches in the vicinity of Kingston; but of all of them, our favorite local retreat remained the isolated splendor of the beaches of Lime Key.

Back on the ward on Monday, the nurses processed a new batch of patients for admission.

Sister M commented that they looked like they came from "a better socioeconomic class," but we ended up with the usual cross-section of the population. Several of the patients came from wealthy families, and alliances within the batch seemed to form mostly along class lines.

Not all of the beds on the ward had been filled, and I assessed a few addicts who'd been added to the waiting list for potential admission. One of them, Morris, appeared to be a good candidate—a bright, young professional who seemed sincere about quitting crack cocaine. The interview revealed a sly wit and a subtle air of superiority. ("I want to be in the prograhm, but nobody cahn programh *me!*") He seemed quite candid for an addict, citing transgressions against friends and family, and ruefully admitting that his wife would leave him for good if he couldn't stop using. He described having holed-up in the sticks for the last ten days, to stay clean—other than smoking ganja.

Another candidate from a "good family", Lance, was only eighteen. A cocky kid, he presented as being so confident of recovery, that I knew he was in deep denial. He seemed more focused on resentments he felt toward his family than on the morass of his addiction. He frequently visited Miami and seemed very receptive to having an American counselor. He expressed concern that his girlfriend, a beauty contest winner, "had Miami in her eyes," and might dump him if he remained in treatment too long. He claimed that she was no longer using crack, but I had my doubts.

John, who'd spent years in Boston, came across as effeminately gay and admitted freely in his interview that he had AIDS. He'd left his green card—his key to re-entering the U.S.—with someone he owed a lot of money to, as security. He wanted more than anything to return to Boston, but his family wouldn't give him the money to redeem his green card. His application for admission to the program appeared to be a devil's bargain with his parents. Although he asked for my assurance that his sexual orientation and his illness would be kept confidential, he went on to practically advertise both to everyone on the ward.

Max was a distinguished-looking investment broker who claimed to have made and lost several fortunes in recent years. Although he admitted to cocaine addiction, he didn't see himself as having much at all in common with "those other addicts." He acted supremely confident that he'd never use cocaine again and came across as God's gift to women. There was, he would tell you, no woman that he couldn't seduce.

Bruce came from a family of middle-class merchants. Although he had just gotten over the DTs and had cirrhosis of the liver, he completely denied being an alcoholic. He just liked to drink beer, he said. He lived for the prospect of inheriting his mother's grocery store someday, drinking Red Stripe all day and running the business.

Peter had come from humble beginnings, but had gotten himself a good job on the crew of a cruise ship. He'd done very well for himself until someone had offered him a lot of money to smuggle a little crack on the side. Eventually, he'd started using. All he wanted, he told me, was to get clean and to get his job back.

Two men who'd lived their whole lives in poverty rounded out the initial batch. James, a fisherman from the north coast, claimed that his crack habit had begun when he'd found a wrapped brick of crack that had washed up on the shore—more than enough to get himself addicted. Max was labelled a ganja addict by the staff, and he certainly showed features of the space cadet stereotype of a "pothead." Much of the time he could barely stay awake, and when he could, he came across as permanently stoned. He usually wore a blissed-out smile, and had trouble getting his thoughts together.

Although ganja tends not to be seen as a hard drug by most Jamaicans, Jamaican psychiatrists use two diagnoses that do not appear in the Diagnostic and Statistical Manual of the American Psychiatric Association: "Marijuana Addiction," and "Marijuana Psychosis." However, the APA manual *does* list "Marijuana Dependence" as a substance abuse disorder, and many experts believe that marijuana use can trigger psychotic episodes in persons with psychotic disorders.

Addiction Alert referred a young man to me for assessment, suspecting psychosis. He'd missed his first appointment, but was brought in for his second appointment by his parents. At first he seemed rational enough and very bright, although nervous. He readily admitted to smoking from one spliff to a quarter ounce of ganja a day and he didn't see that as a problem. I found him quite likable, but noted that he smiled at odd times, as if at a private joke. He gave direct and coherent responses to my initial questions, but I knew that some people with psychotic delusions can appear to be quite normal until you ask just the right question.

He'd referred several times to "my commitment," so I asked him just what his commitment was. It was then that he started flaking at the edges. He spoke in vague terms about some metaphysical pact that he'd entered into with a friend, involving their "spiritual and mental well-being." (Smile.) It had something to do with "vibes." It turned out that he believed he could read the minds of certain people and that he had enemies who intended him harm "of a spiritual nature." (Smile.) Asked if he believed he had a special destiny, he gave an answer that I liked: "Everybody does."

Although his parents believed that his ganja smoking impaired his functioning, he told me that it helped his concentration. When I asked why he'd missed his first appointment, he gave a novel explanation: "I was without shoes." (Smile.) He wasn't motivated for treatment of any kind, and I concluded that he wasn't likely to benefit from the program in his present state of mind.

Not all of the men referred for possible admission to the ward were as pleasant and benign as he. One scruffy-looking candidate for the program buttonholed me in the hallway and begged me to help him get admitted. I arranged for him to be seen by Dr. W. Later in the day, the doctor popped into the office where I did my assessments, cheerfully informed me that the man was a "notorious psychopath, who killed ten people," and then exited with his customary alacrity.

I spoke to one of the nurses and learned that the man had been some Don's henchman during a bloody political upheaval in 1980. After his murder spree, he'd been spirited off the island by friends in high places and sent abroad. He'd later been deported back to Jamaica, but was never taken to court. The nurse told me that he loved to spook anyone who'd listen to him, describing his enjoyment of the act of murder—the fear in the intended victim's eyes, the pleas, the blood, the death throes. A real sweetheart.

Deemed unsuitable for admission to the ward, he was referred to Peter's Lane. The Major first told him he could stay, then gave him the runaround as to when he'd be admitted. He came back to the ward and asked to see me, again asking me to advocate for him. He attributed his treatment by The Major to class discrimination, saying angrily that he'd had about all he could take. By this time, he'd come to rely on me for straight talk; so I was the one to tell him that he had no recourse—it was The Major's program. During the course of his rant, he told me that he respected me, "for a white man." I felt relieved to know that he didn't see me as an enemy, and withheld my honest opinion as to the kind of institution I thought he should reside in.

I took care to memorize his face. He wasn't somebody I wanted to run into on the street.

Group therapy with the new batch got off to a rousing start. One of the patients got caught smoking ganja on the ward and, contrary to policy, wasn't discharged. I confronted him in group, saying "If I ran this program, you'd be *gone*."

"Bot Jeff, is ohnly ganja I used. Ganja isn't my prohblem, crock cocaine is my prohblem!"

"Ganja," I replied, "may not be a problem for everyone who smokes it. But you admit you're an addict. Any drug an addict substitutes for his drug of choice is called a 'bridge drug', because it's often a bridge back to his drug of choice. As long as getting high remains a part of your lifestyle, you're at risk for relapsing on crack."

Several group members came to the defense of the patient who'd used. One suggested that I'd given up on the man, whom he thought was benefitting from the program.

"No, I haven't given up on him. But help me to understand your belief that he's benefitting from treatment. If he's choosing to *use* here on the ward, how am I to believe that he'll stay clean for even a half hour once he's back on the street?"

Nobody answered me, so I addressed the man in question. "You signed a treatment agreement that included a pledge not to use *any* drugs while you're here. You chose to violate that agreement. That suggests to me that you don't take the ward rules seriously. So...is this program a joke to you, or is it your recovery that's a joke? I'm as serious as a heart attack. It's got to be one or the other. Which is it?"

I'd made my point and, since it had already been decided that the patient would stay in the program, we went on to other topics. As far as I know, nobody else in the group used drugs on the ward during the course of treatment.

Of the several patients who would initially test my leadership in group, Morris was the most clever and subtle. He tried to sidetrack from our dialogue on addiction and recovery by questioning my motives for being in Jamaica. I took his challenge in stride and soon seemed to gain credibility in his eyes. But, in the course of a rant on government authority (which Rastafarians refer to as "the Babylon System") and societal hypocrisy, he mentioned a belief which some Jamaicans hold, that Peace Corps Volunteers are actually CIA agents.

Morris didn't really think I worked undercover, he just wanted to test my reaction. I replied that, since secrecy is essential to CIA operations, I couldn't possibly *prove* to a skeptic that I didn't work for the CIA and I wasn't going to try. We had more important things to discuss, and if anyone in the group seriously believed I was a covert intelligence agent, I'd just have to live with that.

When it became clear that Morris' diversion hadn't undermined my credibility, Peter tried another tactic. He asked me if I'd ever smoked ganja.

Every therapist who works with addicts runs into this kind of question from time to time, and I gave my standard response. ""Peter, I'm not going to answer that question, and I'll tell you why. If I were to answer you, I'd be in a no-win situation. If I said I hadn't ever used an illegal drug, some of you would dismiss me as being hopelessly straight and say that I can't possibly understand drug use if I've never used drugs. If I said that I *have* used marijuana, some of you would say, 'See, *he's* smoked ganja, and he seems to have his act together. Ganja can't be that bad.' "

My response elicited appreciative nods and chuckles from some of the group members. Morris laughed out loud and said knowingly, "He's smoked. He was in college during the hippie era. He was probably a hippie, himself."

I didn't bother to explain that I'd been a straight Citadel cadet at the time of the Summer of Love and Woodstock. I simply smiled and said, "You can suspect whatever you want. We have more important things to discuss. Like how you guys got yourselves lost in the jungle of addiction and how you're going to find your way back out."

Many crack-addicted Jamaicans believe that marijuana (and/or alcohol) use can help them to stay off of cocaine, and this was to be a frequent issue in my work on the ward. My main arguments against it were the bridge drug theory and the fact that many crack addicts find that smoking an intoxicant can trigger cravings for crack. I often said in my groups, "You can't solve a chemical dependency problem by using chemicals that give you a buzz."

One of the biggest problems I faced, working on the ward, was the absence of a coherent treatment model. The program used a loose combination of the medical model and the twelve step model, both of which treat addiction as a disease. In order to be effective in my assignment, I had to adapt to local norms to some degree. So, although I consider myself an eclectic, existential therapist, I decided that I needed to work within the existing framework, at least until I could gain credibility and start to serve as a catalyst for improving treatment on the ward. To this end, I adapted my treatment approach to the disease model of addiction. As time went on, I'd start to develop a psychoeducational relapse prevention curriculum, to complement the program as I'd found it.

By late December the tropic heat had abated noticibly, with highs only in the high eighties. No falling leaves or other visible signs marked the coming of the tropic winter. As Christmas approached, Maria and I eagerly awaited the arrival of our first care package from my parents, and we combed local shops for inexpensive gifts to give each other.

In search of the elusive Christmas Spirit, we joined five other PCVs at Bustamonte Childrens' Hospital, to go carroling on the wards. Maria brought her saxophone to accompany our singing. Jennifer and Shirley worked there and warned us in advance not to expect much in the way of the holiday spirit.

Indeed, the hospital proved to be a pretty cheerless place. With Christmas only a day away, nobody had put up any holiday decorations. Some of the desperately ill children we saw on the wards had been abandoned by their families, as many rural Jamaicans view hospitals as the place you go to die. The best of the staff came across as matter-of-fact, while others seemed downright surly. Few seemed to care that we'd come to sing for the patients and not many of the children smiled back at us.

One exception, a pretty, ambulatory ten-year-old girl with a permanent tracheotomy tube protruding from her throat, followed us around from ward to ward, smiling and singing along with us. Her contagious high spirits re-ignited our waning enthusiasm. I don't know how many people at the hospital cared that we'd come, but our performance seemed to brighten the spirits of at least a few who joined in the singing and thanked us for showing up.

Our care package didn't arrive in time for Christmas, but that didn't matter. We ate corn porridge for breakfast, then exchanged gifts. I gave Maria a set of coloring pens and a bespangled shirt; she gave me a book that I'd expressed an interest in, a University of the West Indies tee shirt, and a set of dominoes. We talked about the historical Jesus and the meaning of his life. Borrowing a Gnostic metaphor, I said that Jesus had a twin sister, and it was she.

Few buses ran on Christmas, but we and some of our friends had an invitation for a pot luck dinner with two women from Group 58 who lived on the grounds of a convent. We managed to get a bus to Halfway Tree right away but, once there, we waited and waited for a bus to take us to our destination. Three other Volunteers who'd also been invited to the Christmas dinner eventually joined us at the bus stop. While waiting, we were briefly entertained by a band of costumed children, celebrating the custom of Jonkunnu.

A survival of the days of slavery, Jonkunnu bands combine Christian and African traditions. The children wore bright, raggedy outfits and stylized masks, dancing and frolicking to the beat of a drum. They cavorted among us, their hands held out for money. One especially pushy celebrant almost knocked Maria's sunglasses off with his wooden sword. She was not amused.

The bus finally came and we arrived at the convent in time for dinner. Our groupmates lived in a rectory on the grounds and we saw no nuns during our visit. We feasted on roast beef (our first in Jamaica), scalloped potatoes, green bean salad, our own garden salad, garlic bread, and cake.

We all left around twilight and caught a bus to the home of the Country Director, Ed Hughes, for his Christmas drop-in. This was the first of what I came to call "embassy parties" to which we were invited. Volunteer parties tended to be pot luck, bring-your-own-bottle get-togethers. Embassy parties were catered affairs in richly-furnished homes, with uniformed bartenders tending well-stocked bars. This party was attended not only by PCVs, but also by Jamaican guests and embassy diplomats. As Maria and I were among the last to leave, Ed drove us home.

Jamaicans celebrate Boxing Day on December 26—another holdover from the British Empire. Although we were never quite clear as to the origins or meaning of Boxing Day, we'd decided to celebrate by attending an all-night reggae concert called STING, at the National Stadium. Nobody else we knew was planning to attend, but we could walk to the stadium from our house and the show featured some of the biggest reggae stars on the island. We hung around the house all day, resting up for the music marathon to come.

We ate a light supper and set off for the concert just after dark. Soon we joined a steady stream of concert-goers out on the highway, heading for the stadium. By the time we bought our tickets and got out on the playing field, the music had just started up. Hundreds of fans crowded around the stage and thousands milled around on the field. Unlike the annual REG-GAE SUNSPLASH music festival, STING doesn't draw many tourists and features mostly dancehall performers. We saw few white people in the crowd, and never did see any other PCVs. The highlight of the concert, a competitive showdown between dancehall superstars Super Cat and Ninja Man, wasn't scheduled until well after midnight.

During the evening we listened and danced to the music of such reggae artists as Junior Reid, Beres Hammond, and Freddie McGregor, as well as dancehall performers Professor Nuts, Lady G, and Cutty Ranks. But we felt a whole different vibe than at the White River show. Fans threw fire-crackers (which Jamaicans call "clappers") wildly in the crowd. Between the raucous behavior on the field and hours of hearing the driving rhythms of dancehall music blaring from the stage, by midnight we agreed we'd had enough, and left. The next day, we read in the paper that the crowd had gotten mean during the superstar showdown, throwing bottles onto the stage when Super Cat performed. We decided that one STING was quite enough for us.

On New Year's Eve we caught a bus to a house shared by several Volunteers, for a party. Maria brought her saxophone along. Several Jamaicans had been invited and during the course of the evening I had my first long conversation with a Rastafarian—the boyfriend of a Volunteer. We talked about drug addiction. He had no respect for crack addicts and saw ganja as a sure cure for any addiction. However, he knew that smoking ganja was grounds for immediate dismissal from the Peace Corps, so alcohol was the only drug in evidence at the gathering.

We ate, drank, talked, and danced to reggae music until midnight. Maria broke out her saxophone and played *Auld Lang Syne* to herald in the New Year. The party continued, but people began to leave around one o'clock. We'd been invited to stay over, as buses were likely to be scarce. Connie, a fiftyish woman from Group 58, had drunk one Red Stripe too many but didn't know it. Although unsteady on her feet, she insisted that she could get home. Several of us took turns trying to talk her out of leaving. Just when we feared we might have to resort to physical restraint, she sat down and, before long, passed out. The few remaining guests made pallets on the floor and went to sleep.

In the morning, Connie denied having been drunk, but didn't seem resentful that we'd persuaded her to stay. We all had coffee then breakfasted on boiled green bananas and rundown, a Jamaican speciality made with mackeral and coconut milk. We thanked our hosts for their hospitality and left to wait for a bus that would take us to Halfway Tree. From there it was easy to get a bus to our neighborhood. For the rest of the day we hung around the house and took it easy, writing in our journals and reading. Toward evening, Maria gave me a haircut—something she'd just learned to do since we'd come to Jamaica, but which she's continued to do ever since. It's become one of our familiar rituals, like taking walks and playing backgammon.

The next day, as we walked to the intersection where we'd wait for Dorothy to pick us up, we saw a grandmotherly neighbor dressed in a pink housecoat and slippers, out tending a trash fire on the curb in front of her house. She waved at us with her machete as she returned our greeting. The first few times I'd seen machete-wielding strangers approaching me on the street, I'd been a little unnerved; but it had become a commonplace sight, as many men make their living cutting brush and doing gardening work.

Once I'd even seen a man walking down the road with his machete balanced on top of his head.

In the car with Dorothy, we told her about all the cheerless children we'd seen when we'd gone caroling at Bustamante Hospital. In reply, she told us about the tonic effect of reggae music on sick children, how they just naturally respond to the rhythms with smiles and movement. "Nex' year, sing de cahrols to a reggae beat, an' see if you don' mek dem smile."

Once on the ward, I immediately noticed tension in the air. There had been a disagreement between Sister M and some of the ward nurses, one of whom believed that she was owed an apology. In addition, Sister M had taken a dislike to one of the patients and had said that she wouldn't come on the ward as long as he was there. In Group, several of the men complained that she'd been giving them the silent treatment. "She nah even ahnswer when we say, 'Good Mahrning, Sister.'"

Things only got worse as the day went on, with patients complaining about their treatment on the ward and two of the nurses talking about resigning. To make matters worse, Dr. W—well-liked by all—had come on the ward and cheerfully announced that his rotation would soon be over and that he'd be replaced by another resident. He seemed relieved that his tenure was about to end. The tension between Sister M and the ward nurses had been growing and, like me, he'd felt pressure to take sides. I'd begun to wonder if I could continue in my present assignment.

So far, Dr. W had managed to stay on good terms with Sister M, despite his popularity with the nurses. When he saw the depths to which staff morale had sunk, he reassured us that all was not lost. Then he set about using his considerable energy and charm to patch things up.

Our Christmas care package finally arrived at the Peace Corps office in early January. I took a taxi home and we had a second Christmas. Along with clothes, books, and cassette tapes, the package included two things we'd asked my folks to send: a small AM/FM/shortwave radio, and a tiny black-and-white television.

At the time, Jamaica only had one TV station, which we'd watched while living with Alvira. The programming consisted of a mixture of locally-produced broadcasts, as well as re-runs of American TV series and old movies. For the most part, I hadn't missed TV; but I *had* missed my ritual of watching the evening news. We saw having a TV as a way of broadening our exposure to Jamaican culture. Our shortwave radio gave us access to BBC and other international news broadcasts, and to a wider range of music than we found on Jamaican stations. We felt re-connected to the wider world.

The one channel we got on the TV was operated by the Jamaican Broadcasting Company, or JBC. In addition to news broadcasts, the local programming included ongoing series such as "Lime Tree Lane", a daily fifteen-minute soap opera, and a half-hour sitcom called "Oliver!"—both with dialogue in patois. The JBC station also broadcast sporting events, but neither of us had much interest in cricket or soccer. One program we watched regularly was a Saturday evening entertainment show called "Reggae Strong," whose title requires a little explanation.

Rastafarianism has its own quirky linguistic conventions, including the frequent substitution of "positive" sounds/words for words or phonemes with "negative" connotations.

The hard "i" sound is considered positive, as Rastas refer to themselves and others as " I and I", and also use the term to erase the Christian boundary between God (Jah) and man. Sounds are negative when they're euphonious with words deemed negative: <u>ded</u>icate/dead, <u>sin</u>cerely/sin, <u>ass</u>embly/ass, apprec<u>iate</u>/hate. Thus, *dedicate* becomes *idicate*, *sincerely* becomes *icerely*, and *assembly* becomes *isembly*. Similarly, positive antonyms can be substituted for negative parts of words, as in *livicate* for *dedicate*, *apprecialove* for *appreciate*, and *overstand* for *understand*. Since *oppressor* is considered a negative word, the "up" sound is out of place, and the word becomes *downpressor*.

Ordinarily, a weekly broadcast about reggae music and musicians might be called "Reggae Week" but, as the announcer intoned at the beginning of each show, "Reggae not weak; reggae STRONG!"

In mid-January, Dr. Lui came by the house to invite us along on a trip he'd planned for the following Sunday. He and some friends would be driving to a beautiful waterfall in the interior of the island and spending the day there. We gratefully accepted and agreed to bring some chicken as our contribution to the picnic lunch.

On Sunday we got up before five, having cooked the chicken the night before. We'd barely finished breakfast when our gregarious landlord arrived in his Citroen—one of only ten still running on the island, he told us. He insisted that we call him by his first name, Kai Meng. We set out without delay and soon rendezvoused with some of his international friends, with whom we'd caravan to YS Falls in four cars. His friends consisted of an Indian family, an American diplomat and his Jamaican wife, a middle-aged English couple, and a Syrian Jamaican named Habib. Dr. Lui led the convoy, with Habib riding shotgun and Maria and me in the back seat. As he and his Indian friend had CB radios in their cars, the Indian family took up the rear, so that the two ends of the convoy could stay in touch.

We got in the cars and set out for St. Elizabeth parish, a "county" on the south coast. The sun rose as we cruised the potholed highway between Spanish Town and May Pen. Maria and I had never travelled this far west on the island before, so everything was new to us and we rubbernecked like tourists. The road followed the coastal plains, winding through farmland and lowland palm forests, occasionally passing through country towns and hamlets.

Kai Meng popped a Ferrante and Teicher tape (movie themes and show tunes) into the cassette player, sometimes whistling along when he wasn't talking. But mostly he talked, keeping up a running commentary on the scenery and on landmarks familiar to him, when he wasn't talking on the

CB. "Oh, look at the rocks. They're limestone, you know. All those rocks! They're all over the place."

Occasionally he'd get very excited about some historic building or minor tourist attraction that he knew would soon come into view. He'd get on the CB and chatter away to his Indian friend, whose call sign was Sugar Mike. "Third church...fourth church...I don't see the red church! Maybe we already passed the red church. Oh, no, THERE IT IS! Coming up on the right, Sugar Mike, the red church! Ten four." Then, to us, "The bauxite in the rock makes it red."

Habib, who added his own dry commentary to Kai Meng's observations, said, "It's not bauxite. It's *painted* red."

Kai Meng had an expensive 35mm camera and loved photography, so every once in a while we'd stop to take pictures. Maria had her Ricoh and I had my trusty twenty-year-old Canon along, so we joined in the ritual of pointing and clicking when we'd stop. We never lacked for interesting shots, but decided to save most of our film for the falls.

Late in the morning , we stopped for lunch on a bluff overlooking Red Lake. Actually a lifeless ex-lake, it was a large expanse of rust-red bauxite sludge—the leavings of the aluminum refining process from a nearby factory. Kai Meng told us that the aluminum industry kept promising to clean up—and further exploit—the waste someday, using new technologies to extract other metals and minerals from the vast, red mud puddle. All of us in the caravan pooled our picnic foods, sharing sandwiches, chicken, Indian goat rotis (curried goat in a wrap of flat bread), and fruit. Then we re-loaded the cars and took off again.

Kai Meng always wanted to know precisely where we were, with Habib serving as his often-frustrated navigator. "Have we passed the turn-off to Maggotty? See, on the map there? We should have... oh, no, there it is. See, up ahead? Sugar Mike, Sugar Mike, this is Sugar Tango. We're coming up on the road to Maggotty, on the left. Don't turn, though. Straight on. Ten four."

At one point he became convinced that we should have come to a dot on the map labeled Liliput. By this time we'd driven up into jungle-clad hill country, with steep hillsides above and below the narrow road. He stopped the car in the middle of nowhere to ask a boy where Liliput was. The boy pointed down at his feet, and said, "Yahso."

"Apparently, Liliput is just too small to see," I observed as we got back underway. Habib guffawed and Kai Meng flashed a wide grin. Maria groaned.

Shortly afterward, we saw a crudely-lettered sign indicating the turn-off for YS Falls. We turned onto a dirt road, which we followed for several miles. Straight lines of small, twisted trees lined both sides of the road, serving as fenceposts, the strands of barbed wire absorbed by the wood. We came to a country store, where a large sign proclaimed that tickets to the falls cost $J40 (less than $2) for residents, $J140 for tourists. We parked the cars and removed our gear.

After buying our tickets, we waited outside until a canopied lowboy, fitted with seats and drawn by a diesel tractor, pulled up in front of the store. We loaded our packs and coolers, then climbed on board. Within minutes we were on our way, being carted through farm fields where cows grazed in the company of egrets, toward green hills in the near distance. We forded a stream fed by the falls and passed through a gate into the picnic area, where we caught our first glimpse of falling water and heard the roar of a cascade further up the hill.

We disembarked from the lowboy and carried our gear over to one of several wooden picnic tables that stood at random intervals in the tropical gardens at the base of the falls. Other than a few tourists and the proprietor of a snack shack, we had the place to ourselves. Crotons, hibiscus, and other colorful trees and bushes dotted the landscaped lawn. Some of our party started unloading our picnic supplies onto the table, but I was eager to explore the upper falls.

I got my swimsuit out of my pack and looked around for a place to change. Seeing no dressing room, I looked around and found a tree over by the stream with a trunk wide enough to afford me some concealment. As I changed clothes, I leaned my bare butt up against the tree, for support—a mistake! Almost immediately I noticed a burning sensation where my skin had contacted the tree bark. It got worse as I headed back to join our party, so I doubled back and dunked my butt in the cold waters of the stream until the burning sensation abated. Maria, who'd worn her swimsuit under her clothes, found me squatting in the water and got a laugh at my stinging tale.

We followed the trail that wound upwards from the picnic area, beside the lowest of the falls. This first cataract was only a few feet high but well worth a photo, framed as it was with palm trees and hibiscus. As we climbed, the roar of falling water grew louder ahead of us. We soon emerged from the forest, back into the sunlight. A fine mist from the waterfall cooled our skin and filled the air with fleeting rainbow colors. A torrent of water cascaded over the cliff that towered above us, falling into a rock pool where a few people already swam. Two people had swum around to the side of the falling water and sat on a wet ledge behind the falls.

A long rope hung from an overhead tree branch, dangling just over the highest point of the lip of the rock pool. You had to walk carefully over the rocks through shallow but fast-moving water to get to the spot, but a young Jamaican man and woman—apparently employees—were there to help. We watched as several visitors waded out to near the middle of the minor cataract downstream from the rock pool and were handed the rope, then swung out over the pool and let go, splashing into the water. It didn't take us long to join them.

We swung on the rope and swam, feeling like teenagers. Maria had brought along her snapshot camera, and we took the obligatory Tarzan and Jane shots of one another swinging out over the water. We swam around the falls and sat on the cave ledge on the other side, feeling that strange sensation of lightness that you can feel while watching a curtain of falling water, up close. I've read that tribal shamans have considered such places power spots and that the cascade effect can induce trances in which the shaman "flies."

When we got tired, we sunned ourselves on the rocks and watched the other visitors having fun. The roar of the falls couldn't drown out the squeals, the laughter, and the other sounds of people—adults and children—playing. Even Kai Meng put down his camera long enough to swing on the rope a few times.

After a while we all walked back down to the picnic area and had a second lunch. One of our party said that she'd wanted to take a walk in the cow pastures just outside the park gate, but had been stopped by a farmhand, who'd said it wasn't allowed. When she'd asked why, he'd simply said, "Mahd cows."

The lowboy transports came and went every half-hour or so throughout the afternoon. When we decided to leave, we loaded up our gear and waited for the next one by the gate. Kai Meng told us that YS Falls got its name from the initials of the original owners of the plantation surrounding the site.

It had been a long day and by the time we got back to the cars and started back toward Kingston, I was pretty tired. But we drove back by a different route, through the mountaintop city of Mandeville, and I didn't want to miss anything. I managed to keep from nodding off, listening to Kai Meng's running commentary and taking in the sights. Occasionally Kai Meng would stop talking, to whistle along with Ferrante and Teicher's arrangement of the "Theme from Exodus," or "Some Enchanted Evening." Luckily for the rest of us, he whistled on key.

We'd begun to get into a routine, and things that had seemed strange and new were now becoming familiar. My weekly my trip down to Peter's Lane on Thursdays remained something of an adventure, though, because of the dungtung area's high crime rate. I could catch a bus three blocks from our house that took me to the corner of the Parade square. From there, it only took five minutes of brisk walking to get to Peter's Lane; but I knew that I stood out in the crowd and always stayed alert and vigilant until the gatekeeper locked the gate behind me.

On one of my first visits to the shelter, I had a session with a young man who'd spent most of his life in Brooklyn and had fled to Jamaica because of drug debts. I knew he was a con from the moment he opened his mouth. His charming persona concealed a desperate addict who'd lived by his wits in the mean streets for years. He studied every encounter with an eye toward exploiting it to his perceived benefit. He'd be whoever he thought you wanted him to be if he thought he could get something from you. With me, he played the sincere counselee, while avoiding any disclosure of authentic feelings or any discussion of his dire situation. Articulate, upbeat, and witty, he turned on the charm, never missing an opportunity to praise my acumin and sensitivity. Finally, a counselor who *really* understood him, who could give him helpful insights. I quickly called him on his act.

"You're *always* on stage, aren't you?" I asked, smiling appreciatively.

The abruptness of my amiable confrontation caught him off guard. He looked blank for a moment, as he ran through his repertoire of masks to see which one he should don next. He opted for a mask of sincere contrition: I'd caught him. Now he'd get real with me.

I tried my best to provoke authentic responses and he dodged like a quarterback. I attempted to engage him in a dialogue about the price one pays for being a con. For a while he even seemed to drop his act and be himself—dead-broke, alone, scared, clueless. He might have even told the truth a few times. But soon he lapsed back into the ingratiating charmer he'd been before my confrontation, praising my insight and my ability to cut through the bullshit.

I grinned at him.

He stopped. "What?"

"Oh, no. Please keep on flattering me. I can use all the praise I can get."

"I guess I'm doing it again, aren't I."

I just nodded.

During the bus ride home I got "picked" for the first time. Although I stayed vigilant and held my rucksack in front of me, in the press of bodies someone managed to unzip a side pouch and remove my glasses case, probably mistaking it for a wallet. Whoever did it must have been disappointed when he discovered he'd only gotten a pair of bifocals.

Until the Peace Corps replaced my glasses, I had to make do with an extra pair I'd brought. Wire-rimmed bifocals with round lenses, they had been manufactured in the thirties and had belonged to my Uncle Ellie, who died before I was born. I'd heard stories about him from my father and his parents, with whom he'd shared his NYC apartment for several years during the Great Depression. He'd been described to me as a kindly bachelor with a zest for life and a twinkle in his eye. More than once, I'd heard myself compared to him. I'd felt a connection and had asked for his glasses when family mementos were being distributed after my grandfather's death. As luck would have it, while preparing for Peace Corps I discovered that his prescription was near enough to my own that his glasses would serve as a spare pair. So, often during my tour, I imagined myself looking at Jamaica through Uncle Ellie's eyes.

Within the space of a week I witnessed two separate little bus melodramas involving 'ductors and fares. One involved a raggedy old man who boarded my bus and immediately started trying to beg his fare. The other riders ignored him and he gave up. When the bus stopped at the bustling Crossroads terminus in the heart of the city, he darted out the door, past the 'ductor, without paying. The 'ductor chased him to the curbside, demanding "two dollah." The old man copped an attitude: he shouldn't *have* to pay in the first place! So the 'ductor called him a "blohdclaht," and probably would've let it go at that, except that the old man called him a "blohdclaht" back. Then the 'ductor, probably having seen one too many Bruce Lee movies, attempted an awkward karate kick. The old man easily dodged it, then clumsily tried to imitate the kick, almost falling over in the process. By this time the bus driver, tired of the public spectacle his 'ductor had created, pulled out. The 'ductor had to run to get on board, but yelled back at the old man, "You nevah ride ahn *dis* bos again!"

On another day I gave my seat on a dungtung minibus to a little old lady, who chatted amiably with her seat-mate until the 'ductor tried to collect her fare. She was positively indignant at being asked for money—or that was her act, anyway.

"Me got a pahss, you *know* mi got a pahss!"

I'd never seen anyone use any kind of pass on a bus and she made no attempt to produce one. The 'ductor just shook his head and laughed, but the old lady wouldn't let it go.

"Why you bodda an ol' lady like me? Huh?" She continued to carp loudly, while many of the riders laughed along with the 'ductor. Embarrassed, her seatmate jumped up and exited the bus, apparently a few stops early, muttering "Me c'yant tek dis!"

Not long after this, Maria and I had a little adventure involving the *absence* of buses. At around eleven o'clock one balmy night, we left a party in Liguanie and went to the nearest bus stop, on Hope Road. Police, some of them armed with semi-automatic rifles, patrolled the sidewalks on both sides of the street. They'd set up a semi-roadblock, to slow down traffic for inspection. Most cars they waved through, some they stopped and searched. We had no idea who, or what, they were looking for; but they'd clearly scared off the buses. We waited for most of an hour, without seeing a single bus or taxi. The police had ignored us, but we got a little apprehensive as the hour grew later.

Then some constable gave an order, and the police cleared the road and began to disperse in various official vehicles. Our fear that we'd remain stranded on the street was allayed when a Land Rover carrying four policeman drove up and the driver asked us where we lived. We told him and he invited us to get in the back. I rode in the middle, with Maria on my lap, flanked by silent police corporals holding M-16s. It was to be our only escort home by Kingston's Finest, and we were soon delivered safely to our doorstep. In retrospect, I'm sure the only reason we got the ride was the color of our skin.

When I went back on the ward, I quickly noticed that the atmosphere had lightened. Dr. W had managed to smooth Sister M's feathers. When she joined us for our morning meeting in the nurses station, she was all sweetness and light. She even made reference to her Silent Treatment, saying that she'd found some of the last batch of patients annoying and that it's better to be silent than to get angry.

One of the potential candidates for admission came from a small village on the north coast. He balked at the prospect of staying "in hospital" for twenty-eight days. He said that he thought we'd give him medications to flush the drugs out of his bloodstream and send him home, cured, in a week. We admitted him, but he never stopped looking for a quick fix. He ended up dropping out of the program early. He'd heard of a Jesus cult that could wash out his bloodstream with the Holy Spirit.

During an interview with a well-educated patient diagnosed as suffering from Ganja Psychosis, I managed to write down some of what he said, verbatim. Dreamily, he told me that smoking ganja "mek you feel like deah sahmwahn else wit you…. God com to me in de night. When I sleep, my cahpillaries are like videotapes, like my vision, my sclera. My pupils ahct ahs brain organs…. My body reverses, to show me what I need to see in my sleep…. My mind is noht togedder."

While I had my own frustrations to deal with at work, Maria's job had rapidly gone from its extended orientation phase to a daily grind. Not only did she teach classes at the School of Nursing, but she also supervised eight student nurses on the Psychiatric Ward. This meant not only having to write lesson plans, but also keeping up with her students' work logs, and writing and grading tests. She routinely had to bring work home, just to keep up.

Doctor R had replaced Dr W as the Detox Ward Resident, and everything I thought I knew about the structure of the treatment program went out the window. My January 29 journal entry read, in part:

My greatest continuing frustration remains the disorganization at every level. Regardless of what is put on the ward schedule, things get decided arbitrarily. We're supposed to have a structured four-week program, but under Doctor R new patients are being admitted *ad hoc*, after other patients drop out. I see no consistent rationale for who is admitted and who isn't. There's no telling how things might change, with new residents rotating through every few months.

Dr. S keeps on reminding me that he wants me to do 'formal psychological testing' with all new admissions, but I have no psychological tests available for my use. He responds to my doubts about the reliability and validity of U.S. tests in the West Indies with comments about needing to do a literature search, but so far he's done nothing.... I have to figure out every discrepancy between what's said and what's done on my own, without any maps to go by. When I lead groups, the nurses feel freed-up to go about working on their own agendas. They aren't motivated to co-lead groups, or even to acknowledge that there might be something they could learn from working with me. So much for the "transfer of skills" part of Peace Corps service!

Since there's no coherent treatment model for the ward, I'm reading up on the materials available to me and keeping notes, hoping that my research will eventually lead to some meaningful input, to help in creating a structured program. Currently I'm working on reconciling cognitive-behavioral models and relapse prevention with the medical model. For what it's worth.

I still seemed to get along well with the ward staff, and the nurses appeared to genuinely appreciate my contributions. However, I got no unsolicited feedback about my role on the ward or my performance. If I needed help in figuring something out, I had to ask *just* the right questions. I decided to be proactive, to submit a proposed job description in order to get some clarification of my role. Part of it read: "to facilitate implementation of psychoeducational and psychodynamic components of the ward's comprehensive treatment program." I'd begun to narrow down the scope of a proposed psychoeducational curriculum to three topics: Anger Management, Stress Management, and Relapse Prevention. After Sister M read and approved my job description, I felt like I had permission to proceed with my plans.

In the last week in January, Group 58 reunited in Kingston for our Early Service Conference. Even though Maria and I could have easily commuted to Bamboo Pen, we took advantage of three nights free lodging at the funky old Sandhurst, to be near our friends. The conference was our first opportunity to compare notes on our on-site experiences and to continue the unending PCV dialogue on what it means to be a grass roots development worker. We all had stories to share and soon learned that almost all of us had had *something* picked or otherwise stolen during our first three months of service.

We had presentations, we split up into work groups, we had panel discussions, and between these activities we hung out and caught up. By this time, about five of our number had ET'd, leaving twenty-seven of us, plus the five who had joined us from Haiti. We learned that Group 59 would be arriving in early February, replacing us as the newcomers. To them, we'd be experienced PCVs to whom they could turn for advice.

Jimmy, a Jamaican member of the training staff with a degree in sociology, gave the most interesting presentation of the conference. Among other things, he told us about rural burial, healing, and religious traditions. He told of an extended kind of wake called Nine Nights, where the community celebrates the life of the deceased with prayer, dancing, singing—and rum. Lots of rum.

By custom, the family of the deceased (at least in the case of the impoverished majority) never had to pay a cent toward the burial. Men in the community built the casket and dug the grave; women prepared the body, sewed the shroud, comforted the kinfolk, and cooked. Not everyone in the community attended the wake nightly, but nine nights allowed each local family who wanted it an opportunity to grieve with the bereaved, as well as allowing time for distant relatives to travel to the home of the deceased. By the ninth night, the soul of the departed was assumed to be at peace.

Some Jamaicans believe that if a soul isn't properly laid to rest, it may hang around as a duppy, to torment the living. There are a myriad of customs and superstitious practices in the folk tradition to ward off duppies, evil spirits, and obeah hexes. Magic and medicine are inextricably intertwined in many peoples' minds. A sick man who can't afford a doctor may seek out a healer at the local *balm-yard*—a fenced and festooned yard where faith healing rituals are performed.

Africa looms large in the Jamaican psyche. Although most Jamaicans are nominally Christians, African animism has combined with elements of Christianity to produce several syncretistic cults which still survive. *Kumina* derives from the Africam *myal* cult and involves the use of drumming and dancing to induce ecstatic trances and invoke the protection of spirits. *Pocomania* ceremonies take place around an " altar" (poco) decked with candles, flowers, and offerings. Participants engage in rhythmic movement and sing Christian hymns to lively African rhythms, inducing trances that they believe have healing and protective powers. Some celebrants may speak in tongues and experience spirit-possession. *Obeah* is the Jamaican analogue of Haitian voodoo. Someone may visit the obeah-mon for divinations, protection against spells, bush medicine, or sympathetic magic. Obeah involves the use of charms, roots, powders, potions, and spells. Some obeah-mon-dem claim to be able to be able to raise the dead.

Jimmy told us about the role of Dons and posses in Jamaican society, about how the competing gangs collectively provide a structure to absorb the constant flow of young people who flee rural poverty for the dream of making money in Kingston or Montego Bay. He also told about the national standardized test administered to school children at age eleven or twelve. A score at or above the 85th percentile means that the child can attend "college" (high school).

Thus, a large majority of Jamaican children get stigmatized as academic failures by age twelve.

Another topic discussed at the conference was Jamaican racism. Unfortunately, the old racist adage, "If you're white, you're all right; if you're brown, stick around; if you're black, get back" describes the attitude of a lot of Jamaicans. Many light-brown-skinned Jamaicans would take offense at being called black. There's a whole spectrum of classifications one hears on the street: white man, brown man, Chinee man, Indian man, Syrian man, red man, yellow man, and, at the bottom of the list, black man. Although some rich and prominent Jamaicans have dark skin, general society observes a pecking order along the lines of the adage quoted above. And among Jamaicans with aspirations to climb the social ladder, there's a tendency to marry someone whose skin is no darker than one's own. I'm sure that many a light-skinned Jamaican Juliet has been pressured by family and friends to break up with her dark-skinned Romeo, or at least not to bear his children.

Sadly, some of the same racist stereotypes found in the U.S. also persist in Jamaican culture. Dark brown skin and "negroid" features are associated with lower intelligence, laziness, and so forth. Jamaicans would joke with me about about someone's tendency to fall asleep after lunch, referring to it as "niggeritis." (My usual reply was that they'd used a word that's not in my vocabulary—that in "psychologese" we call the condition postprandial lassitude.) Many stories in Jamaican folklore also reflect this tragic legacy of Colonialism.

Lest I give the impression that most Jamaicans tend to be ashamed of the African origins of the great majority, I need to clarify that the residual racism one finds in Jamaican culture is not identical to American racism, and that many younger Jamaicans are being taught by their elders to be proud of their African roots. Although not mainstream in the Jamaican culture, Rastafarianism is an instrumental force in educating the young to celebrate their African heritage and in helping older Jamaicans to overcome the wounds of their upbringing in an inherently racist Crown Colony. In direct contrast to the above-cited examples of racism, one also sees in the streets a re-birth of pride in the Afrocentric culture, similar to the Black Pride movement in the sixties and seventies in the U.S. There also exists in Jamaica a spirit of solidarity with African and other Third World liberation movements. The chorus of a reggae song popular at the time went, "By the ballot, by the bullet/ By the Bible or the gun/ Any which way/ Freedom will come."

One of the benefits of living in a foreign culture is that it tends to make you reflect on your own culture and its values. Seeing the Jamaican values regarding parentage reinforced an impression formed in my teenage years, that "bastardy" is merely a Teutonic (or European) social invention. In high school I observed that if a white girl got pregnant, she generally either got an abortion, or disappeared for a few months and returned babyless. On the other hand, if a black girl got pregnant, she generally carried the baby to term and her family helped her to raise it. And that baby was born into its mother's family, carrying the family surname, with no stigma attached. If the unwed black girl's family felt any shame, it was eclipsed by other, more positive feelings and by values that said, "you concieved that baby, she's one of us now, and you're responsible for her upbringing." Noticing this was an early lesson in the relativity of values and one of my first appreciations of Afrogenic cultural values.

The concept of a "fatherless child" is absurd to Jamaicans, and a child born out of wedlock carries no stigma of bastardy. It's commonplace for a "babymother" to have children by several different "babyfathers."

Sometimes the child will carry the father's surname, sometime's the mother's. Some babyfathers financially support their out-of-wedlock children and play a role in their raising, and others don't.

Having multiple lovers seems to be more tolerated in Jamaica than in the U.S., and Jamaicans are generally less prudish than most Americans I know. (While it's not unusual to see a rural Jamaican washing, naked, at the community standpipe, the only topless women/naked people you'll see at the beaches are tourists.) Many Jamaicans shed all inhibitions when they dance, and popular dances like "The Dollah Wine" and"The Butterfly" raunchily mimic the sex act. Even children do these dances, and spectators laugh and think it's cute.

The last night of the Early Service Conference, most of us walked from the Sandhurst to what had become our favorite rum bar in Liguanie, Matilda's Corner. Fairly large as such places go, it had a front bar room with tables and a square bar built into one corner, and a dimly-lit back room for dancing. The two regular bartenders were an immensely fat woman and a dwarf who had to stand on wooden boxes placed at strategic intervals behind the bar so he could reach the customers.

I got Maria a Red Stripe and myself a Dragon Stout, and we went back and joined some of our group who'd already started dancing. The Americans and the Jamaicans in the bar mingled freely, talking, laughing, and dancing the night away. When I got tired, I went out to the sidewalk to cool off and breathe some fresh air. The only Viet Nam vet in our group, Bob—whom we'd nicknamed "Bad Bob," because of his profane language and wild stories—already sat on the curb. I joined him.

We got to talking about our respective assignments and Bob waxed enthusiastic about his. He lived in a small village deep in the bush, probably the most isolated work site of any Volunteer on the island. He knew everyone in the village and everyone knew him. He spoke of the dire poverty in the area and of his attempts to help individual people he'd met.

"One of my neighbors," he told me, "a young woman, is dying of cervical cancer. She's single, but she has two kids. She's all they've got and she doesn't want them to go into an orphanage. She's so *brave!* They told us in training not to try to be a one man-rescue mission, but I guess I've taken her and her boys on as a special project."

For the first time, I got to see his sensitive side. As we got up to go back inside, I remarked, " You'd better watch out, Bob. You're going to ruin your bad reputation."

Maria liked the winter, not only because the temperature only rose into the high eighties, but because it's mango season. I love mangos, too, but she'd become a real connoisseur. One Saturday, shopping at the dungtung Coronation Market, she got her shoulder bag slit by a teef. He didn't get anything, but when she got home she expressed dismay that he had cut into her prized mango! She regretfully threw it away, saying, "You never know where those knives have been."

A mango tree grew in a vacant lot across the street from us and Maria eyed the ripening fruit, hoping that we'd get to it before the neighborhood boys. I'd climb the tree, carrying a stick to knock down ripe mangos, while Maria stood below to catch them. It was also my job to harvest and shell the gunga peas that grew on the tree in our yard.

On a Friday night in early February, we got invited to our first party given by our next-door neighbors, Vasanth and Shiv. The invitation came on short notice and we'd already eaten supper, but we ate again around eleven, which seemed to be the traditional time to eat at an Indian party. They served spicy-hot curried chicken, rice, and cucumber salad with a minty yogurt dressing. Most of the guests were Indian, and Vasanth went out of his way to make us feel at home. He wouldn't take no for an answer when it came to refilling an empty glass with rum, so I nursed my drinks.

During the course of the evening, I got into a spirited discussion with an Indian doctor about the arrogance and excesses of the U.S., as a world power. I agreed with him on much of what he said. He was quite opinionated and we drew something of an audience. I became concerned that we were monopolizing the conversation and tried to disengage more than once, but he was on a roll and persisted. Other than my concerns that we'd taken center stage, I enjoyed our dialogue. Maria and I bowed out and went to bed sometime before one o'clock, with the party still going strong next door.

The next day, Vasanth apologized repeatedly for being an inadequate host. I didn't understand at first, but it had to do with my conversation with the doctor. Vasanth clearly had no judgements regarding my behavior, but was very critical of his friend. Several people at the party, it seemed, had shared his embarrassment at the doctor's criticisms of my homeland. Apparently he'd been seen as having violated the rules of propriety regarding a foreign guest. I assured and reassured him that I had taken no offense, and had enjoyed the give-and-take of our debate. He finally desisted from his apologies and accepted my thanks for his kind hospitality and his sensitivity to the feelings of his guests.

The new Peace Corps Trainees (Group 59) arrived and, as was the custom, Group 58 held a party for them one evening at Bamboo Pen. We answered their questions like seasoned veterans, remembering our own, recent, days of culture shock and anticipation as Trainees. ("It'll get even hotter in a month or so, but you'll be swatting mosquitos year-round.") When the beer ran out, we took some of the new group to Matilda's Corner and introduced them to "Dollah Wine" dirty dancing and deejay reggae.

As an example of West Indian humor, I told some of the newcomers my favorite Jamaican riddle. "Why de mohnkey im fahll out de tree?"

"I don't know. Why *did* the monkey fall out of the tree?"

"Im dead."

One of the the Trainees, a silver-haired grandmother named Celine, was an art therapist, scheduled to be assigned to the University Hospital, part-time on the Detox Ward. I told her something about the ambiguities she could expect to encounter and invited her to join us, if she could, for a "coffee morning" the ward staff had planned for the following week.

The next few weeks would prove eventful. A new treatment cycle was about to begin on the ward, but before it got underway we had a few days scheduled for staff meetings and training. I'd volunteered to do an afternoon training session on therapeutic communication, to complement a morning session on communication by a guest speaker known throughout the West Indies as an expert on counseling. I hoped my presentation wouldn't be redundant.

I arrived before his scheduled start time, only to find that he'd called and said he'd be "a little late." ("Soon com.") As we awaited his arrival, I noticed an air of tension in the nurses' station. This time it didn't involve Sister M, but rather a perceived slight by one of the nurses toward another. Sandra—who had no official supervisory role on the nursing staff, but had a gift for leadership—was clearly trying to patch things up between June and Martha. Nobody clued me in as to the nature of the conflict. I wrote about it in my journal that night:

> June announced she was going for a walk. As soon as she'd left, Martha started complaining about her unjust treatment by June, whom she presumed doesn't want her working on the ward. Angry, tearful. Sandra, Francine and Inez placated: "Don't let it get to you!" Not wanting to get pulled in, I excused myself to go and work on the flip-charts for my session.

> The guest presenter didn't arrive until noon. He expressed regret at his lateness but, although the nurses still expected his full presentation, he hovered between justifying his immediate departure and doing a sorry excuse for his planned talk. What was it we wanted him to discuss? He clearly hadn't prepared anything, but went on to give a ten minute extemporaneous speech—all platitudes and generalizations. We must do this, we must always do that. Exit, stage left, to applause.

Expressions of appreciation followed his departure: wasn't that inspiring, timely, etc. Anything to avoid the chill between June and Martha. Then Sandra leapt into the breach and tried to fix things, with a deft segue from the non-presentation to the morning's rift. Certain people who'd gotten their feelings hurt might need to speak up; certain people who might have said certain things they might have regretted might want to apologize. Certain people were under certain pressures that might cause certain difficulties.

Martha sat there, sphinxlike. June wore a poker face, said nothing. Someone suggested it was time for lunch and the tension broke. I split for lunch, still clueless.

I returned at two and gave my presentation, flipcharts and all. It seemed to be well-received. I later learned that June had apologized to Martha—for whatever—over lunch. The Theme For the Day was clearly communication.

The next day everyone seemed quite amiable. Celine had gotten permission from the PC training staff to attend our coffee morning on the ward, and I introduced her to the nurses. Staff members from other wards attended and we all chatted and laughed, as if nothing untoward had happened the day before.

Celine had to get back to Bamboo Pen by noon, so around eleven o'clock I took her on a tour of the hospital. Cilantro grew on the grounds and, as we walked across the yard between buildings, the distinctive smell hung heavy in the air. Celine had told me that she wanted to see the Childrens' Ward, where she'd be working part-time. On our way there we noticed an entourage heading toward us, following some dignitary around. As we got closer, I saw a tall, tanned, distinguished white man at the head of the flock and suddenly recognized who it was.

"That's Michael Manley!" I said to Celine, awed. "The Prime Minister!"

We stood to the side of the walkway to let the group pass, gawking. Manley noticed us, probably because our white skin made us stand out, and stopped to shake hands with us. He had a firm handshake, smiled at me, and made direct eye contact. I can't remember what pleasantry came out of his mouth, and I was too surprised to even say, "We're Peace Corps Volunteers." He turned and went on his way, leaving Celine and me to congratulate one another for being in the right place at the right time.

The following Sunday we went on our second outing with Dr. Lui. He drove us up to an herb farm up in the Blue Mountains above Kingston. A talkative friend of his named Roy rode shotgun on this trip. He kept touting this and that about Jamaica, stating that the old chestnut about its having the most churches per square mile (alternatively, per capita) of any country in the world had been authenticated in the Guiness Book of World Records. Kai Meng immediately said it hadn't; he'd checked for himself.

But that didn't dampen Roy's penchant for hyperbole. God, he assured us, vacations in Jamaica. After a conversation about the rights of the mentally ill and the difference between mental illness and eccentricity, I quipped that Jamaica has more eccentrics per capita than any other country on earth.

The herb farm, perched on the crest of a hill, was owned by Pam and Audrey, two middle-aged white women. Before giving us a tour of the terraced plots of organically-grown herbs, they showed us around the estate house on the hilltop. Audrey described Pam as "practically a daughter" of Jamaica's best-known artist, Edna Manley; and, indeed, the rustic, wooden house contained several of Mrs. Manley's original sculptures and prints. Among the sculptures was her only work in resin. She'd learned while making it that she had a severe allergic reaction to resin.

Pam, who'd come to Jamaica from Australia, gave us an introductory lecture on the farm, which seemed to be run on almost mystical ecological principles—something like a West Indian Findhorn. They fertilized only with compost and used no insecticides, working on the principles that you don't "force the soil" and that healthy plants naturally resist pests and diseases. They hadn't even attempted to repair damage to the hillsides from Hurricane Gilbert or from a fire several years earlier, but worked with what nature had given them. They believed in the restorative power of time and "the natural balance."

As they walked us around the terraced plots, amid the rich smells of tilled earth and pungent herbs, they explained that they sold most of their produce to restaurants and resorts. From the hillside gardens we could see Kingston far below us to the South. To the North we saw Blue Mountain, its peak shrouded in drifting clouds. The temperature at this elevation was pleasantly warm. Johncrows rode the thermals, soaring with the beauty of eagles.

As the daily temperature started to rise back into the nineties, the political heat also rose. We read in *The Daily Gleaner* about riots dungtung, and there were fears of growing social unrest in some neighborhoods, related to the impending extradition to the U.S. of a gangster named James Brown. (I'd seen graffiti saying "Free James Brown," and had at first thought they referred to "the Godfather of Soul," then serving time a South Carolina prison.) Like many Jamaican outlaws belonging to gangs with either Peoples National Party or Jamaica Labour Party connections, Kingston's James Brown was something of a folk hero in certain neighborhoods. Just as the date of his impending deportation had been rumored to be drawing near, his son, known as "Jah T," was murdered by a rival gang.

While working at Peters Lane the Thursday after his death, I received a message to call the Peace Corps Health Sector supervisor, Elizabeth. She informed me that, effective immediately, PCVs were forbidden to go dungtung until further notice. Volunteers had been further advised not to travel outside of Kingston and to stay in their homes to the extent possible, until things had calmed down. The anticipated unrest, she said, was likely to be unfocused and concentrated in the poorer dungtung neighborhoods for the time being; but if the word got out that Brown's extradition had been finalized, Americans might be targeted.

I assured her I'd go right away, made my excuses to The Major, and left. Even warier than usual, I made my way across the National Heroes Park to the part of the terminus where buses on the 22-A route parked. A 22-A would take me to the Olympia neighborhood on main roads, unlike the local minibuses I usually rode on Thursdays, that wound through the narrow dungtung streets directly between Olympia and Parade. The 22-A at the stop had only three or four passengers aboard, so the driver sat in his seat and read the newspaper while the 'ductor killed time outside, waiting for the bus to fill.

I took one of two sideways seats just behind the driver's seat and sat facing the door. Within a minute, a short, stocky man took the first forward-facing aisle seat, sitting catty-corner from me. He leaned forward and mumbled something to me. I didn't understand him and, with a friendly, smiling countenance, asked him to repeat himself.

He repeated, "You move, you die."

Then I noticed the icepick in his hand, pointed at my heart. An accomplice stood beside him, brandishing a knife. Heart racing, I slowly raised my hands to shoulder level and let the teef rifle through my shirt pockets. As he searched me, he dropped the folded, plastic bag he found in my left breast pocket, containing my Peace Corps ID card and $J20 "walk around money" on the floor. Although scared, I heard myself ask him to please leave me my ID card. At that point the driver noticed what was going on behind him and confronted the teefs.

They'd been trying to pull off the robbery unnoticed. Knowing that they could be identified, they backed off. Then the 'ductor entered the bus, straight razor in hand, and told them to leave. The teefs reluctantly got off the bus and the one with the knife ran away. But the one with the icepick wouldn't let it go. He yelled, "'Im a Yahnkee! Why you 'elp a Yahnkee?"

He tried to drum up support from the growing crowd of curious onlookers, claiming that I was a CIA agent. I picked up my ID from the floor but stayed put, thinking, *he could have killed me*! My mind raced, sorting through my limited options.

The teef ran over to a higgler's cart, where he stashed his icepick and grabbed some empty bottles. He came back and started to throw them at the bus, breaking a glass panel on the bus door, still trying to whip up the crowd.

A few nervous passengers had gotten out of their seats and moved toward the door. Nobody exited, though, and that may have saved my life. I certainly wasn't going anywhere. It began to resemble a riot scene from the movie, "The Year of Living Dangerously." I got up and stood in the aisle, alert for a possible attack from any direction, as some of the windows were open. No police had arrived on the scene and the teef kept up his harangue. The 'ductor held his ground at the door.

Finally, the bus driver decided to pull out, realizing that nobody else would be boarding his bus in this near-riot. I breathed a deep sigh of relief, noting with some surprise that my legs hadn't gone rubbery on me. I gave the driver and the 'ductor my heartfelt thanks. When we pulled up at the first bus stop on the far end of Parade and took on new riders, some of the passengers already on board told them indignantly about how the white man almost got teefed. I heard one of them say of me, "An' im jost a workin' mon!"

I felt moved by this affirmation. White man or not, I rode the bus; I was one of them.

The driver stopped at the first Constabulary Station on the route to report the incident. It only took him two or three minutes and I saw no indication that anything would be done in response to his report. After all, it was just another robbery attempt in dungtung Kingston.

I called the Country Director as soon as I could and reported what had happened. He told me to take a taxi to the Peace Corps office and write an incident report. He wanted to get it to the embassy as soon as possible, due to the possible political aspect of the assault. He told me that James

Brown's extradition had been postponed, but that things might remain edgy until after Jah T's funeral the next day.

Partly as a result of what had happened to me, most dungtung Peace Corps projects were curtailed shortly thereafter. I never went back to work at Peters Lane on Thursdays again.

A few days later I boarded the very same 22-A at the Papene terminus after work. The 'ductor recognized me and came over to me, saying, "You know de man ahlmos' teef you de odder day? Im dead." He explained that the man had been shot in the head during another robbery attempt. I felt shocked and, to my surprise, profoundly saddened to hear the news.

In the days that followed, the press referred to the unrest dungtung as a war between the posses of competing Dons. I knew that some Kingston neighborhoods had Peoples' National Party Dons, and others had Jamaican Labour Party Dons. "PNP ZONE" and "JLP ZONE" were painted on walls in some neighborhoods in the respective party colors of orange and green, and even wearing clothes of the wrong color in the wrong neighborhood could get someone killed.

A rising PNP Don nicknamed Bogle, after one of the official National Heroes, had a dance named after him. Dancing the Bogle in a JLP neighborhood could bring a death sentence. In a newspaper interview, Bogle made the comment that he's PNP *because of* the neighborhood he was born in. "If me born in Tivoli Gardens, me would be a Labourite."

In dungtung Kingston, geography is destiny.

After Jah T's funeral, the dungtung war quieted down for a while. Brown never did get extradited. A few days later someone fire-bombed his cell and he burned to death. To the best of my knowledge, nobody ever got indicted or tried for his assassination.

While the countryside tended to be safer than inner-city Kingston, we'd had it drilled into us in training to avoid going to isolated places. Two Volunteers who'd ignored that rule almost paid dearly. John and Cathy had bicycled out to an isolated beach on their Peace Corps trail bikes and had been joined by a seemingly-friendly young Jamaican man. John chatted with him on the beach, while Cathy went for a swim. John turned his back to keep an eye on Cathy and the man hit him on the head with a piece of driftwood, knocking him unconscious. When he later told me about it, he said he didn't even remember what followed; but Cathy told John that when he came to, the man was trying to drag her off into the bush. John struggled with him and chased him off.

Lest I give the impression that Peace Corps service in Jamaica is two years of living dangerously, I will hasten to add that most Volunteers aren't ever assaulted during their stay and that no Volunteer serving in Jamaica has ever been murdered. But the State Department has maintained a tourist advisory for years, cautioning tourists against exploring dungtung Kingston unaccompanied. You're generally not in danger when there are witnesses around, but to be safe you have to know the rules.

When Jamaican friends leave to go their separate ways, they often wish one another safe travel by saying, "Walk good!"

When I say that Jamaicans have a culture steeped in violence, that is not to say that it is necessarily any more violent than our own culture; the violence just takes other forms. The worst Kingston neighborhoods are no more dangerous than certain neighborhoods in big American cities, with their gang wars and drive-by shootings.

Because gun ownership is illegal without a permit in Jamaica, the ubiquitous machete seems to be the weapon of choice. One frequently reads about "choppings" in the newspapers, and vigilante justice is as common in Jamaica as it was in the Wild West. The local version of the Neighborhood Watch sometimes serves as judge, jury, and executioner. When teefs, rapists, and other criminals are chased down by mobs of local citizens and get hacked or stoned to death, the authorities only rarely hold anyone accountable.

The book Maria had given me for Christmas was titled **Men at Risk**, by Dr. Errol Miller, who'd been the guest speaker at our swearing-in. The theme of the book was the "marginalization" of economically disenfranchised men. When men feel powerless in their lives, they sometimes overcompensate with strutting, banty rooster displays of machismo. The lyrics of many deejay rap songs extol the performer's sexual prowess and capacity for violence. Some of this is rooted in African traditions, but it also reflects the frustration felt by men trapped in modern conditions of economic powerlessness and hopelessness.

One Saturday at the Courtley swimming pool, I spoke with a young, dreadlocked defense attorney named Eve. She gave me several examples of the informal administration of justice in Jamaican society, such as the "bag and tag." A man believed to have raped a woman might be found dead in the street, "tagged" as a rapist. I said that, surely, sometimes the wrong man is killed. She replied that when this is found to be the case, the community chips-in for the innocent's funeral and pays his family something for its mistake. Fair is fair.

Janet spoke of the recent "chopping" of a man in a rural community, for teefing goats. A small herd of goats, she explained, is viewed as someone's livelihood, not "just a few goats."

She told me about a murder case. She defended an innocent-looking, soft-spoken young man who had killed another man at the behest of his neighborhood political "garrison constituancy," for the crime of switching his party affiliation. When he was arraigned for the murder, the community rose up in his defense, incensed. After all, he'd just carried out the sentence decreed by his people!

She successfully defended him, then lectured him: "Now don't go killing anyone else. I won't defend you on another murder charge." He ran afoul of the law again, on lesser charges, and she continued to serve as his attorney. Recently he'd come to her, asking her to defend his brother, whom he said had been accused of a murder he didn't commit. She told him she couldn't just take *his* word; she'd have to hear the brother say that he hadn't killed the victim.

"Bot me *know* im nah do it. Is *me* kill de mon!"

From time to time I had to deal with the violent aspect of Jamaican machismo on the ward. More than once I had to stand between two angry addicts to prevent a fight. Although I seldom tried to speak in patois under normal circumstances, I soon developed a set of stock phrases for use in hot situations: "*Chill*, Pahtrick, nah let im get to you! *Trevor*! Nah t'row petrol ahn de fire!" (That is, "don't egg Patrick on with taunts.")

Sometimes, especially during my first few months on the job, I had a hard time following the rapid- fire patois in group. One day, during a heated exchange between two group members, I wondered, *was that a death threat I just heard?* I listened harder. *It sure was!*

"*Chill*, guys, chill out! QUIET! I don't tolerate threats in my group! Look, if you don't stop this, someone's gonna get discharged. Me *serious*, mon!"

It took me a while to regain control. By that time, the nurses had entered the room in response to the noise. The fracas had started with Andrew accusing Cliffton of stealing a shoelace. At first, Cliffton had refused to talk about it. When he finally spoke, he voiced an angry threat to kill Andrew. I started talking about group rules and the need to use group process to resolve the conflict.

"What you tahkin' 'bout, group prohcess," Andrew interrupted. " We tahkin' 'bout me *life*!"

"I hear you," I said. "And we're staying here until Cliffton takes back his threat."

A group member named Larry spoke up, trying to reassure Andrew. "Look, me a lot more bahd dan Cliffton, an' me *gahrantee* you im jos blowin' smohke. You nah got to wohrry 'bout im t'reat."

"Me wan' hear dot frohm Cliffton, noht you," Andrew replied.

"And we're not going to lunch, " I added, "not leaving this room, Cliffton, until you not only withdraw the threat, but *mean it*!"

In a diplomatic gesture, Andrew took back his accusation about the shoelace. This allowed Cliffton to save face and he retracted his threat. The two of them shook hands. We did a little processing about what had happened, then broke for lunch.

It wasn't to be the last time I'd have to deal with death threats in groups, but I think the way I handled this first one helped me to "earn my spurs" in the eyes of the nurses. Although they didn't shrink from confrontation when it became necessary, they acknowledged that some conflicts between Jamaican men required the intervention of an assertive male.

Carnival, in the Trinidadian tradition, hasn't been celebrated in Jamaica until recently. The official Jamaica Carnival was held in late April, but some Kingstonians warmed up for the big celebration in early March at the University of the West Indies Carnival. The students formed into bands—not the musical kind, but groups of people that wear the same theme outfits—and held parties ("fetes") and costume competitions. They also elected band leaders, who would lead the band formations in the Carnival parade, wearing especially elaborate costumes. The parade was the culmination of the week's activities: a slow march around the circular road that rings the main campus.

Interspersed between the costumed bands of marchers, musical bands rode on long flatbed trucks, their music amplified by gonzo sound systems. The two main bands at the UWI Carnival parade consisted of a Trinidadian steel drum band and a soca band. Soca music is a popular Caribbean/South American hybrid with a frenetic Salsa beat, and with a frequent theme of "wine down" (i.e. wind down)—of which the "Dollah Wine Song" is an example. To wine down is to dance wildly to a fast beat, mimic-ing sexual activity in a variety of imaginitive ways.

The afternoon of the University Carnival parade, I walked over from the ward to Maria's office at the School of Nursing. I was thinking we'd go home and return later, as I'd been told that things wouldn't really get jumping until at least eight. However, she told me that we'd been invited for drinks by a Canadian colleague, Lucy, who lived in the nurses' quarters on the hospital grounds. She also planned to check out the parade and wanted some company.

Profane and irrepressible, Lucy proved to be good company and quickly warmed to us as we sat in her room and helped to polish off her gin. She was around our age, divorced, and she loved to party. She looked like she could hold her own in a bar room brawl. Her favorite expressions were, "not too shabby, ay?" and "you (do that) and you're *toast!*" She owned a VW beetle that she'd named Mary Lou, and when the gin ran out we drove down to Papine to buy beer and snacks. Back in her room, she asked us if we might like to take some trips around the island with her, and we knew we'd made a new friend.

After it got dark, we set off on foot across the campus for the Carnival parade. Maria usually doesn't drink much, but by then we all had a bit of a buzz from the gin and beer. It's said that "nobody in his right mind celebrates Carnival," so we were in the right frame of mind for the spectacle to come.

By the time we got to the ring road, the celebration was in full swing, the brightly-outfitted bands following behind strutting Carnival Queens in fantastic costumes. Chicken wire frames decked with blossoms, feathers, and streamers transformed them into spider women, butterflies, goddesses. The band outfits were mostly in African and Caribbean motifs—bare, brown skin set off by glittery fabrics. The revelers moved in a slow procession to the sounds of steel drums and soca music, but the dancing was fast, wild, and erotic.

Nobody who doesn't want to has to remain a spectator at Carnival. Anyone can join in the snaking, carnal conga lines of pelvic-thrusting party people. I'm talking human hero sandwiches of twitching, gyrating dancers, stacked male-female-male-female, bumping and grinding and sweating their way down the road in the hot, tropic night. It was intoxicatingly pagan. Casting our normal inhibitions aside, the three of us joined the parade and danced ourselves silly.

Lucy had promised us a ride home but as she kept knocking back the Red Stripes, I became concerned about her ability to drive safely. By eleven-thirty we'd had about all the revelry we could take and trudged back across the campus, encountering a horde of incoming celebrants along the way. Lucy turned out to be sufficiently sober to navigate the pot-holed roads safely. At home, I made us a late supper of hamburgers. Exhaustion quickly set in and our new Canadian friend accepted our invitation to spent the night in the guest bedroom.

True to her word, Lucy invited us to ride up to Port Antonio with her the next weekend. Several Volunteers we knew, including Rick, Jennifer, and Nancy lived there; and it turned out to be our favorite vacation spot on the island. Unlike the big tourist destinations of Ocho Rios, Montego Bay, and Negril, it had no high rise hotels or all-inclusive resorts. It had a lot of small hotels, guest houses, and tourist-oriented clubs and businesses, but had the look and feel of a typical coastal Jamaican town.

We arranged to get off work early on Friday and Lucy picked us up at the house in the mid-afternoon. Instead of taking the mountainous cross-country route from Kingston to Annotto Bay, Lucy opted for the scenic route around the southeastern coast. We drove east through Morant Bay and through foothills of the Johncrow Mountains that come right down to the sea. The roads were in terrible condition, but the roadside sights were the real Jamaica we'd come to love—jungle-clad hills, fishing villages, ocean vistas, vast sugar cane fields, and groves of banana and coconut trees.

One of the first sights we saw, approaching Port Antonio on the north coast, was a white, European-looking palace, bright in the tropic sun, incongruous amid the tall coconut palms. It had been built, we learned, by a German contessa. The town itself curves around the shore of a crescent bay, one of the prettiest on the island.

We secured lodging at the Sunny Side Hotel, an inexpensive guest house on a hill just beyond the clock tower square at the town's main intersection. Maria and I got a room with a queen-sized bed for $J200 (about $8) and Lucy got a single room, with a faded print of "September Morn" hanging over the headboard of the bed, for half that. The rooms were spartan but clean, with a bathroom down the hall. At night the hallway lights shone through the slats in the wall.

After settling in, we sat out on a porch overlooking the bay to drink rum and bitters and watch the colors fade from the sky. Lucy was fun even when sober, but got quite outrageous when she'd had a few drinks. We swapped tall stories and dirty jokes, and laughed until our sides ached. Then we set out to find Daddy D's, a restaurant that Rick had recommended, only to find it closed.

However, we ran into Nancy in town—as we had in Ocho Rios. She seemed to have a knack for showing up at just the right time when we were on the north coast. She told us that Tim and Teresa would be arriving shortly from Montego Bay and staying with her. We all agreed to meet at the clock tower at ten in the morning, then Nancy left us to meet the bus.

We dined at the Golden Happiness Chinese Restaurant, sharing our entrees. Then we walked back to the Sunny Side for a nightcap and a few hands of poker on the porch before going to bed.

Saturday morning we explored downtown Port Antonio before meeting our friends at the appointed time. Tim and Teresa told us that their bus from "MoBay" had broken down the day before. Luckily, it happened near the driver's home and he'd fulfilled his contract with his remaining passengers by driving them the rest of the way in the back of a truck.

A kid had washed Lucy's car, unasked—a common street hustle—but when we got there he wasn't in sight. A raggedy old gray-bearded man tried to collect money for the job. He bowed and winked, one hand going through the motions of polishing windows with his handkerchief, the other extended in the universal gesture for *give me money*. The kid showed up, protesting that we owed *him*, not the old man. But Lucy said, "Ay! no one asked you to wash my car," and nobody got paid.

With four of us crammed into the back seat, we headed east from town to Boston Beach—which lays claim to being the birthplace of jerk. It had a safe parking area, changing rooms, showers, and access to two stretches of beach, all for free. We walked over a rise and down steps of crumbling concrete to the further of the two beaches, which was bigger and more secluded. Seaward, two promontories bounded the cove, with the expanse of the Caribbean visible between them. Low waves rolled in, beckoning us into the blue-green waters.

A Volunteer from Group 59 named Sam joined us briefly on the beach, but I sensed that he took some kind of hint from Nancy, and he left as abruptly as he'd come. I knew Nancy to have an easy disposition and, indeed, most PCVs I've met have been likable. But Sam turned out to be the exception that proves the rule—someone who joined the Peace Corps for all the wrong reasons, yet managed to make it through the screening process. Nancy described him as arrogant, self-centered, insensitive, sexist, and condescending. She said that during Community Orientation Week he'd managed to alienate himself from all of the other Volunteers in the area. We were to learn more about him later.

We swam, beachcombed, and lay in the sun for several hours. Lucy fit right in with our PCV friends, swapping stories and telling jokes. She drank four or five beers to my one as the afternoon went on, but obviously had a high tolerance for alcohol. She never seemed to get drunk, just *wild*.

By three o'clock we'd all had enough sun, so we dressed and walked up the road to one of the "jerk centres." The place we chose attracted far more Jamaicans than tourists. Like many roadside eateries, it was made of weathered boards, bamboo struts, and a thatch roof. Jerk chicken and pork sizzled away on grills in the open center of the structure, the distinctive smell of pimento wood smoke filling the air. We ordered a round of Red Stripes, jerk pork and chicken, and festival (cornbread fritters).

Sun-reddened and sated, we crammed ourselves back into "Mary Lou" and headed back to Port Antonio. We dropped the others off at Nancy's house and returned to our rooming house to shower and nap.

That night, we found Daddy D's open, and it lived up to its reputation for delicious and inexpensive food. Afterward, Lucy wanted to check out the nightlife. We prowled the rum bars downtown for a while, then came upon a night spot called The Roof Club that Lucy couldn't resist. We paid the $J10 cover and walked up the stairs to the club.

We found a big, open room with a bar along one wall. Neo-hippie tropical tourist "primitive" designs in bright colors covered the walls and ceiling, illuminated by blacklights and strobes. None of the tourists danced to the disco-style deejay rap emanating from the sound system. They lounged or dozed in the chairs that lined the walls, tall,colorful drinks on the small tables in front of them. A few Jamaicans danced, going through the motions of lust to the staccato beat of the deejay lyric flood. The atmosphere was one of forced gaiety against a background of ennui— the only touristy episode of the weekend. Happily, we didn't stay for long.

The next day we checked out of the Sunny Side around ten and started for home. This time we drove to Annoto Bay and took the mountain route back to Kingston. Lucy dropped us off at our house in the early afternoon, parting with the comment, "Back to the daily grind, ay?"

For our next little weekend adventure, we took a day trip with our group-mate Linda to Hellshire Beach on a Saturday. We met her at Halfway Tree and got on a bus that took us across a causeway to Portmore and on to Naggo Head, where we caught a taxi out to the beach. The most popular beach near Kingston, Hellshire was dotted with thatch hut restaurants, featuring mostly fried fish, festival, and cold beer. One bore a sign that said, "Food prepared to your likeness." A bank of mega-speakers secured to palm trees and pointing seaward blasted out deejay reggae nonstop, resulting in much boogying on the beach.

We met Bamboo Bob, who tried his best to sell us tourist trinkets carved from bamboo. Other beach hustlers offered locally-caught lobster, salty snacks, ice cream, beverages, and even Three Card Monte. A goat strode over the blanket we'd laid out on the sand, almost taking my sunglasses with her. Fishing boats came right up onto the beach, selling their fresh fish, lobsters, and squid right on the spot.

People danced on the shoreline and, when they got too hot, in the water. You could walk, in chest-deep water, to a bank of rocks about 200 meters out, where the waves broke. The rocks were slippery but, even so, people danced and played in the surf.

The heat forced us into the water every twenty minutes or so. We stayed until we'd gotten our quota of sun for the day, cooled down with beers in the shade of a thatch roof, then headed back to Kingston.

That night JBC News announced "the end of an era" on TV: Michael Manley had announced that he'd retire at the end of the month, due to health concerns. This would end fifty years of a PNP dominated by Norman and Michael Manley (father and son). Michael had been Prime Minister for twelve years, off and on, and Leader of the Opposition for eleven. At the very least, it would be the end of a dynasty.

We considered ourselves fortunate to have found the house we lived in. Although our neighborhood was on the border of what the Peace Corps considered safe, we felt secure, had a good relationship with out landlord, and a guest bedroom that made our home a haven for PCVs from out of town. All Volunteers had to come to Kingston at least four times a year for their "GGs" (gamma globulin injections, a prophylaxis for hepatitis), so we often played host to friends from Group 58, and eventually to some from the new training group.

By that time two neighborhood cats had adopted us. Hopeful, the tom-cat, had always been a pig for affection. The other cat, whom we'd at first called Shy Guy, turned out to be a female, and Hopeful's mate. It took her awhile to come around, but with patience and a lot of table scraps and milk, she'd taken to hanging out in our yard and even allowed us to pet her sometimes.

We re-named her Miss Kitty. She'd already been pregnant once since we'd moved in, but had apparently lost the whole litter to neighborhood dogs or other predators. When we noticed her belly swelling again, I wired a grate I'd found to the front of the enclosed space beneath the concrete laundry sinks, creating a fortress/nursery. I left an entry hole just big enough for Miss Kitty and started conditioning her with food to nest on a blanket, inside.

On one of my frequent trips to the neighborhood grocery store, I met two retired men—Mr. Pendergast and Mr. Watson—who frequently hung out together at the snack bar beside the store. They invited me to join them for a Dragon Stout and I learned that they were both well-off for pensioners, and well-travelled. Both had served in World War II. Each having subsequently made a career in England, they'd returned to their native land upon retirement, where their hard currency pension checks went a long way. Their accents were more English than Jamaican.

Mr. Pendergast would never settle for a word like "speed", when he could say "alacrity."

Mr. Watson sometimes came across as a bit senile, but his friend covered for him as best he could. ("Yes, Cologne was spared by the British, but it was bombers, not Spitfires, that flew the sorties.") They enjoyed talking to foreigners and expressed their delight in having Peace Corps Volunteers in the neighborhood. They wanted me to stay for another round, but I had to get home. On my way, I got blessed by a man walking with a Bible balanced on top of his head.

One Sunday morning a man came through the neighborhood selling brooms. He chanted as he walked, reminding me of the stories my mother had told me about growing up in Charleston and hearing street vendors singing the praises of their wares. His chant went, "Coarsebrrm, finebrrm, housebrrm, yahrdbrrm, cahrpetbrrm....brummmmmm!"

Only weeks after our first trip with Lucy, she invited us to accompany her to Negril, on the island's west coast. We arranged lodging with Tim and Teresa in Montego Bay for the first night, and with Group 58's other Jeff, once we got to Negril. We arrived in MoBay without incident but, when we tried to leave the next morning, the car wouldn't start. This turned out to be for the best, however, because by the time a mechanic came and got it going again, Jeff showed up. He'd found himself stranded overnight in MoBay and needed a ride back to Negril. We boarded Mary Lou and took off.

Most of Negril is clustered beside the coastal highway. It's a long, thin town whose economy thrives on its seven-mile stretch of beach. We passed a few resorts and a lot of small hotels, rental cabins, guest houses, restaurants, and craft shops. After the beach the road climbs, running parallel to seaside cliffs. Jeff lived just down the road from the famous clifftop restaurant, Rick's Cafe. ("Where the tourists go to watch the sunset.")

His house was made up of three linked, circular rooms, and stood in a paradisical glade set well back from the highway, surrounded by crotons, lime trees, soursop trees, and palms. All kinds of birds flew around in the area, including tiny, green hummingbirds.

When you find yourself in Eden, why go anywhere? That first evening, we mostly stayed put, only leaving to cross the highway and watch the sunset from the cliffs overlooking the sea. We'd bought groceries on the way in and fixed tacos and salad for supper.

The next morning Jeff made omelettes, throwing in the leftover taco fixings. Then we set out to explore. First we went to the craft market, just landward of the beach. I didn't like hanging around in Jamaican craft markets, as I'd quickly tired of phony hospitality and hard sell pitches.

We didn't have much money to spend and some vendors get surly if you didn't buy anything. I accused Maria and Lucy of teasing the merchants cruelly, as I knew that they weren't there to buy, either.

A few men smoked fat, conical spliffs openly, letting the tourists know that ganja was for sale. If you bought a dope pipe, the vendors told you, they'd give it to you already loaded. We also got offered hashish and psilocybin mushrooms. More than one dreadlocked man introduced himself to me as Farmer Brown (wink, wink). I was tempted to say, "What do you grow, Farmer Brown? Cucumbers perhaps? Organic squash?"

We went down to the beach and found a spot to lay out our stuff. We'd all worn our swimsuits under our street clothes. After taking a dip, I slathered on some sunblock and went jogging along the beach. To my surprise, I ran across Jennifer, sitting under a thatch-roofed shelter, sipping frozen daiquiris with her father. Her family had come for a visit and had rented a beach cabin with all the amenities, including air conditioning and a blender. They invited us to join them, so I jogged back and fetched the others.

We spent the afternoon sunning ourselves, swimming, and drinking daiquiris made with pineapple, with mangos, and with papayas. By the time we got back to Jeff's place, we were all feeling pretty good. We showered and changed clothes, then walked up the road to Rick's Cafe.

Having been there once, I have no interest in going again. It's not just *a* tourist bar, but *the* tourist bar. Now, I've got nothing against white folk, being one myself; but this place was just *too white* for me. I wasn't accustomed to being around so many white people and it felt strange. Most of them wore "country club casual" attire and, although Maria and Lucy had dolled themselves up for the occasion, Jeff and I looked like beach bums compared to most of the men on the veranda outside the bar. The only attraction was watching drunken tourists in swimsuits hurling themselves off of a forty-foot cliff nearby, into a tidal pool.

We ordered a round of beers and watched the sun set over the Caribbean Sea, but decided we'd look for supper elsewhere. You had to buy tokens to order at the bar and the drinks were expensive. One would have been fine with me, after all the rum I'd consumed that afternoon; but Lucy ordered another round. By the time we left to look for food, we were, although sunburned, feeling no pain.

When we came upon a roadside bamboo and thatch hut called "Felix and Roy's Serious Chicken," we knew we need look no farther. We'd no sooner settled in at a table when Lucy ordered a round of Red Stripes. She even ordered one for Roy—the inventor of Serious Chicken—who joined us at the table after taking our order. Felix cooked our meals.

I ignored the beer in front of me and got into a conversation with Roy about Rastafarianism and spirituality. Lucy initially got a bit loud while bartering for a favorable rate, explaining that we weren't tourists. After that, she mellowed, and even Roy seemed to enjoy her company.

Serious Chicken turned out to be a different kind of barbeque than jerk, and was delicious. I told Roy and Felix that if they could set up a Serious Chicken franchise in the States, they'd provide *serious* competition for Colonel Sanders. Lucy ordered more rounds of beer and by the time we'd finished eating, the table was crowded with bottles. Still high, the four of us pooled our money and paid the bill, then set off down the road.

The ladies were giggly with drink. Lucy hugged more than one tree. Along the way up the drive to Jeff's house, they conspired in whispers and started collecting palm frond "fans." We two Jeffs didn't have a clue. When we got to the house, Maria and Lucy disappeared into the bathroom long enough to shed most of their clothes. They emerged, posing coyly behind the palm fronds, and did a fan dance. Jeff and I ran for our cameras. To avoid the possibility of blackmail, the ladies called us cowards until we'd stripped down to our skivvies and posed for their palm frond peekaboo snapshots.

I've hidden the negatives.

We'd begun to sober up by then. Still laughing at one another, we got dressed again and played some poker. Penny ante poker. Strip poker would have been anticlimactic.

The next day we bid goodbye to Jeff and headed for home—a five-hour trip. The only hairy moment came after we'd stopped by the seaside for Lucy to catch a catnap, and the car wouldn't start. We were practically broke. Fortunately, Lucy had watched as the mechanic had worked on Mary Lou in MoBay and knew roughly where to troubleshoot. Maria found the loose wire and fixed the problem. We got back underway and drove overland from Ocho Rios to Kingston without any further problems.

If you ask Jamaican children to name the seasons, some will start off with "mahngo season," or "rainy season."

As the days got hotter, they also got wetter. We got caught in cloud-bursts and endured days of constant drizzle. Power outages sometimes accompanied the heavy rains. We spent some soggy Saturdays and Sundays at home drenched in sweat, praying for the electricity to come back on so we could use the fans again. We passed one more than one evening reading and playing backgammon by the light of our hurricane lamp.

Tom, the Volunteer who'd introduced me to Peter's Lane, went back to the States "on vacation" and never returned. Some of the old-timer Volunteers we'd met completed their two years of service and departed. We were starting to feel like Old Jamaica Hands, to use a term from the island's colonial days. As we approached the six month mark of our own service and the economic turmoil continued to worsen, we heard serious speculation among Volunteers as to whether we'd be able to complete our two-year commitments. We wondered if we'd end up being evacuated in the midst of a political upheaval, like the Volunteers from Haiti.

The swearing-in for Group 59 coincided with the thirtieth anniversary of the Peace Corps' presence on the island; so the agency's new director, Elaine Chou, would be attending the ceremony. The guest speaker was to have been Michael Manley, but now that he'd left office, the address was to be given by P.J. Patterson, who'd succeeded him as Prime Minister. The U.S. Ambassador, Glen Holden, would also be there.

All the Volunteers who were in Kingston got to meet with Director Chou on the day of the ceremony for a question-and-answer session. Then we hung around in Liguanie until evening.

The Prime Minister delivered all the expected platitudes in his address, then promptly departed. Director Chou administered the oath to the new Volunteers. The rite left me feeling renewed, hopeful that Jamaica would endure its latest crisis and that we'd all get to complete our terms of service.

A journal entry from around this time began," I awoke this morning with a lingering dream image of the Detox Ward spontaneously combusting."

Dr. W had told me that nurses, not doctors, ran the wards. Over time, the nurses I worked with began to take me into their confidence and I started to understand more about ward politics. While there was no ward sister (i.e. head nurse) to oversee the daily operation of the ward, and Sister M made it clear that she was an Administrative Sister, apparently she'd unofficially appointed June to run things for her. This had put June in an awkward position and had led to her run-in with Martha. While it seemed to me that June got along well with the other nurses when I first joined the ward staff, as tensions grew between Sister M and the duty nurses, June was increasingly viewed as Sister M's deputy. I tried my best not to take sides in the running conflict, but sometimes I felt like a tightrope walker.

Dr. S continued to pressure me to administer MMPIs to all new patients, responding to my objections about the reliability and validity of American tests with vague references to research done concommitant to this book, that study. I started combing through the *Index Medicus* and other resources in the medical library, trying to find the sources he'd cited. I couldn't find any evidence of the MMPI having been normed on West Indian populations and felt ethically bound to refrain from participating in research based on invalid data.

On the positive side, I felt more comfortable in my role as a group leader. Most of the patients seemed to accept me despite my white skin and foreign accent, and I'd gotten better at understanding patois. Sometimes a nurse would even sit in on a group session. I didn't like the fact that they only observed, and came and went as they pleased, but this didn't seem to distract the patients.

Some of the "batches" of patients showed a higher level of motivation than others to really take advantage of the group setting to work on their problems. There were sessions where some patients made candid and painful disclosures, once they knew they were in a safe setting. When this happens in a group, the members can learn from one another and, in their empathetic responses to honest disclosures, provide a balm of support and acceptance to those who took the risks.

I developed new therapeutic metaphors as time went on. Starting from Abraham Maslow's, "If the only tool you have is a hammer, you tend to treat everything as if it were a nail," I compared the process of recovery to collecting new tools to carry on your toolbelt, there to be used when you most needed them. Starting a lifetime in recovery, I said, is like going through a door, not knowing what life will be like on the other side. Some might fear that living a lifestyle of sobriety would be like moving from Jamaica to Iceland; but the only way to learn the difference between true happiness and mere intoxication was to live "clean and sober," one day at a time.

I compared the addict to Gulliver, bound and made helpless by a multitude of tiny strings: reflexes, habits, memories, associations, and cravings. Not only does recovery consist of becoming aware of each string that binds you and pulling each one out of the ground, you have to keep on doing it; because when you awaken from sleep, you find yourself having to deal with strings you thought you'd already freed yourself from.

When the day of the Jamaica Carnival parade arrived, Maria felt wiped out from the heat, so I went by myself. The procession would be moving down Hope Road, from Liguanie to Halfway Tree and beyond. I went on my recently-issued trail bike, and the ride uphill to Liguanie left me weak-kneed and sweaty. I stashed my bike at Bamboo Pen, resting and rehydrating myself until I heard the sounds of the approaching parade. Out on Hope Road, I bought a Red Stripe from one of the legion of higglers selling their wares to the excited throng that lined the parade route. I found a spot on the curb and waited for the party to come to me.

The parade was a movable feast for the senses. If you stood still, the cavalcade took nearly forty-five minutes to pass you. Then you could walk through the crowd at a fast clip to the beginning of the slow-moving procession and watch it again. Or you could walk, shimmy, gyrate, or bump and grind along with the costumed celebrants. The party went on and on, and you were part of it.

Talk about your cast of thousands, this cortege of carnal delights was bigger and more spectacular than the UWI Carnival. The heat and the effects of bright sunlight on the shimmering, spangled, multi-colored, extravagant costumes made this a very different experience—quite unlike anything I've seen before or since.

Loud soca and calypso music filled the air, emanating from giant speakers on the flat-bed trucks that bore the musical bands. Theme-costumed bands of revelers strutted and danced in loose formation or rode on floats festooned with vibrant blossoms, sweat and glitter sparkling on their exposed flesh. Skin shades ranged from black, through all shades of brown, to white. Some participants were tourists who'd come to Kingston for Carnival and paid to join the frolicking bands of masqueraders—all race, class, and national distinctions made irrelevant by this celebration of fun and fantasy.

Some band floats and costumes evoked images on the theme of Nature's Fury: The Hurricane, The Volcano, The Earthquake. Others were based on "Something" themes: Something Musical, Something Mystical, Something Tribal, Something Exotic, Something for the Birds. Most marchers carried scepters in the band theme design. Some strutted and some sauntered, while most danced variations of the raunchy "wine down" dance as they advanced slowly down the street. Some broke ranks to dance with the people who lined the road or to buy a beer from a higgler, then boogied back into formation.

Each band was led by elected "kings" and "queens" in ornate costumes embodying the band's theme—here a Bird of Paradise; there Anancy, the African spider god, his eight waving legs controlled by a "puppeteer" who walked behind him. There were giants, monsters, tribal chieftains, pirates, goddesses, stylized animals—colorful, larger-than-life creations that had to be seen to be believed.

Nobody was merely a spectator. Even the police along the parade route smiled and bobbed in place. The fantastic sights, the rhythms, and the frenzied dancing intoxicated you and drew you into this vibrant, moving celebration of universal aspects of humanity, from the carnal to the mythic. You can't stand still at Carnival.

After a few hours of this joyous spectacle, I decided I'd had enough. I'd used up all the film in my camera. My legs were weak from dancing, my wet clothes clung to my body, my ears rang from the music, and my face hurt from grinning and laughing. I let the colorful, gyrating, humping procession pass me, bought a Red Stripe to cool myself down, and headed back through the gradually thinning crowd to Bamboo Pen to get my bike.

The roads went downhill most of the way from Liguanie to Olympia, so I mostly coasted, the breeze cooling the sweat that ran down my body. Traffic was light and I rode home, dodging potholes, without incident. I found Maria watching the parade on our tiny black-and-white TV, regretful that she hadn't felt up to going with me.

"There's always next year," I consoled her.

Part III

June–November '92

Every two years or so, Peace Corps Jamaica staged an All Volunteer Conference for all the PCVs on the island. It provided an opportunity for us to share experiences and ideas, and some of us were asked to do presentations on topics relevant to projects other than our own. The 1992 conference was held at a resort called Dragon Bay, near Port Antonio, where the Jamaican scenes in the godawful Tom Cruise movie, "Cocktail" had been filmed. The round, thatch-roofed beach bar was now known as the Tom Cruise Bar.

The Volunteers living in Kingston congregated at the Peace Corps office and boarded a charter bus. We rode east along the coast, stopping along the way to pick up PCVs who lived and worked in rural areas along the way. During the ride, I kept notes on some of the colorful names of roadside establishments: Total Experience Headquarters, Mikey Puss Tavern, New Illusion Video, Faith in God Drinking Saloon, Fish Soup Joint, First and Last Bar, Moo's Patty Place, Cool Rock Headquarters, Sufferer's Jerk Pork, John Bull's Cow Cod Soup, and Chippie's Lounge.

When we arrived at Dragon Bay, we checked into our rooms and ate lunch. After a plenary session in a pavillion facing the beach, we split up to attend the presentations and workshops of our choice. Elizabeth, the Health Sector Supervisor, had asked me to do a presentation on dealing with the families of chemically-dependent persons. I'd signed up to give it during the first session, to get it out of the way. Then I was free to do what I wanted the rest of the evening.

The resort had satellite TV, so I went back to our room and watched Headline News. I learned that President Bush was in L.A., to show his concern about the Rodney King beating and that Marlene Dietrich had died. Would the space shuttle Endeavor take off on schedule? Tune in end-lessly and see. Tomorrow and tomorrow and tomorrow, with last syllables and burning candles and poor players strutting and fretting, and dusty deaths.

After supper, some of our number played volleyball in the bright moonlight. Others of us sat under the stars, drinking and talking, while a so-called calypso band played passable reggae and pitiful country and western. Imagine "I'll Be There Until the Next Teardrop Falls" done with a hint of a calypso beat.

Some of the conference sessions were work-oriented, while others were just for fun. The next day I attended a workshop on making fish-print teeshirts. The process involved covering dead fish with paint, then care-fully pressing the teeshirt onto the fish, to imprint the shape and texture. My first effort turned out well and I got lots of compliments on it. I can't recall what *serious* presentations I attended that day.

Free time started at three thirty. Maria and I had gotten some requested Groucho Marx glasses—the kind with a big nose, eyebrows, and mustache attached—in a care package. We had a photo project in mind, entitled "What Do Peace Corps Volunteers Have In Common?" We took pictures of clusters of our friends, engaged in leisure activities, all looking like Groucho.

I also took snapshots of Maria leading a group of Volunteers in Tai Chi, on the lawn. We took in some sun on the beach, then borrowed some snorkling gear and went for a swim in the azure bay. We didn't see many fish out in the reefs, but enough to make it an enjoyable snork.

The resort crew had stacked bamboo on the beach for an evening bon-fire, but shortly after dark a torrent of rain began to fall. It rained all night and, off and on, well into the next day. Maria was in the pavillion when the deluge began, while I got stranded at the Tom Cruise bar. I waited for a lull in the downpour and made a mad dash for shelter and supper.

Although it wasn't that hot, the humidity made up for it. On this night we had a good reggae band playing in the pavillion. Primed to boogie the evening away, we stayed drenched in sweat as we danced. Maria and I retired to our air-conditioned room around eleven, but the party went on for hours after we left.

Apparently unaware of the legendary thirst of partying PCVs, the pavillion bar ran out of beer. The beach bar still had some, though. Everyone was soaking wet anyway, so the party moved outside, as the rain continued to fall. Later, some of those who'd sought the cool shelter of their rooms got lured out on false pretexts and thrown in the pool. I watched the madness from our balcony.

Sam, the misfit of Group 59, didn't show up for this mandatory conference until the next day. He bragged that he'd hitched a ride from MoBay on a yacht. We learned that the Jamaican agency he'd worked for in Port Antonio had asked that he be reassigned, and he'd been sent to work with Bad Bob in his isolated assignment in Seaford Town. Bob told us that Sam only showed up for work two or three days a week, then left for long weekends in MoBay. He'd obviously joined the Peace Corps for an extended vacation in the tropics.

While the new ward resident openly acknowledged that she saw me as the real expert on therapy in the program and consulted me from time to time, I continued to experience the same sense of helplessness and frustration on the job. We had no official "chief" and nobody was ultimately accountable. The buck stopped…nowhere.

We had no treatment model. Patients continued to smoke on the ward and to break other rules without consequences. I no longer felt that I could credibly claim, in group, that we had a systematic treatment program, as every alleged standard eventually got ignored or violated on someone's whim. I saw no point in claiming that there was a price to be paid for breaking the no-smoking rule and decided to stop playing the enforcer role.

I'd combed through the meager resources of West Indian psychiatric literature in the University library and the medical library without finding

any evidence that the MMPI had been normed on the Jamaican population. Still, Dr.S cited references that only led me to more dead ends, and
he continued to urge me to start testing our patients.

The one area where I saw some progress was in my informal secondary
project of organizing the mounds of dusty books in the unused wing of
the Psychiatric Ward. I finished my initial sort, getting all the thousands of
books stacked and separating the fiction from the non-fiction. I started
breaking down the fiction into categories: mainstream, literature, juvenile,
mysteries, science fiction, and so forth.

Here, I could feel a sense of accomplishment. It was my therapy. I'd
gotten permission to distribute the books as I saw fit. I posted a message
on the bulletin board at the Peace Corps office, offering them to
Volunteers who worked in schools and literacy projects. I soon got a reply
from a woman who was trying to establish a library for teens in her community, and let her know that she'd get first pick of the juvenile literature.

An exerpt from my journal entry of June 23<u>rd</u> will illustrate my frustrations on the job:

> Today was one of those days when I spent several hours on the
> ward in a controlled state of shock, watching the chaos spread
> while all the staff did was to comment on it and suck their teeth
> (a common Jamaican expression of displeasure). No attempts at
> any kind of strategic intervention. How could there be, with
> nobody in charge?
>
> I heard allegations of death threats and brandished kitchen
> knives on the ward last night, of patients allowed to go off the
> ward without supervision at 5 a.m., "to go jogging." The no-
> smoking rule is being routinely broken, with no consequences
> being imposed. In this context, my attempts to help create a
> more therapeutic environment seem pitifully inadequate.
>
> The patients, by the second week, have studied the system
> enough to test the limits. What they usually find is that there *are*
> no effective limits. Chaos blooms. Predictably.

I don't usually do a Tuesday group, but it looked like some crisis management was in order. All I had to go on was second-hand accounts of who-did-what-to-whom, when. After group, things seemed a little calmer. Later, I spoke to some of the staff about my frustration, suggesting than non-enforcement of stated rules *invites* contempt for staff authority. The ward resident overheard some of this and simply commented on the difficulty of the problem.

Who can I turn to? Dr. S sees me as a technician who can help to generate research and is probably annoyed with me for not dancing to his tune. He has no apparent interest in my professional judgements or recommendations. The resident doctor acknowledges my expertise in behavior management but is stuck between Dr.S (her supervisor) and chaos. Sister M and the ward staff don't know what to do with me. Yet.

I've heard other Volunteers cite similar problems at their own job sites: disorganization, lack of accountability, administrative tyranny and neglect. I'm at the point that I think most PCVs get to at some time or other in their tours, asking *what am I doing here?*

Even some of the new batch of patients were asking for more structure and enforcement of rules. To a certain degree this could be viewed as a cop-out (i.e. *you* be responsible for my behavior), but it was also a cry for help. Many addicts are arrested adolescents, who both crave and hate limit-setting. Although I felt helpless as a change agent much of the time, some days I felt like I might be making a difference, at least for some of the patients—a handful of the thousands of addicts on the island who needed drug treatment.

Celine had started working part-time on the ward. A trained art therapist, she'd scrounged a small cache of art supplies for the patients to use and was good at what she did. Most of the patients enjoyed her sessions, where she encouraged them simply to express themselves in drawings. Then she would help them to interpret their own and each others' creations, in a very down-to-earth manner. Having another PCV with me boosted my morale.

Howard, a gifted professional dancer from Guyana, had also proved to be an asset to the program. A volunteer, who got a small stipend for his work, he had no training as a therapist but seemed to me to be a natural. I'd have thought it near-impossible to get a group of Jamaican men to engage in "movement therapy," but Howard had a knack. I'd watch from the nurses' station and see him leading the patients in movement exercises resembling free-form dance. Unlike Celine, he didn't try to get them to interpret their expressions; but I soon came to regard his efforts as legitimate therapy.

Howard performed as the lead male dancer in a dance troupe named *L'Acadco*. In July Maria and I got to see the premiere of a show that they'd be presenting in Cuba. The electric performance incorporated elements of ballet, modern dance, African dances, and reggae. For the finale Howard did a solo that he'd choreographed himself, based on Guyanese "Indio" dances, exhibiting amazing energy, stamina, and grace.

When Howard returned from the tour, he described Cubans as a warm, hospitable people who don't seem to perceive themselves as living under a dictatorship. He said that only those who'd travelled abroad and seen prosperity knew how impoverished the island was. Cubans, he told us, greatly valued education, had excellent medical care, and extolled artists. Dance was very popular. With Cuba only forty miles north of Jamaica, I felt disappointed that we couldn't visit, due to the State Department's ban on travel to the island.

In the "round robin" letters we wrote to be copied and circulated among family and friends, we'd invited anyone who wanted to come visit us, promising them an opportunity to see the real Jamaica. Only two friends from our years in the South Carolina Lowcountry, Pamela and Ben, and (later) Maria's father, took us up on our invitation.

In July Pamela and Ben flew to Montego Bay and took an air shuttle to Kingston, arriving at our door in a taxi. They brought gifts and requested supplies, including a mosquito net for the guest bed and snorkeling gear. After they'd unpacked and napped, we took them uptown, by bus. One bus ride was quite enough for them; after that, we took taxis.

We first went to Devon House, once a manor house, now a tourist center with a bar, restaurants, and shops. Maria and I sometimes went to Friday happy hour at the bar, a favorite meeting place of PCVs from out of town, as you could walk there from the Peace Corps office in ten minutes. Drinks were expensive by our standards, but it was a classic expatriate bar with a colonial-era feel to it, and our friends had offered to pay our way while they stayed with us. We sat outside at a table on the patio in the twilight, beneath stately old trees. Maria and I could usually only afford beer there, but on this evening we sampled exotic rum punches. Afterward we walked over to the upscale New Kingston business district and ate at a fancy restaurant specializing in West Indian cuisine, then took a taxi home.

The next day was Saturday, so we took Pamela and Ben out to Lime Key for a day of sun and snorkeling. Sunday it rained all morning, but when the skies cleared we toured the Hope Botanical Gardens. Ben, a landscaper by profession, was disappointed at the scarcity of signs identifying the flora; but the gardens were a riot of color, with exotic blossoms everywhere.

Pamela and Ben were travelling, not romantic, companions and Pamela wanted to have some time by herself on the north coast. We recommended Dragon Bay and she drove there in a rental car. Ben had a pilgrimage to make: he wanted to visit Bob Marley's gravesite, a Rastafarian shrine up in the hilly interior. Maria and I not only had to work, but didn't know where Marley was buried, so Ben was on his own. A resourceful traveler, he walked down to the nearest taxi stand and hired a cab to take him on a day trip into the country. He paid a lot for the ride but hit it off with his driver, who also served as his guide. He got what he'd wanted—a memorable trip into a part of Jamaica that few tourists ever see.

When Pamela returned, Maria and I took a day's leave and Pamela drove us all up into the mountains north of Kingston. We lunched at a hilltop restaurant/resort called Pine Grove, from which we could glimpse Blue Mountain Peak through breaks in the drifting clouds. Our friends departed on Friday, having spoiled us rotten during their week's visit.

On the Fourth of July we attended a traditional American picnic at Bamboo Pen. An embassy-sponsored event, it featured burgers and hot dogs and an Air Force Reserve band that mostly played rock'n'roll favorites. The few PCVs who attended hung around together for the most part, as we seldom got invited to social events with Diplomatic Corps types and saw ourselves as a separate breed.

We learned that day that the embassy staff got hazardous duty pay for serving in Jamaica. Word had it that they'd been about to lose it, but had offered statistics on incidents involving PCVs in order to justify its continuation. As my informant put it, "they're relying on us to continue to be victimized."

Jeff had some bad news to pass on. For one thing, he was about to ET, planning to ship out the following week. Then he told us that Les, one of the older members of Group 58, had been attacked and subsequently medically evacuated to the States. He was okay, but would almost surely ET as well.

Jeff had been with him at the time of the assault. He and his girlfriend Joanne (also from Group 58) had been walking with Les through a middle-class neighborhood in MoBay around twilight, when a berserk man clad only in shorts had come out of nowhere and chopped Les on the side of his head with a machete. Jeff didn't see the actual attack, but heard Les cry out and turned to see him rolling down a grassy slope.

"I thought he was dead. I was in shock, I wasn't thinking, but I yelled and ran at the attacker, who fled. We never did find out who he was or why he did it. Just a madman, I guess. Les was conscious and it was just a scalp wound, but he was bleeding pretty badly. It took seven stitches to close the wound."

Jeff said that he'd already been thinking about early termination, but what he'd seen happen to Les was the last straw. Sure enough, he left the following week—but this wasn't the last we'd be seeing of him. He had unfinished business in Jamaica.

The next Detox Ward crisis began with Sister M storming into the nurses' station and loudly berating Martha over a misunderstanding about a phone message. Her rant disrupted the morning devotional the patients held in the group room, next door. The storm blew over as quickly as it had come up and Sister M acted as if nothing had happened.

This occurred during the last week of treatment for the patients in residence, so it wasn't as disruptive as it could have been. The next week had been set aside for training and administrative catch-up, and the ward nurses requested a meeting with Sister M and Dr. S to discuss the problems in the program, on Monday. They seemed to have finally resolved to tackle the issues affecting staff morale.

One especially interesting patient in the current batch was a well-educated and cosmopolitan businessman, who'd seen it all. He'd only recently come to realize and admit that his twenty-odd year pattern of heavy drinking constituted alcohol addiction, and spoke ruefully of all he could have accomplished had it not been for his drinking. He told me of an Old Boys Club of alcoholic Jamaican wheeler dealers with whom he'd spent most workday afternoons drinking. He said he'd finally come out of denial regarding his alcoholism when he'd noticed that there were only four of his eleven original "rumpanions" left in the circle. Four had died of alcohol-related causes, the rest were in recovery and attending AA meetings instead of getting together with the old crowd.

This batch seemed to get a lot out of group work and gave me plenty of positive feedback about my role in the program. We'd even gotten around to discussing values and ethics as they relate to recovery issues. I'd posed, as a theoretical issue, something that a patient in an earlier batch had claimed actually happened to him.

"What if, sometime in your recovery, you were to come across a kilo of crack, washed up on the shore? What would you do?"

Most of the crack addicts in the group denied that it would lead to a relapse and said that they'd deep six it or otherwise destroy it, to remove temptation. Harold, however, had a different plan.

"Me nah *use* it, meself. Bot me sure *sell* de stoff!" His eyes lit up at the prospect.

"How many of you think that keeping the crack to sell would lead to a relapse?"

Everyone but Harold agreed that it probably would.

"Okay, Harold. Separate issue. Even if you *didn't* relapse, would you feel okay about making money off of the coke trade? You've talked about the misery that crack causes and said you wished you'd never come across it. What about the harm putting that crack on the market would do?"

"Nah me business, dat. Me nah mek nobohdy use de stoff."

I told the group about a short story I'd read that posed an interesting question. A stranger comes to a man's door and offers him a box with a button on it. He can keep it as long as he wants. If he pushes the button, two things will happen. He'll get a million dollars and someone he doesn't know will die.

"What would you do? Would you even *take* the box?"

Most group members caught the analogy right away, and it strengthened their conviction that they'd dispose of the crack. Harold didn't budge from his claim that he'd feel no pangs of conscience about selling the "rock." Then I asked how he'd feel if his little brother were to get hold of some of the cocaine, become addicted, and die of an overdose.

That seemed to give Harold some pause. I wound up the discussion by saying that probably none of them knew what they'd *really* do with a kilo of crack if they actually came across one, but that I thought it would probably put any cocaine addict's recovery at risk if he kept it to sell. I said that I hadn't brought the subject up to judge anyone, and thanked Harold for his honesty, concluding that we're all responsible for the results of our actions.

The next Monday the ward staff met with Sister M and Dr. S around the table in the group room. Dr. S knew something was up and encouraged us to speak our minds, but nobody broached the subjects of Sister M's tirades on the ward or the ambiguities about leadership. Sister M took the offensive, claiming she had been slandered by unspecified persons and that the ward nurses spent the workday "socializing." She spoke of a conspiracy to demean her reputation at the hospital. Still, nobody said a word about her recent attack on Martha. Celine and I looked at one another and kept our silence.

Dr. S seemed to realize that something important had been withheld, but had to attend another meeting. He suggested that we get together again the following week. Knowing that we'd be constrained by having patients there, I spoke up for the first time, suggesting that we really needed to meet again *this* week. I mentioned no names, but added that sometimes the angry vibes were so thick on the ward you could cut them with a knife. He agreed to another meeting the next morning.

To my surprise, the second staff conference started on time. When I'd spoken to Sister M earlier, she'd indicated that she'd have nothing to say at this meeting. This suggested to me that she may have some insight into her tendency to reveal more than she'd intended when she *did* speak up. Dr. S again encouraged us to air any grievances we might have. To my chagrin, everyone continued to pussyfoot around, avoiding the important issues.

Once more I rushed in, where angels might have at least hesitated. I simply said there'd been an incident on the ward last week and that I'd been surprised nobody had mentioned it.

Martha had told me that she didn't feel she should be the one to bring it up, but that once the subject had been broached, she'd talk. But the staff went on in generalities and I began to think I'd taken a risk for nothing.

Nothing got past Dr. S, though. He asked to know more about the incident and at that point Martha spoke up, much to my relief. Francine added what she'd witnessed, then mentioned that it hadn't been the first time such a thing had happened.

Despite Dr. S's repeated invitations for her to speak her piece, Sister M initially answered, "I have nothing to say." After several long, awkward pauses, she finally spoke up.

She implied that there was a conspiracy against her and referred to the other nurses present as "only staff nurses"—which immediately drew exclamations and strong nonverbal responses of offense from them. Sister M said that she was accountable only to her supervisors, not to her supervisees.

Dr. S had finally seen and heard for himself how Sister M dealt with the members of her staff. They went on to challange some of her allegations, but her own words and demeanor had revealed all he needed to know about the nature and extent of the rift.

I felt compassion for Sister M. Beneath her anger I could sense her hurt feelings about having been excluded from the comradery shared by the ward nurses, but she didn't seem to have any insight about how her attitude and actions had led to her exclusion. After all, sometimes she came on the ward all smiles and "my Dears," and once she'd even ordered a pizza for a staff luncheon. She apparently had a selective memory about the other times, when she'd worn her "Sister Hyde" persona.

Dr. S had a big professional investment in the success of his fledgling Detox Ward and knew that the ward had its opponents in the hospital hierarchy. He must have sensed that some of the staff nurses would resign if the situation didn't improve. He encouraged the staff to rise above personal enmity and try to patch things up.

After the meeting ended, I left feeling pleased that everything was finally out on the table; but I knew I needed to check out how the encounter might have affected my relationship with Sister M. After all, she was my nominal supervisor. I went to her office on the Psychiatric Ward (Ward 21) and knocked on her open door. She sat at her desk, going through the motions of doing paperwork, her face a tight mask. She didn't look up.

"Sister, do we need to talk?"

She in no way acknowledged that I existed on the same planet with her, but continued rustling papers. I tried again to address her, to no avail. So I said, " Sister, I'm open to talking with you whenever you feel like it."

Silence.

Giving it one last try, I said, " I don't want you to think of me as your enemy," and left.

Later in the week I arrived at Ward 21 at the same time as Dr. S and asked him if I'd commited any errors of judgement or timing—if I'd misspoken in any way. He said no, in fact he wished I'd said more. I admitted that I'd held my tongue and avoided specifics, but that I nevertheless needed to make repairs with Sister M, who was giving me the silent treatment. He said he'd talk to her and try to smooth her ruffled feathers.

On Friday the ward staff had an open discussion, with June present, about the confusion over her "deputy" role on the ward. My introduction of the word "ambiguity" seemed to help clarify the situation, and I asked her if her job description was any different from those of the other nurses.

Taking no evident offense from my question, she said that it wasn't. I liked her as well as I liked any other nurse on the staff and sensed that, like me, she felt under pressure to take sides. With important things having been discussed, the tension seemed to have abated somewhat. Sandra and Martha said they'd spoken to Dr. S since the Tuesday meeting and that he understood how serious the circumstances in the program had become.

The following Monday I managed to patch things up with Sister M. When I saw her in her office and knocked on her door, I initially got a cool response.

"Can we talk?"

"About what?"

I told her that I hoped we could still work together, and she invited me to sit down. She indicated that she'd listen to whatever I might have to say, but no sooner had I gotten started than she took over and said her piece. She said she'd thought we had a good relationship, until I'd spoken up at the meetings. Despite Dr. S's statement that nobody was on trial, she'd *felt* like she was on trial. She'd heard that Martha had "flippantly" told a senior administrator that she *never* came on the ward. Convinced that the ward nurses had dragged her name down, she related self-serving stories about other "staff nurses" who'd deservedly felt her wrath in the past, but had gone on to become better nurses for it.

When she'd finished I reminded her that I'd mentioned no names in the meetings, but had just referred to an incident that I'd felt had affected patient care. "Dr.S said we needed to share our thoughts and feelings honestly. I'm a candid person by nature—maybe to a fault. So when he asked how things were going and nobody else spoke, I felt obliged to speak up. But I'm enough of a professional not to presume that I knew everything that had happened, nor to assume that anyone was the 'good guy,' and someone else the 'bad guy.' If I spoke out of turn, I apologize."

That seemed to soothe her hurt feelings. She said that when I'd mentioned an "incident," she'd honestly not known to what I was referring. She'd thought it had all blown over. She admitted that her temper got the best of her sometimes.

That having been acknowledged, I took a risk before leaving her office. I said that sometimes she left wounds behind her on the ward.

"Wounds? What do you mean?"

"Wounded feelings."

Apparently that was news to her. We parted on amicable terms.

Later in the day I began to run a fever. At home that night I had a headache, my joints ached, and blotches briefly broke out on the backs of my hands and feet. Maria and I suspected I'd gotten dengue fever, a mosquito-borne virus common in the Tropics.

By the next day my fever had climbed to 103 degrees. Maria said she'd drop by the ward and tell the staff I was sick. I read and slept for most of the day. That evening Maria administered chicken soup therapy, accompanied by the appropriate soothing noises and caresses.

When I awoke Wednesday, still feverish, I took a taxi to the Peace Corps office. I described my symptoms to the staff nurse and she immediately pronounced that I had dengue fever. She told me to treat it with aspirin, fluids, and bedrest, and to just ride it out. Typically, she said, the aches and fever subside after a few days, followed by a week or two of fatigue. I picked up our mail and took a cab back home.

That night we had overnight guests, Rory and Rachael, a young couple from Group 59 who'd stayed with us twice before. The first time they'd been stranded in Kingston unexpectedly, and had been most apologetic for imposing on us, until we'd reassured them that we had a spare bedroom and that such things were part and parcel of the "Peace Corps experience." It turned out that they, too, had stayed with Alvira during training and that we had other things in common. Like me, Rory was an Army veteran who'd served in Germany, a writer, and a cinema buff. Like Maria, he played the saxophone. Rachael was well-travelled, having lived in China for a year as a student. Maria had lived in Korea for a year, during her first marriage.

Rory was an African American who dressed the part of the "peace warrior": camouflage or fatigue pants and a bandanna headband. Rachael was white and Jewish—a lovely, *zaftig* Earthmother-type. Unfortunately, they had not hit it off with Alvira and thought that she was prejudiced against interracial couples. (Alvira later told us they'd been fussy and hadn't liked all of her rules.) Their dislike of Alvira didn't stand in the way of our getting along, however. We just stopped mentioning her. We'd talk books and movies late into the evening, and Maria and I taught them both to play backgammon.

This time they were in town for a reggae concert at the National Stadium, commemorating the hundredth anniversary of Haile Sallasie's birth. Because of their remote assignment, they were among the few PCVs who'd been issued motorcycles. It was just as well that they had plans for the evening, because we'd run out of cooking gas, Maria didn't get home until late, and I wasn't likely to be very good company. I gave them a house-key, as they didn't plan to get back until the wee hours of the morning.

The next morning before they took off, they told me that the concert had still been going strong when they'd left at three. I used the telephone next door to order gas and forced myself to stay awake until it had been delivered. Miss Kitty had recently given birth to three kittens out in the shelter beneath our laundry sinks, so I kept her supplied with saucers of milk and watched her nurse her brood. By now their eyes had opened and they'd started to explore the world outside their nursery.

By Friday the aches in my joints had begun to subside, but my temperature still hovered around 101-102 degrees. Never in my life had I kept a fever for this long, and the tropic heat made it even worse. Bored from staying at home all day, every day, entertained only by strange fever dreams, I didn't have the energy to do much more than read, write, and sleep. I consoled myself with the knowledge that dengue isn't contagious, so Maria couldn't catch it from me, and that it usually confers immunity for a year or two, so I wasn't likely to have to endure it again during our tour of duty. I wrote in my journal, "I'm sick of being sick, tired of being tired."

Over the weekend the fever finally broke, but I still had no energy. Although I wanted to go back to work, I couldn't in my exhausted condition. I was missing the first week of a new batch on the ward. I felt alert enough to work on the relapse prevention handouts I'd begun to develop for the patients in the program, but the slightest physical exertion left me drained.

Toward the end of the week I started to feel more myself. We'd hoped to attend two or three nights of the REGGAE SUNSPLASH music festival in MoBay that weekend, and I began to think we might be able to go. I felt good enough that we went to a performance of the National Dance Company on Thursday night.

It energized me to watch the exuberant men and women of the troupe dancing in their colorful costumes. They danced to jazz, blues, and reggae, winding up the show with choreographed version of a traditional Jamaican kumina dance, performed to a frenzied beating of drums. I left the theater feeling invigorated, but Maria told me she thought she was running a fever.

Sure enough, the same dengue-bearing mosquitos that had infected me had gotten to her. She encouraged me to go to MoBay by myself, but I knew the reggae festival just wouldn't be the same without her, and that she'd need to be comforted and cared for. On the evening of the day that we would have left for the north coast, I was listening to a blues tape and fixing supper, when she joined me in the kitchen and asked, "May I have this dance?" I put down my spatula and slow-danced with my febrile ladylove in the tropic twilight.

When I returned to work the following Monday, I soon learned that there were two unique things about the new batch of patients. For the first time in the program we had the correct ensemble that the ward had been designed to serve—four men and four women. The ward resident, however, had been absent during the first week, the patients hadn't had the usual admissions assessment, and there hadn't been a single "ward rounds" (i.e. staffing) since they'd been admitted. Without the usual structure my groups provided, things had deteriorated to the point of anarchy.

One patient, Winston, a bright young sociopath, had managed to alienate the entire staff and to sow the seeds of discord among the patients during the week of my absence. He'd lived half his life in Canada, where he'd been a one-man-walking-crime-wave: car theft, burglary, armed robbery, con games, and God knows what else. Eventually, he'd been deported.

So far, he'd broken just about every rule, without consequence. He'd left the ward without permission, he'd made out with his wife in his hospital bed when she'd come to visit him, he'd smoked (and probably gotten high), he'd lied-to and manipulated staff, and he'd stolen food from the other patients. Two of the other men had come close to the point of a physical confrontation with him and others had said, "either he leaves, or I do!"

A consummate actor, Winston could go from tears, to charm, to rage in a heartbeat—whatever he thought would work to get him what he wanted at that moment. He talked as if his recovery from crack addiction was a *fait accompli*: he'd seen the error of his ways and would never use cocaine again, honest! When confronted about something, he played the victim, the injured innocent. The whole staff agreed that, not only was he not benefitting from treatment in any discernable way, but that he'd effectively sabotaged the other patients' treatment as well.

The patients had requested a group session. When I rounded them up, Winston absolutely refused to attend, saying he was sick. The rest of us assembled and I asked the patients, "what's up?" After an initial sullen silence, they poured out their complaints.

"Im tek me cheese bun widout ahskin'!"

"Im got no respect fi nobohdy bot imself."

"Im say me jost a 'opeless jonkie ahn mi fi die soon frohm de crock cocaine!"

"If im nah get 'is way, im blow op an' t'reaten you!"

"Im disrespeck de nurse-dem ahn ahlways wan' be de center ob ahttention."

With their permission, I took back what they'd said to the nurses. We all agreed that Winston shouldn't ever have been admitted and should be discharged—the sooner, the better. However, only the ward resident could discharge a patient. I called her at her office in Ward 21 and appraised her of the clinical crisis. She agreed to come and interview him for possible discharge, asking me to sit in with them.

The interview turned out to be neither an intervention nor a confrontation. Winston proved to be an expert at diverting attention from himself, blaming, denying, contradicting—responsible for nothing he'd been accused of.

Validating a patient's perceptions in service of the therapeutic relationship is one thing; gullability is quite another. The resident seemed to be in over her head. Not only did she not confront him, she gave him every benefit of the doubt. He played her like a hooked fish.

She *sincerely* tried to convince him that he needed long-term treatment. He calmly informed her that he surely did not. She asked him earnestly what he saw as his biggest problem. He psyched-out what she wanted to hear to the degree that he admitted to having been an addict, but went on to assure her that he was no longer at-risk of using drugs. He told her that she was the only staff member whom he could still trust, because she still listened. The rest of us had proven ourselves untrustworthy.

The resident let him go on with his attacks on staff and patients alike. I could no longer hold my tongue. I used the therapist's technique of reflecting his current ploys back to him, in the hope that the doctor would see through his tactics.

"You seem to be convinced that you're the only person on the ward in possession of the truth. You persist in playing the role of the injured innocent, no matter how much evidence there is to the contrary. You refuse to take even the least bit of responsibility for the actions that have led to this meeting."

"See, doctor! Is what I said. Im against me, too!"

The doctor allowed him to rant on and on about all the injustices that had been heaped on him by the unprofessional staff members, to the point where I completely lost my patience. I felt like asking the doctor, *Can't you see this is all just a game to him?* I got up and walked out.

I left because it was the only appropriate expression my mounting anger allowed me. I was immediately angry at myself for allowing Winston to push my buttons as he had, but I needed to cool off. I recognized that my behavior had been an accumulated response to the whole context—the ward and the program—as much as the immediate situation. While I wasn't pleased with my behavior, neither was I ashamed. I may have rewarded the patient's pathological behavior, but it came to me that I'd never felt as powerless in a job as I did on the Detox Ward.

I resolved that if things didn't improve in the program I'd request reassignment. While I perceived that the staff increasingly relied on me as a troubleshooter and a catalyst for change, I still felt ineffectual with so many variables beyond my control.

I walked around the hospital grounds, my mind and heart racing. As I gradually calmed down, it occurred to me that I really needed to go back to the ward and make the necessary repairs. Feeling a little sheepish, I returned.

The ward clerk let me in the locked door and I saw Winston in the hall. He smirked at me. I met his gaze, but otherwise ignored him as I walked by. The nurses all looked at me solicitously as I entered the nurses' station, but nobody spoke. The ward resident looked up from where she sat at the desk, writing up her notes. Winston had followed me as far as the doorway, not wanting to miss anything.

"Doctor, sisters, I want to apologize for my unprofessional behavior. It was uncalled for, and it won't happen again. I shouldn't have let him get to me, but I did."

The resident smiled understandingly and said, "No problem." She didn't indicate whether or not she'd be discharging Winston. The nurses made sympathetic noises. One said, " He could upset a building."

At home, I found Maria in bed, tired despite all the sleep she'd gotten and running a fever of 102 degrees. She listened to my account of how I'd lost it in front of the whole ward and empathized, as she felt similarly powerless in her job. That night I wrote in my journal, "I see the ward as a potentially seaworthy ship, with a more-or-less competent crew, but no rudder, no compass, and no captain."

The next day at work I learned that the resident had decided "to give Winston another chance." She let me know that she essentially agreed with my assessment of Winston as a sociopath in deep denial, but apparently Dr. S had pressured her not to discharge him. She said she'd told him he was "on probation."

As she seemed receptive to staff input, I argued against her decision.

"I don't think we'd be doing him a favor by letting him stay. We'd just be reinforcing his entrenched notion that he can do as he pleases and bullshit his way out. He's stuck in denial. To hear him talk, he's already recovered. He presents a paradox: he won't cooperate with treatment and he says he *knows* he'll never relapse, but he still wants to stay on the ward.

"He role-models non-compliance to the other patients and his behavior interferes with their progress. With no system of consequences in place for breaking rules, this program isn't designed for patients like Winston. It's designed for people who have some motivation to work on their problems."

The resident didn't disagree with anything I'd said, but it was clear that the decision had already been made. Then June said something that blew my mind—that *all* the other patients had changed their minds about Winston since the day before! I knew then what the focus of the day's group meeting would be.

"Good morning ladies, gentlemen. Normally, we'd get started with introductions and a discussion of group rules, but there seems to be higher priority today. Yesterday you all agreed that Winston needs to go. So, what's happened to change your minds?"

Nobody spoke. Winston just sat there, smiling. Finally, one patient said, "Well…his ahttitude has changed." Someone else made excuses for him, but as others began to talk, expressions of ambivalence, frustration and, finally, resentment came out.

One man said, "Me nah really trost im, but me cahn ignore im."

Winston began to glare at the other group members, but stayed silent. It seemed likely to me that he'd somehow put pressure on the others to support him. I tried to keep the focus on whether he could fit in as a group member, or if his continued presence would interfere with the others' progress. Winston could no longer contain himself and went on the attack, loudly denying that he'd done anything to anyone.

"I jos' say what I t'ink! I nah brownnose, like de res' ob you. I am ME!"

At that point I saw the ward resident standing just outside the door, listening. After group ended, one of the nurses beckoned to me. She informed me that because Winston had again displayed his true colors, the doctor was in the process of discharging him from the program as we spoke .

After his departure, order was restored and we got down to business in group. One of the patients—diagnosed with "ganja psychosis"—proved to be too delusional to benefit from treatment. He told me that his is the *real* voice you hear singing on Jamaican radio stations. You may think you're listening to Michael Jackson, or Bob Marley, or Shabba Ranks, but it's really him. One of the women, whom we'd thought was simply an alcoholic, finally admitted to being a "huffer"—a user of inhalants. Not only had she gotten high from sniffing glue and gasoline fumes, she'd recently taken to sniffing *and drinking* turpentine.

One of the crack addicts in the group admitted that he'd gotten to the point in his addiction that he'd do almost anything to support his habit. He said that he was afraid that if he relapsed again, he might even become a gunman—a "dogheart" killer—for a posse. If he ever sank that low, he said, he wouldn't consider himself fit to live.

One day when I'd walked to the Papine market/terminus for my usual ride home, I found standing room in a packed 22-A bus, but there was no sign of the driver. Usually buses would depart as soon as they got filled, but this driver had gone off somewhere on an extended break. Apparently the riders had been waiting for some time, as they'd started grumbling impatiently and complaining to the 'ductress.

Another 22-A pulled up to the stop. As soon as its passengers got out, all the riders on my bus—including me—piled off and boarded the other one, much to the 'ductress' dismay. The newly-arrived bus took off right away, leaving the first bus to fill up all over again, and the 'ductress cursing the tardy driver. We riders laughed and joked, sharing a rare, heady sense of victory in the daily grind of commuting.

Walking towards home through the neighborhood, I saw goats rooting in a trashpile and a man walking with a chainsaw balanced on top of his head. I reflected on how the sights and sounds of Jamaican life, once so new and different, had become familiar to me. Along with this realization came the thought, *but if a friend or family member were looking through my eyes right now, how strange and rich it would all seem*! It was like a new layer of appreciation of my being there settled into place, a sense of being at home in Jamaica.

Maria recovered from the dengue fever and returned to work. Sometimes she spent her days supervising her student nurses down at Belleview, the national psychiatric hospital. She returned one evening, horrified by what she'd learned. We knew of the severe shortages of medications and hospital supplies, but she now knew that patients there routinely died of starvation.

"It's horrible!" she told me. "Most of the patients only get *cocoa* for breakfast. For lunch they get a small ration of soup. And for supper they usually only get *tea*—maybe a little bread, if they're lucky! The other day they ran out of soup for lunch and some of the patients only got sugar water. No wonder they're always begging!"

Tired of seeing their patients die, the nurses had threatened to strike, so we knew the press would soon report on the deplorable conditions. Sure enough, the dire situation at Belleview was the lead story on the JBC Evening News. In an interview, a hospital spokesman denied any cases of death by starvation but allowed that when patients die of "pneumonia or senility" (die of *senility*?) "their poor nutritional status is helping them to pass on more quickly."

I grabbed pen and paper to record the fat bureaucrat's outrageous PR euphemism verbatim. The next day the newspaper had nothing to report about Belleview, but the evening news showed truckloads of food being delivered to the hospital. Maria later told me that nothing had really changed—the patients were still on starvation rations.

In Jamaica, the families of hospital patients often keep them supplied with food, clothing, and linens. While the stigma attached to mental illness is probably no worse there than in the U.S., in such a poor country it sometimes results in the literal dehumanization of the "mad." Many of the patients in Belleview had been abandoned by their kin and were consigned to live out the rest of their lives on the back wards, forgotten by society. The underpaid nurses and orderlies had become understandably hardened by the conditions in which they worked, and some stole food to keep their own families fed.

Maria felt angry and helpless, but as a PCV she couldn't become active in "local political issues." We got begged every day on the street and knew we could do nothing to alleviate the terrible poverty we saw all around us. Anything we might have given would just be a drop in the bucket, and we'd learned early-on that giving money to beggars would only call attention to you as a "rich American" or as an easy mark.

One of the goals of the Peace Corps is to increase the awareness and sensitivity of U.S. citizens to the problems facing developing countries. Serving as a Volunteer can be both educative and humbling, as you learn the limits of what you can expect to accomplish during your two years of service.

I'd quickly gotten over any feelings of being hard-hearted when I turned down beggars. Most of them left you alone when they saw that you weren't going to give them anything. I soon developed a standard answer, in my best patois, for those who persisted and asked me why I refused their requests. "Me get beg ahl de time, mon. Me nah give you mohney fi de same reason me nah give mohney to de las' mon who beg me. If me give *you* mohney, wha' me gwan say to de nex' mon?"

The view that many Jamaicans hold of North Americans can be illustrated by their attitudes toward having their pictures taken. While some didn't mind being photographed, others demanded money. One man helped me to understand a common perception when he said to me, "You go bahck an' sell me picture to Nahtional Geograhphic an' is *you*, nah me, get de mohney!"

One thing I got from my Peace Corps service was a profound sense of gratitude for my good fortune at having been born a citizen of a prosperous, industrialized nation.

Les returned from his recuperation back in the States. He told us he'd considered asking for reassignment in Poland but, to our happy surprise, he opted to stay in Jamaica and got a new assignment, in Kingston. Together with Jackie and Paul (from Haiti), and Celine, he'd gotten an opportunity to rent a very nice, large house in Liguanie. It even had a swimming pool! But in order to afford the rent, they needed more tenants. They invited us to look at the place.

We would have had our own bedroom and the run of the spacious house. We got along with all of the prospective co-tenants and would have been considerably closer to our work sites.

It was tempting at first, but we considered ourselves fortunate to have a nice house to ourselves and decided that we hadn't joined the Peace Corps to live with Americans. We declined their invitation and they soon found other PCVs to move in with them.

We were mostly just on waving terms with our neighbors, but occasionally had visitors. Willard continued to bring us fruits (which Maria concluded were probably filched) and do yard work for us. Lorna, a young, single working mother with three children, whom we'd met at the bus stop, occasionally came by on Sundays with one or more of her kids. Shiv had moved out from next door, to be replaced by a friend of Vasanth's named Prakash. Our friendship with Vasanth had continued to grow.

Vasanth and Prakash both spoke English more articulately than some Americans I know, although with heavy Indian accents. Maria invited them to pick mint and herbs from her spice garden and they, in turn, treated us to samples of southern Indian cuisine. One Saturday breakfast consisted of pan-fried bread and quartered limes pickled with hot peppers and salt.

Maria gave Vasanth the occasional haircut, and we would often sit out on the patio between our respective front doors in the twilight, sipping drinks and talking. We discussed politics and culture, and I found that Vasanth was much more knowledgeable about America than I was about India. He observed that although the American ethic of hard work seemed to have lost ground, many Indians still see the U.S. as the Land of Opportunity for people who are willing to work hard and to save. Like some Jamaicans, many middle-class Indians expected to immigrate as soon as relatives became citizens and could sponsor them. Our dialogue gave us yet another window on international perceptions and opinions regarding our country's role in the world.

Although Hopeful and Miss Kitty just hung out in the yard, the three kittens loved to climb through the open louvers on the back door and explore the house. We'd named them Raggamuffin, McGillicuddy, and Thelonia. They especially liked to hang around in the kitchen when we cooked, and we had to be careful not to step on them. We'd leave out cardboard boxes, bags, and other things for them, and enjoyed watching them play.

I remember one of them watching with rapt attention one evening as Maria practiced her Tai Chi to the flute music of a "zen meditation" tape, in the living room. Barefoot, wearing only a tee shirt over her underwear, she glided gracefully from stance to stance, naming them to herself as she went. "Carry tiger to mountain," she intoned. "Parting the horse's mane …parry and punch…grab the peacock's tail…snake creeps down…repulse monkey."

It reminded me of a skit from Monty Python, featuring a commercial service called "Confuse a Cat."

One day Hopeful showed up in the back yard, scratched up and with a festering wound behind one ear, apparently from a fight with another neighborhood tomcat. His ostensible owner was out in the yard next door, doing her wash, and I remarked on Hopeful's injury. She replied that she hadn't seen his head wound, but that the other day she'd noticed an injury "to his balls." She was out in her yard again the next time I saw Hopeful, whose wound now crawled with maggots. She told me she'd just sprayed the wound as best she could with some disinfectant, but that he'd jumped the fence to get away from her. I borrowed the dishsoap squeeze-bottle she'd used, coaxed him near, and managed to squirt him behind his ear once again before he ran off. I knew she wasn't going to take him to a vet and that he'd probably scratch the hell out of anyone who tried to hold him and treat the wound properly. I wondered if he'd survive.

I didn't see him for almost a week and when I did, he was in bad shape. He'd been scratching at the abcess, which looked worse than ever, and he'd lost weight. Maria and I tried to get him to eat, without success. For the first time we saw his nemesis, a yellow tomcat, standing by Miss Kitty in the yard. Hopeful kept his distance from the other tom, meowing pitifully.

I tried to tell myself that this sort of thing happens every day; it's called natural selection. But I hurt for Hopeful, whom I'd come to care about. He still loved affection and kept trying to rub up against me. I petted him gingerly, avoiding touching his awful-looking lesion. He started coming in the house, which he'd never done when he'd been well. We wondered if he didn't want us to put him out of his misery. Our neighbor told us she'd been treating him with some kind of "bush medicine". We hoped for a miracle.

We saw Alvira at the swearing-in for Group 60 and she invited us to her house for Sunday dinner—our second such invitation since we became Volunteers. I felt nostalgic on the bus ride out to Greendale, remembering our days as Trainees. We arrived a little early to find Alvira still getting ready. But—no prohblem, mon—she broke out three Red Stripes, and we sat out on the back porch and caught up, as she finished combing and braiding her hair. It was good to be back with our Jamaican Mama.

She went on and on about Rory and Rachael's pickiness and disrespect for her house rules; they had clearly *not* become family during their stay with her. As usual, she griped about the rising prices and declining social values, and she listened with great interest to our stories about life and work as Volunteers. When we got on the subject of Jamaican "rough justice," she waxed enthusiastic as she endorsed the practice of neighbors banding together to kill teefs caught in the act of stealing. The teefs *deserved* it!

Before we ate she offered us the customary Sunday "hoppitizer" of Johnny Walker. Then we sat down to a feast of spicy fried chicken, cold roast beef, salad, yams, rice and peas, and soursop juice. Before we left she invited us to come back sometime during Christmas week. We hugged her goodbye and walked out to the bus stop.

Lucy's contract at the School of Nursing was about to expire, but before she sold her car, Mary Lou, and prepared to leave Jamaica, she invited us to take a final trip with her. This time we went to a south coast resort called Treasure Beach, on the western end of the island. On the way we drove through a picturesque stretch of the southern highway called Bamboo Alley, which is almost like a tunnel beneath overarching bamboo stalks, and passed dozens of roadside vendors selling packets of peppery boiled shrimp.

The last part of the trip was through a part of St. Elizabeth Parish known as the San Pedro Plains. Sheltered by the mountains to the north, this area gets little rain. We saw no more jungle-clad hills, and cactus plants dotted the limestone outcroppings. As we neared our destination, we couldn't see any indication that we were near the sea. Then a blue haze replaced land on the southern horizon, gradually resolving into the clear blue of the Caribbean. There was no village of Treasure Beach that we could discern—just homes, beach cottages, and the occasional store, eatery, or rum bar.

We stayed in a small hotel that catered mostly to Jamaicans. While it didn't offer all of the amenities of the big north coast resorts, it was (more-or-less) air-conditioned, had hot running water, and offered satellite TV in the lounge. We arrived in time for an afternoon swim. The waves were high enough for good body surfing. We swam and I jogged on the beach.

We retired to our rooms to shower and rest, met on the front porch for cocktails, then had a leisurely dinner in the hotel restaurant. Lucy didn't drink as much as on our other trips and didn't get wild. I think we were all feeling somewhat subdued, knowing this would be out last time on the road together. After dinner the ladies got to talking shop, so I retired to the TV lounge, where I got my first look at the Sci Fi Channel.

The next morning after breakfast, we sunned and swam until check-out time, then packed and hit the road. On the way home, we stopped at what is probably Jamaica's least-developed tourist attraction, a 1,500-or-so-foot cliff called Lovers' Leap. We followed the signs off the main road and ended up driving past it. When we found it, all we saw marking the spot was a small lighthouse, a tiny Jamaica Defense Force camp with a truck-mounted, rotating radar dish (set up to scan for drug smugglers' small planes, we heard), and the concrete block shell of what appeared to be a club or restaurant under construction. The best view we could find of the shore at the base of the scrub-covered cliff was from the porch of this building.

Remarking on the fact that the cliff wasn't a sheer drop, Lucy commented, " At a *real* lovers' leap you should be able to fall all the way to the bottom. A leap from here would *kill* you all right, but you'd just disappear into the brush. They'd never find the body, ay?"

On our way back through Spanish Town, I saw a restaurant named "Quail-o-rama." Shortly afterward we came across what appeared to be a small parade. Led by strutting cheerleaders, a small marching band played "Onward Christian Soldiers." Then we saw the yellow hearse bearing a casket draped in purple velvet, heaped with flowers. A procession of mourners followed.

The night before I'd dreamed that Hopeful had recovered from his abcess. When we got home it wasn't long before the cats showed up and, sure enough, Hopeful looked like he might make it after all. Although he was still scrawny, he'd gained back a little weight and the wound seemed to be on the mend. There was no sign of the yellow tomcat. We broke out a can of mackerel and gave the cats a feast.

Lucy ate supper with us and stayed until after ten. Maria and I thanked her for asking us along on her trips and we drank to our friendship—with Red Stripes, of course. I quipped that Jamaica's breweries would notice a decline in sales when she left.

"Ay!" she said, "another crack like that and you're *toast*."

By the time I got to work on Monday, two of the new batch of patients admitted over the weekend had "eloped" from the ward. One had left a scrawled note saying he wasn't "mentally prepared" for the program and would be sending someone to pick up his things. I presumed that meant he'd headed straight for the nearest crack house. The other, a well-educated man named Daniel, apparently came from a family that had connections in the medical community. He'd been admitted to the program for the second time as a professional courtesy, having dropped out shortly after his first admission.

The nurses speculated that he'd probably be readmitted if he showed up soon, professing ignorance of his violation of ward rules. Francine made noises about quitting, for the sake of her sanity. I replied that I'd given up my sanity before joining the Peace Corps.

The next day I learned that Daniel had been brought back by friends during the evening and, sure enough, had been admitted again, despite the fact that he showed no motivation to participate in the program. He'd refused to attend either the morning devotional or Celine's art therapy session. I was scheduled to hold my introductory group meeting, but knew that his special treatment would be a subject of group focus, and went to see the resident to get her rationale.

She said that, because he had either bronchitis or pneumonia and was suicidal, and because no other ward would take him, she had no choice but to keep him. When we spoke to him, he sat slumped like a despondent child, refusing to answer our questions about his willingness to cooperate with treatment. To my dismay, Dr. S came in at this point and suggested that Daniel be excused from ward activities for the time being and be coddled by the nurses. Perhaps, if he was treated like a small child, he might come around in a week or so. This made no sense to me at all—I saw it as rewarding his petulant behavior—but it was out of my hands. I'd just have to deal with the group's questions as well as I could.

Group was late getting started and it became clear from the outset that one patient, Norman, had decided to take me on as to who would be the *real* leader. A self-descibed "group therapy veteran" who'd been in several drug treatment programs, as well as prison in the States, he made no attempt to soften his hostile attitude. He repeatedly interrupted my standard introductory presentation and tried to lock horns with several group members. I used my reflection technique to point out his disruption tactics to the others. Then I addressed him directly.

"Look, if you're angry, that's okay; you don't have to hide it. But I won't tolerate *destructive* confrontations and attacks in these meetings."

"Hey," he replied, with only a trace of a Jamaican accent, "if some asshole is bullshitting, I'm not going to let him hurt *my* recovery! I'm going to tell him to pack his shit and get the hell out of here!"

"It's clear you have a lot of pent-up hostility to deal with, Norman. But if you can't keep from attacking other group members, the consequence will be that you'll stay on the hotseat, and the group will focus on your hostility. So far, it seems to me that you want to lock horns and prove you're the toughest ramgoat here."

That seemed to slow him down, but not for long. He used sarcasm to goad another man into getting up and advancing on him angrily. I stood up and intercepted the man, positioning myself between him and Norman.

"Look at what he just did, mon. He baited you and you bit his hook. Now he's trying to reel you in. Don't give him the satisfaction. Check out that grin on his face! Do you think he's *really* amused by all this? He's grinning like that to try and piss you off. It's all part of the game he plays when he's in a situation where he doesn't feel in control. This is your chance to show him he can't control you, that *you* control you."

Several group members backed me up and helped me to calm-down Norman's target. Norman knew his tactic had been exposed and retreated into sullen silence.

When we got around to personal introductions, a group member named Edmond used the opportunity to voice his objections to the ward's no-smoking policy. "Me com here becahs me got a problem wid ahlcohol, noht to quit de cigarette-dem. Me nah got time fi dese Nazi rule-dem! De rule nah mek sense, it ohnfair!"

I tried to get him to look at the fact that he'd known about the rule before he'd entered the program, but that didn't get him off his soapbox. I validated his right to speak out, made empathic statements, and said I'd try to help him cope with the stress of nicotine withdrawal; but that didn't work, either. He didn't think he should have to follow a rule if it didn't make sense to him. I tried a new tack.

"What's the difference between this situation and being shipwrecked on a desert island with everything you need to survive, but no cigarettes. Let's say you *know* you'll be rescued in twenty-eight days. Couldn't you accept, early-on, that you're just going to have to do without, and not make the situation worse than it had to be with your thinking? Or do you think you'd be just as upset on the twenty-seventh day as you were on day one?"

"Is different, dot."

"How?"

He grudgingly conceded that, while he wouldn't be on the island by choice and simply wouldn't have any cigarettes to smoke there, he'd chosen to be in a no-smoking program but knew that there *was* access to tobacco on the hospital grounds.

"I want to suggest to you that the only real difference in the two situations, when it comes to the question of how difficult it would be to do without tobacco for twenty-eight days, is in your thinking. You have the same choice of attitude on day one *here* as you'd have on day one on the island. You can either accept that you're in a no-smoking situation by choice, or you can spend the next twenty-seven days torturing yourself with thoughts like, 'it's not fair,' or 'people are smoking *right now*, not fifty feet away from here.' We can't change the hospital's rule, but you *can* choose your attitude about circumstances you can't change. That's what the Serenity Prayer is all about."

Edmond seemed to get my point—at least he stopped railing against the unfairness of the rule. The dialogue during the rest of the session was fairly calm and reasonable, but I could tell that group work was going to be challenging with this batch.

As the group continued to meet, a member named Everett began to compete with Norman for dominance. Norman continued to verbally attack others and Edmond kept obsessing about cigarettes. Daniel finally started attending group, but had a *prima donna* attitude, and came and went as he pleased. I had my work cut out for me.

I started seeing Norman for individual sessions in addition to group. One-on-one, he acknowledged childhood abuse, having a problem with residual anger, and being abrasive in his interactions. He told me that he'd learned to use his anger to survive in prison. He said he'd gotten hooked on phenobarbital while being treated for a head injury in the States, and that he'd gone on to abuse alcohol, speed, heroin, Quaaludes, tranquilizers, LSD, ganja, and crack. You name it, he'd used it. In our sessions he alternated between candid disclosure and defensive denials. He said that he'd try to work on his tendency to attack and dominate others in group.

One day in a group session, Edmond admitted he'd realized he wasn't only addicted to alcohol, but also to nicotine. In fact, he said, he was probably even more addicted to cigarettes than he was to rum. He thought that he could probably leave the program anytime and not return to drinking.

"I'm scared for you, mon," I replied. "First, it's not a contest as to which you're more addicted to. You're addicted to both. As for your belief that you're already out of the woods as far as any risk of relapsing on alcohol, that just shows me that you're at a different stage of denial.

"You've progressed beyond the bedrock stage, where you don't even admit that you're an addict. Now you're at a stage a lot of addicts get to, where they say, 'I may be an addict, but I'm not like those *other* addicts. Now that I'm sober, I know I'll never relapse.' The next step back toward the bottle is usually convincing yourself that you're a *recovered* addict, or an *ex*-alcoholic. In my experience, people in early recovery who become convinced they'll never relapse are usually setting themselves up to do just that."

The following week, things fell apart on the ward. The staff heard allegations that "certain patients" had been using over the weekend, but no details. Ganja? Crack? On the ward or off the ward? Nobody was talking.

A nurse on the night shift had passed on her suspicions to Francine. She'd smelled smoke on the ward, but didn't know what it was. All she knew was that it wasn't cigarette smoke. When confronted, some patients admitted that something had happened, but nobody would say exactly what. The nurses seemed to expect me to get to the bottom of things in group.

Once we'd assembled I got right down to it. "Okay guys. Information has come to us that some of you have been using. What gives?"

Nobody spoke.

"Listen, anyone who uses in this program is *not* benefitting from it, and they're putting everyone else's recovery at risk. You won't be doing anyone a favor by enabling. And to address anyone here who might have used, if you can't manage to stay clean and sober for twenty-eight days…please have the decency and the respect for the others in the program to pack your bags and leave before you use."

That broke the deadlock. Edmond first said that he'd smelled smoke on the ward last night, but said he didn't know what crack smelled like. Then he admitted that he'd smoked a cigarette in the bathroom during the weekend, himself. Another patient admitted he'd smoked ganja.

Everett was the first to admit to smoking crack, but said he'd been off the ward when he'd done it. Then Daniel said that he'd brought crack onto the ward with him and smoked it. Eventually, another patient confessed to having smoked crack. Norman said he'd smelled crack and that it had triggered cravings, but that he hadn't given in. "I resent you guys threatening my recovery," he said. "I felt like there was nowhere to run to."

By the end of the day we were down from eight to four on the ward.

I was pleasantly surprised that Norman hadn't relapsed. Despite his hostility, I liked him.

When we met for individual therapy later in the week, I labelled his anger as a defense.

"You rely on your anger because it helped you survive in prison—it was your armor. But a knight only needs armor in combat. Sometimes people cling to tried-and-true defenses even after the need for them has passed, and the price they pay is that they stay stuck where they are. The only way you can learn that you don't always have to be heavily defended in every situation is to take the risk of facing the world without your armor, at least in safe situations. You act tough all the time, but I think that's because you're afraid to face the world without wearing your suit of armor. And that's a pretty heavy burden to carry around all the time."

"You don't know me," he replied. "Everything I do is for a good reason."

"If so, you'd be the first person I've ever known who does. We all have subconscious motivations. Norman, I don't think you *want* to let people see the man inside the armor. I think I know you better than you want to admit. They say the best defense is a good offense, and I see you as a very defensive person."

"You're wrong. I always know what I'm doing."

"Well, *you* may believe that, but don't expect *me* to. Come on, man! Bright as you are, you can probably see things about me when I'm leading a group that I may not be consciously aware of. So don't assume I can't see *some* things about you more clearly than you can."

I struck a haughty pose. "After all, I'm a trained observer of human behavior."

"But so am I," he countered. "That's how I survived in prison."

"Different schools," I acknowledged with a grin.

We both laughed.

Our rapport was off-and-on, and he continued to try and dominate in group. He disagreed with every observation I made about his hostile behavior and his need to control every situation he found himself in. I realized that he was just too defensive to concede anything in a group setting, sometimes finding him more open to insight in our individual sessions. When he knew I was going to confront him about something one-on-one, he'd hijack the conversation, interrupting me and engaging in lengthy monologues—mostly about prison life.

In one session I asked him, "When two people go into a room to talk, how does one of them demand that he dominate the situation?"

He seemed to get my point: you talk and talk, and refuse to engage in a dialogue. But then he launched back into his prison stories—interesting, but an obvious refusal to deal with *my* agenda. I later asked him if I could have one minute for every three of his and, when he agreed, I conspicuously kept my eye on my watch. Gradually he came around and we started to engage in more of a dialogue. I pointed out the change, and thanked him.

I got around to asking him if he thought he already knew everything he needed to know about himself to remain in recovery. He conceded that he probably didn't. I observed that he seemed more open to insight in our individual sessions than in group.

"When I say something about you in group, you seem to react as if I'd pulled down your pants, pointed at your arse, and invited everyone to laugh at you."

"Maybe so," he conceded, "but don't forget—I've lived in your country and I've done time in your prison system. You're white."

The scales fell off my eyes. I'd become so used to being around black people who didn't seem to distrust me because I'm white that I'd failed to take his history into account. I thanked him for his honesty. I told him I felt honored that he'd let me in as much as he had, and that he'd listened to me at all.

Later in the hour I said I could see that he was not only sincere, but "passionately sincere" in his desire to stay in recovery. We ended the session with the gesture used by Jamaican men to signify accord, bumping the knuckles of our right fists and both saying, "Respect."

In mid-September our groupmate Linda, with whom we'd gone to Hellshire Beach, contacted us and asked if we'd like to join her on a "turtle watch" the following weekend. She explained that an endangered species of sea turtle laid eggs at a certain secluded beach on the south coast at the same times every year. These turtles had been hunted to the brink of extinction by Jamaican fishermen, who used them to make soup and collected the eggs, which they considered an aphrodisiac. She knew a biologist named Andrea, who worked for the Natural History Society and organized groups to camp overnight and patrol the beach when the turtles were due, to protect both the turtles and their eggs. It sounded like a free adventure to us, so we agreed to participate.

We didn't have much in the way of camping gear, but on Saturday we loaded our packs with warm clothes, windbreakers, beach towels, toilet articles, flashlights and spare batteries, canteens, and food. I also took insect repellant, my Swiss Army knife (a Peace Corps perennial), and a bota bag filled with wine. We hoped we were ready for anything.

Around noon we took a bus to Halfway Tree and walked to the designated meeting place.

There we met groupmates Linda and Shirly, as well as Andrea and the other members of the expedition. We found them loading several vehicles with their supplies. The party of turtle watchers was mostly comprised of Jamaican teenagers, but also included two Jamaican men named Michael, a white Jamaican woman named Susan, an Englishwoman named Jill, and a United Nations ecologist from the Netherlands named Jan (pronounced "Yon").

Our gear got stashed in the first vehicle to leave, a four-wheel drive Isuzu jeep with a luggage rack mounted on top. We left later, crammed into a car with some of the teenagers, concerned about being separated from our stuff. The car was filled with banter and raucous laughter, and smelled of teen sweat.

We drove through the town of May Pen, then headed south toward Milk River Bath, past sugar cane fields and banana orchards. I spotted a sign that read "Banana Crossing," and another that read "Sleeping Policeman Ahead." (This, one of the teenagers informed us, was the Jamaican term for a speed bump.) As we rode, I again copied interesting names of business establishments in my pocket notebook, including a rum bar called Lilly's Fun Jug, the Cry Cry Bar, the Full Belly Restaurant, Rumour Tavern, Dreamland Tavern and Guest House, Forever Supermarket, Healthy Appetite Cafe, Seekers Pub, and Melon Man Headquarters.

Passing Milk River Bath—a natural springs spa—we followed signs to Alligator Hole Swamp. We stopped at an unattended guest center in the swamp to stretch our legs. It had a small visitors' pavillion. Its only exhibits were ecological posters and a badly-stuffed, scraggly little crocodile. Jamaica's toothy aquatic reptiles are technically crocs, I learned from one of the posters, but are generally referred to as alligators.

From there the rutted dirt road steadily worsened and we all got bounced about in the crowded car. We reached a point where the driver said he could go no further without a four-wheel drive vehicle, let us all out and turned around, leaving us to walk the remaining four or five miles to Guts River, our destination. Swarms of mosquitos attacked us as we made our way down the road, between jungled limestone hills and the swamp.

We arrived at the spot where the Guts River meets the sea. The only human habitation we saw was a rum bar on the landward side of the narrow river, which we had to ford to get to the seashore. A boy ferried us across in a small flat-bottomed boat, and we found Andrea and our packs awaiting us on the beach.

She stationed Maria and me at the central campsite with herself, Susan, and Jan. Linda, Shirley, Jill, and the two Michaels, she told us, were already in place down the beach about a half mile to the west. The teenagers would set up camp about a mile up the beach to the east, where we could see the huge hump of Round Hill—the eastern boundary of the beach—in the distance.

They would patrol the stretch of beach between their camp and Round Hill, the other group would walk from their site to the western end of the beach, and we would watch for turtles coming ashore between the eastern and western camps. Each camp would patrol in shifts throughout most of the night.

As the first shift wasn't until seven and we still had about an hour of daylight in which to explore, Maria and I set out to find Linda and Shirley. We had to cross the river again to get to their camp, but it was only about two feet deep where it crossed the beach, and deliciously cool.

When we located our two groupmates, I broke out a flask of rum and some limes, and the four of us had cocktails on the beach as the sun went down in a blaze of colors.

We got back to the central camp by seven and unpacked, while Andrea, Susan, and Jan prepared to set out. Before they left, Andrea explained our mission. We were to walk the beach at the tideline and look for turtle tracks, which she illustrated in the sand.

"Use flahshlights ohnly if you mohst. Walk to the next cahmp, wait ten minutes, then cohm bahck. If you see turtle trahcks, find out if she'is still on shore, wait ontil she's bahck in the sea, then cohver op the trahcks."

The landward side of the beach was forested, so it would be easy to break off a leafy branch to use on the sand to obscure any turtle tracks. The moon had risen over the sea, almost full. Although the sky was partially obscured by clouds, the moon offered ample illumination for our task.

It sprinkled briefly while the others walked their first patrol. For most of the time they were gone, flashes of sheet lightning backlit the clouds that scudded around the moon. We opened a tin of corned beef and made sandwiches, then lay back to rest on the poncho that Andrea had loaned us—having brought her own sleeping bag.

Shortly after the others returned, we set out under the light of the tropic moon, both of us barefoot, walking a stretch of Jamaican beach that few tourists see, even by daylight. Gentle waves lapped at our feet as we walked, soaking the bottoms of my rolled-up jeans. Part of the time we held hands. Sometimes we talked, the rest of the time we just drank in the beauty around us in silence.

The marker for the eastern camp was the upright tail of a small crashed plane (a drug smuggler who'd barely made it to land?), which glowed with flickering firelight in the brush just north of the beach. We found the youngest contingent of turtle watchers huddled around a small campfire and stopped to chat for a few minutes before heading back. On our return we came across two men coming in the opposite direction, carrying buckets. One of them held a machete. I tensed up. We exchanged "good night"s as we passed each other.

Are they hunting for turtles? I wondered. I'll never know, but I reported them to Andrea when we got back. She'd seen them, too.

After a while the other three set out again, leaving Maria and me to finish our supper. I'd recently resumed pipe smoking, having asked Pamela and Ben to bring me a pipe and tobacco when they visited us; so I lit up a pipe and smoked while Maria lay back on the poncho and tried to nap.

Andrea, Susan, and Jan returned sometime after eleven. They hadn't seen anything of note. We all talked for a while, then Maria and I left for our second and last patrol. We saw no signs of turtles, but enjoyed another sensual trek in the moonlight together. At the eastern camp we found everyone wrapped in blankets, their campfire down to embers. We sat on a driftwood log and listened to the lapping waves for a few minutes before we started back.

This time we came across a man who identified himself to us as the local game warden, although he wore no uniform. He knew about the turtle watch and thanked us for our help. Returning to our campsite, we sat and talked with the others until it was time for them to leave on their final walk for the night. I was still awake when they got back, around two-thirty. I'd put my shoes back on, rolled down my pants legs, and donned my windbreaker in preparation for sleep. Maria had already dozed off, covered in a beach towel. She didn't sleep very well that night, but I slept soundly. I fell asleep looking at the moon.

My next memory was also of the moon, low in the west against against a dark gray sky, set off by three short, horizontal clouds. Sensing another dim source of light in the sky, I looked to the east to see the first hint of dawn brightening above the distant silhouette of Round Hill, which looked like the upper fifth of an immense, dark sun, rising over the horizon.

I had no desire to roll over and sleep any more, but was instantly awake. I sat up and stuffed some tobacco in my pipe, smoking and watching as the sky brightened into shades of salmon and blue, with drifting clouds white against the fading grays of night. Looking shoreward, the greens of the tropic vegetation and colors of the brightly-painted rum bar across the river seemed amazingly intense in the dawn light. I watched as the gray sea gradually brightened into blue, with moving ribbons of white foam. It was one of the finest awakenings of my life. There was no place I'd rather have been. It felt like the center of the world.

Maria wasn't so enthusiastic when she awoke. Her sleep had been light and fitful, and by the time she opened her eyes the mosquitos were out in force. She put her bandanna over her face. I covered her with the part of the poncho I'd occupied, and she snoozed off again.

When Andrea woke up, she drank some tea from a thermos then set off for the western camp. Jan still slept until she returned shortly afterward, reporting turtle tracks a little way up the beach. We followed her to just past the mouth of the river, where we saw the tracks going up and down the beach. It was easy to see where the turtle had laid her eggs, so we raked over her trail with branches until it was impossible to tell she'd been there.

So, while it turned out that none of us turtle watchers had spotted any turtles during our vigil, eggs had been laid during our night on the beach. The trip would have been a worthwhile experience anyway, but this knowledge made it all the more special.

Maria and I had our gear packed by seven-thirty. We forded the river to where the jeep awaited us. This time we got out with the first load, the driver speeding, grousing about needing to get to church on time, in Kingston. I had to ride in the rear, straddling the spare tire—the third perch in a back seat built for two. The first six miles up the rutted, pot-holed swamp road were the worst, as I got tossed around in the back. By the time we got to Halfway Tree, around nine-thirty, I was stiff and sore. Our driver still went on about how he was in a hurry to get to church, but I felt like I'd already been, out on the beach.

When I told the nurses on the ward about our expedition the following Monday, Sandra commented, "I've lived here all my life, and I've never seen some of the things you've seen."

As time went on, I learned more about the "rude boy" culture of posses, drugs, and dancehall music. The term rude boy was a compliment in some circles, signifying a soldier in the turf wars between posses. Some of them were also known as cocaine cowboys, and the gang ethic was glorified in the lyrics of many deejay/dancehall songs. The possession of a handgun earned one great prestige on the street, and the custom of firing off a fusillade of bullets outside of a party venue had become known as the "Jamaican salute." The popular weekday tabloid called the *Star* was filled with rumors and stories about poisoned bullets and acid-throwing.

According to this paper, some people carried vials of acid—known as "monkey lotion"—around with them, to use on enemies or people they felt had slighted them.

One night after supper we watched a JBC talk show whose host, Diana Wright, discussed with guests the topic of "conscious" versus "slack" lyrics in reggae music. Conscious referred to pro-social, uplifting lyrics, or lyrics that reflected pride in the African roots of Jamaican culture. (Bob Marley's "Stand Up For Your Rights" and "Redemption Song" are good examples of conscious songs.) Slack was synonymous with rude, reflecting Kingston's street culture of Dons, gangs, and guns.

Nobody on the show had anything positive to say about slack lyrics. One guest said he feared that slack deejay music could pull down reggae. Another said that most Jamaicans care more about the rhythms than the lyrics. The general tenor of the comments was that reggae lyrics, in the tradition of Bob Marley, should promote brotherhood, react against oppression, and reflect positive values. Someone pointed out that, although many slack songs demeaned women, it was mainly women who seemed to lionize the rude boy performers.

The appeal of the macho ethic and the glorification of guns was understandable in a society with such a mass of powerless, or marginalized, young men. However, one of the panelists expressed an idea popular in this proud nation: that reggae was destined to change the world—reggae in the Rastafarian spirit of Marley's music, not its slack offspring. She said that many Jamaicans hoped dancehall music would prove to be a flash in the pan. But true reggae, she said, *lives*, and would endure, not only on the island, but in such world cultural centers as Capetown, London, Toronto, Tokyo, and New York.

Around this time I'd started going to the Mutual Life Building in uptown Kingston on a regular basis. The building housed not only the U.S. Embassy, but the United States Information Service library, which had videotapes on drug abuse that I could check out for use on the ward.

I did some research at the library on Jamaica's role in the international drug trade and learned some interesting things.

Apparently, in the eighties ganja had been the island's main cash crop and the chief source of income for thousands of subsistence farmers and their families. Many Jamaicans still believed that the only reason ganja remained illegal was pressure from the U.S., in the form of strings attached to financial aid. Jamaicans have exported untold tons of ganja to the U.S. since the seventies, but when crack cocaine came on the scene in the mid-eighties, the drug posses turned to crack distribution and Jamaica became a major link in the transshipment chain from South America. By 1988 "Jamerican" posses had established themselves as some of crack's primary traffickers. Columbians controlled the wholesale trade, but Jamaicans had carved out a major niche in the retail marketing of crack in the U.S.

Operating via self-contained cells, so that no local bust could bring down the larger organizations, Jamaican posses established a reputation for organization, efficiency, and ruthless violence. Operations had branched out from New York to Washington and Miami—earning I-95 the name "cocaine alley" in the process—and from crack distribution to illegal weapons sales. All of this had a profound impact on life in the streets of Kingston and on Jamaican popular culture.

In October I attended a major West Indian symposium on drug abuse at the National Conference Center, down by the harbor. As I recall, it was partially underwritten by the DEA. U.S. representatives as well as by drug experts from all over the Caribbean region attended. Prime Minister Patterson gave the opening address. Presenters discussed all aspects of the international plague of drug abuse, from the economic impact of the drug trade on West Indian economies, to crop substitution programs which could provide profitable alternatives to ganja farmers, to local and national drug treatment strategies.

A speaker from the Bahamas freely admitted that the transshipment of cocaine through that island nation had bolstered its economy from the grass roots level on up. Given the natural bounty of the sea, not even the poorest Bahamians had ever faced starvation; but now many citizens had gone from living in conditions of poverty to buying satellite dishes and wearing high-fashion clothes.

Several presenters addressed the issue of relative accountability for the spread of hard drugs in the Western Hemisphere—the supply-side factors in the equation on the part of developing countries, versus the demand for drugs in the industrialized nations of the north. One speaker made the point that the U.S. doesn't have the right to interfere in the sovereignty of so-called Third World nations by imposing its own standards, via economic and political sanctions, while failing to adequately address the demand side of the equation.

Dr. G, head of the Drug Abuse Secretariat and author of Jamaica's Integrated Demand Reduction Programme (IDER), gave a keynote address on his plan. He'd just returned from giving a pitch for funding at a U.N. conference in Vienna. He touted IDER as a model for not only the Caribbean, but the world, extolling Jamaica's newly formed community action agencies (CODACs) for their alleged accomplishments. He declared that cocaine abuse had been reduced by ten percent on the island, although he cited no research to back up his claim.

Subsequent speakers took over praising the model where Dr. G had left off. I could understand that. It *was*, after all, a Jamaican conference, and Dr. G had distinguished himself as the local lion in the area of drug abuse prevention.

Personally, I hadn't been impressed by what I'd seen and heard of IDER. My cynical assessment had been that, since the government couldn't adequately fund a national prevention program, they'd placed the emphasis on local community action agencies which relied on unpaid, under-trained "counselors" to prevent the spread of drug abuse. They looked like they'd gotten the problem covered, on paper, but I hadn't seen any outcome studies on the fledgling program.

What I heard at the conference made me re-think my own judgements. Like PCVs, the CODACs were trying to make stone soup—to catalyze positive change with limited resources. Dr. G had gotten sizable monetary commitments from the international community, so he'd obviously impressed *somebody* with his model. I had to admit that I had no expertise in policy planning and community prevention strategies. *Admitting your ignorance*, I reminded myself, *is the beginning of wisdom.*

A Canadian speaker praised IDER, saying, "other countries meet and churn out lots of paperwork, but Jamaica is actually *doing* something about the problem." Later in the day, representatives from several CODACs spoke about their local efforts. These included not only drug education in the schools, but organizing neighborhood watches, creating new jobs, and holding community meetings to discuss local problems and solutions. One CODAC organizer admitted, "We are learning dot it is wan t'ing to write a plahn, and quite anohther to make it work. Dis effort is bringing os togeddah as a cohmmunity."

In his address, Dr.G had criticized "the intelligensia"—in whose number he'd included himself—for having a tendency to generate centralized plans that proved to be irrelevant to local realities, instead of working from the ground up. The IDER model proposed evaluation, planning, and implementation phases, all to be carried out at the community level. It recognized that drug abuse doesn't exist in a vaccuum, but is related to other community problems.

I left the conference humbled, a little more aware that I share some of the arrogance of which North Americans are sometimes accused by people in developing countries. *Jamaican problems*, I reflected, *call for Jamaican solutions.* My experiences at the symposium reminded me that I wasn't just in the Peace Corps to teach, but to learn.

As our first year in Jamaica drew to an end, I hoped that things might just work out on the ward. I felt I'd earned my spurs and decided to become more active in my efforts to improve the treatment program. To that end, I began to draft a program assessment, detailing recurring problems and possible solutions.

My secondary project, the small library in the nearly-abandoned Child Guidance Clinic where I had my office, began to have some takers. At the request of a Volunteer who taught school, I loaded some of the juvenile fiction I'd found into cardboard boxes and took it by taxi to the Peace Corps office for her to pick up. A few weeks later, another Volunteer showed up at the hospital in her supervisor's pickup truck and we loaded it with books. Others contacted me over the next few months and the stacks dwindled, as the Volunteers met me at my office, inspected the books, and took what they wanted.

When the ward staff learned that we'd be getting student nurses on the ward, as part of their clinical rotations, I volunteered (through Maria) to teach an orientation class on drug addiction and treatment. I worried that having different student nurses sitting in on my group sessions might interfere with group process, but the decision had been made. UHWI was, after all, a teaching hospital, and I served on the faculty. I developed a lesson plan and, once every few weeks, spent an afternoon teaching over at the School of Nursing.

Since the no-smoking rule continued to create problems on the ward, I took it upon myself to write a pharmaceutical company and request a donation of nicotine patches. The staff liked my idea and agreed that if we had to forbid cigarette smoking in a program for addicts, we should treat nicotine withdrawal medically. I didn't know if the letter would get us anything, but it was worth a try.

We'd started having a family night on the ward once or twice during each treatment cycle. Some got cancelled because hardly anyone came, but others were well-attended and gave me a chance to meet the patients' family members. One evening when I'd stayed at work late to attend family night, who should I see as a guest presenter but Morris, the arrogant ex-patient who'd been one of the first to take me on in group. He'd been clean for almost a year. Active in the recovery community, he'd been invited as one of the program's success stories.

I couldn't believe the changes I saw in him. When he spoke, I heard nothing of his former superior attitude and biting sarcasm. He even admitted that he'd learned the only way he could stay clean was to abstain from *all* drugs, including ganja and alcohol. He spoke freely about how he'd messed his life up with drugs and about the things he'd had to work on to stay in recovery.

After the meeting I congratulated him and remarked on the changes I saw in him, adding, "Morris, humility *becomes* you." He responded with a wry grin.

Yet another ancillary job duty was community drug education. Sister M had asked me if I could give a talk and serve on a panel at an upcoming Healthy Lifestyles Exhibition, to be held on a Saturday at a large church. Similar to a health fair in the U.S., it would have blood pressure testing, displays, and booths from different organizations and health-related agencies, with their inevitable stacks of pamphlets. There would be panel discussions and presentations in the church hall throughout the late morning and the afternoon.

On the Saturday of the exhibition I had no trouble catching a bus and arrived early for my ten o'clock panel. On my way to the Detox Ward table, I saw booths run by Bahais, the Unity Church, the Nation of Islam, Transcendental Meditation, and the Seventh Day Adventists, each pitching its own formula for healthy lifestyles.

The panel discussion didn't start until ten thirty and, except for mine, the "two minute" opening statements ran ten to fifteen minutes each. The panel moderator then *summarized* these introductions for the benefit of latecomers—a common practice of Jamaican moderators—and held a question-and-answer session that dragged on through the noon hour. My presentation on self-esteem, scheduled for eleven, didn't get started until nearly one. It was videotaped for posterity and seemed to be well-received.

I would have left after completing my duties, but decided to stay and watch a performance by a group of young people called The Teen Players. Howard, the movement therapist, had told me about the organization that sponsored the performing group. The Little People trained children and teens in the theater arts and staged performances. Howard had told me to expect a pretty polished show.

Sure enough, the all-acting, all-singing, all-dancing cast proved well on its way to achieving professional performance standards. Called "Positive Vibes," their show was about sexual choices, STDs, and safe sex. One number in particular brought the house down.

I stood behind the stage—which afforded a better view than the crowded floor—so when the performers emerged from the wings and took their places, facing away from the audience, I could see that each one wore a tee shirt with a single letter on the front. The six who'd come in from my right lined up in a row, their respective letters being, " S, M, R,E,P,S." The three girls who'd entered from my left wore the letters, "A,V,O." I caught on just before they turned around.

The six boys burst into action, dancing energetically and singing a song called, "We're The Sperms." *Sounds like the name of a punk band*, I thought.

Then the girls turned around to musically announce that they were The Ova. Just as the boys started bumping and grinding their way over to the girls, out came eight dancers wearing cheap, translucent raincoats over their clothes. Each raincoat bore a sign reading , "CONDOM." The singing condoms linked hands, encircling the eager sperms and keeping them from reaching the demure ova. The audience loved it. I laughed until my sides ached.

Although PCVs and embassy personnel seldom socialized except for special occasions at Bamboo Pen, in late September the Charge D'Affaires gave a party for all the Volunteers in Kingston over the weekend at his grand villa up in the hills overlooking the city. The party was in honor of Ed Hughes, the Peace Corps Country Director, who was about to return Stateside. By coincidence, it also marked the first anniversary of Group 58's arrival on the island.

Maria had gone early, to help with food preparation. When I arrived, the sun still shone brightly, but clouds had begun to slide in over the mountains. Most guests milled around on the spacious lawn that extended downhill from the main house, chatting and drinking beer. Others had gathered around the satellite TV in the sumptuously-appointed downstairs den to watch American football.

I walked from the den out onto the patio, got myself a Dragon Stout from one of the several coolers there, and walked down across the lawn to where some of our number were standing around a cluster of grills and food preparation tables. Maria volunteered me to make hamburger patties and I was soon up to my wrists in mince (ground beef).

Burgers and chicken already sizzled on the grills. We rushed to finish cooking, as the sky began to look threatening and thunder rumbled in the distance. We caught up on current events in the Peace Corp community as we worked. I introduced myself to Richard, from Group 60, who turned out to be the only second-generation Volunteer I've ever met. He literally owed his life to the Peace Corps, his father having met his mother—a Columbian—while serving in that country. I also spoke with Michael, a Volunteer of my acquaintance from Group 59, who told of having recently survived a shootout in the dungtung streets.

"It happened a few blocks from Parade," he said, "on my way to work. At first I didn't even know I'd been caught in a crossfire. I thought I heard firecrackers going off, then suddenly this Jamaican guy grabbed me and pulled me to the ground! I thought he'd attacked me, then I saw these gunmen running, shooting behind them. Then I saw constables shooting back from across the street. I'd walked into a getaway from a bank robbery! I heard one of the robbers got killed, but I didn't see it myself."

Michael wasn't sure at that point if he planned to complete his tour in Jamaica. His local national boss, a neighborhood Don, sometimes assigned him an armed bodyguard. He'd thought about requesting a transfer out of Kingston. He didn't want to push his luck.

Jamaica has two rainy seasons, centered in the months of May and October. We'd recently had some gullywashers and nature wasn't through with us yet. The clouds opened up, pouring rain down on us in a sudden torrent. We grabbed all the food we could carry and rushed up the rain-slick lawn to the house. Already soaked to the skin anyway, some of us went back and rescued the rest of the food.

Everyone crowded onto the sheltered portion of the patio and into the den. White-jacketed servants put out card tables for the overflow of food and took the uncooked meat to finish preparing it in the kitchen. Those of us who'd gotten drenched stayed out on the covered patio, chatting, dripping, and drinking until the food was ready. Maria and I had time to talk to Ed and his wife, and to wish them Godspeed on their impending departure. We had just enough food and beer, so a good—if damp—time was had by all.

I usually went to the Peace Corps office at least once a week, to check for mail and to use the word processors in the Volunteer lounge. I'd also often browse around in the sizable library there—books donated by PCVs over the years. Volunteers in Jamaica often find themselves waiting in lines or idled by circumstances beyond their control, so most of us carried books wherever we went. I averaged at least one book a week, donating some of mine that I'd finished to the PC library, returning the ones I'd borrowed, and picking up new titles almost weekly. If I found a care package waiting in the mail room, or if I did a "major shop" at Wong's Supermarket on the way back, I'd treat myself to a taxi ride home; otherwise, I'd ride the bus.

I felt safe on the streets of Kingston, but only because I never let my guard down completely. Keeping an eye out for potential teefs had become second nature by now, especially in crowds. Human predators, like their animal counterparts, study the herd for likely prey; and I knew I stood out. So I'd learned to look out for men who seemed to be watching me, to see if I was being stalked. More than once in dungtung crowds, I'm convinced that a teef saw me watching him watch me, and backed off in search of easier prey. In a letter home, I claimed to have grown eyes in the back of my head.

One day after I'd been to the Peace Corps office, I was crossing the uptown business district of New Kingston on my way to the bus stop when I came upon a dreadlocked man clad only in a burlap sack, worn as a skirt. He hailed me and asked where I was from. Knowing that this was often a prelude to getting begged, I usually ignored such questions and kept walking; but, in this instance, I stopped and answered the man's question. He asked me what I was doing in Jamaica, and I told him.

Despite his madman appearance, he was bright and well-spoken. He knew the difference between a psychologist and a psychiatrist, which suggested that he'd spent some time at Belleview. We chatted briefly, but when I attempted to disengage, he asked if I was a Christian and proceeded to quote scripture in an effort to persuade me to give him some money. I gave him my standard answer, but he persisted in begging me. So I said, "Respect," and went on. When I continued to ignore his attempts to re-engage me, he called out "God bless you" as I walked away.

Ironically, my walking-around money—about $J20—got picked on the bus ride home. If I'd given it to the beggar, it wouldn't have been in my pocket to steal. Jah, as the Rastas would tell you, works in mysterious ways. Jah giveth and Jah taketh away.

Around this time an article appeared in a Kingston newspaper with the headline, "Jockeys on the Rampage on Hospital Ward." It was topic number one when I went to work, because we were the ward referred to in the story! Kingston had a racetrack and we *had* had jockeys in the program, but the story was a fiction. It said a "highly-placed" source at the hospital who'd "begged anonymity" had described to a reporter how jockeys had "wreaked havoc" and sold drugs on the ward.

Martha told the rest of us that a reporter had called and asked if we had any jockeys in the program. She said she hadn't answered his question, but had referred him to Sister M—who'd recently refused outright to come on the ward and who'd been heard to remark that she didn't care if the ward was shut down. We all had a pretty good idea who the highly-placed source had been. I wrote in my journal, "The article certainly made us look like a big circus...or something more like a circus than we, in fact, are."

On the home front, Vasanth's sister, Rainuke, moved in with him and Prakash. She'd just arrived from India, in hopes of attending the UHWI School of Nursing, but she hadn't yet applied. We didn't meet her until her second day in country, after she'd slept off her jet lag. She came out and joined Vasanth, Maria, and me as we sat out under the overhang in a twilight thunderstorm, talking loudly to be heard over the din of the rain.

We'd been discussing religion—specifically, the difference between deists, atheists, and agnostics. I labeled myself as somewhere between an *a* gnostic and *ag*nostic, depending on where you placed the "a." Vasanth said that he was an agnostic, now living with *two* deists—at which point he introduced us to his slender, shy, sari-clad sister. Rainuke and Prakash, he told us, ate no beef and practiced Hindu prayer rituals daily.

Then we saw what may have been a sign from God. A yellow butterfly flitted about in the downpour, apparently dodging the battering rain-drops, a miracle of flight.

Not long after Rainuke's arrival, we learned from Dr. Lui that some Jesuit seminarians would be moving into another house he owned, next door. He also mentioned that he'd recently joined a Buddhist sect. Something he said jogged my memory. My first wife, Doris, had briefly been involved in a Buddhist sect, Nichiren Daishonin, that practiced a chanting ritual. I asked Kai Meng if his sect was the one that chanted, "nan myoho renge kyo." He lit up and said that it was.

With the Jesuits about to move in next door, it looked like we had the makings of an ongoing religious symposium.

Rick and some other Volunteers who lived on the north coast decided to stage a First Annual Port Antonio Pub Crawl on a Saturday in mid-October and sent out invitations. Maria and I set out by taxi for the country bus terminal on that morning, expecting a two or three hour bus ride. The dungtung streets of Coronation Market were crammed with pedestrians, who parted to let the taxi pass like fish before a diver swimming the reefs. I'd no sooner paid the driver, outside the terminus, than a conman asked us where we were going and promised to secure us seats on the next bus to Port Antonio. I knew not to trust him because he wanted money in advance.

We entered a large, enclosed asphalt square, surrounded by kiosks, snack shacks, and rum bars. From this place you could go anywhere in Jamaica. Sweaty crowds clustered around each newly-arriving bus, shoving and jostling to get on board. We found the area marked for the Port Antonio buses, expecting one to show up any minute. Three hours later we were still waiting.

You really didn't even have to go shop in the kiosks to get anything you might need for a trip. Hustlers roamed throughout the terminus selling box drinks, bag drinks, beer, doughnuts, and other snack foods, tee shirts, sunglasses, hats, toothbrushes and toothpaste, combs and brushes, watches, soap, shoe polish—even packets labelled "Spanish Fly."

Maria and I avoided drinking much, as we realized that once we got on a bus it might be hours before we got a chance to relieve ourselves. I craned my neck and stared as each new bus arrived, hoping. We knew that when a Port Antonio bus finally *did* come, there would be a mad dash and a shoving match to board. I told Maria, "when it comes, *think Jamaican*— every mon fi 'imself." Later I said, "think Malcolm X—*by any means necessary.*" We knew better than to expect to get seats; we just needed to insinuate our bodies on board in the crush. We had ourselves psyched-up like athletes.

When a bus finally arrived, we charged forward with the crowd and managed to get near the door. Hardly anyone got off and we realized that the bus had already loaded up at Halfway Tree. All the seats were filled and standing room was scarce. Young men behind me managed to slip past me through the knot and board, slick as butter. I got separated from Maria, but managed to shove my way up onto the steps. I reached back over the heads of the other hopefuls and grabbed her weekend bag, getting my cheap sunglasses knocked off in the process. Somehow I managed to retrieve them from the floor, but one of the plastic lenses was missing.

Once on board there was no going back, and I prayed that Maria would manage to get on, too. We were the only white people in the crowd, and she later told me that others in the press of bodies practically shoved her onto the bottom step, realizing that she was with me. When the bus door closed, the crowd was packed so tightly that she barely had room to breathe, her sternum pressed up against a hand rail.

I nearly panicked as the bus pulled out, not knowing if Maria had made it. "Did the white lady get on board?" I called out, "*Maria!?*"

"Nah wohrry, mon," someone near the door called back. "She ahn de bos."

I had to take his word for it. Although we couldn't have been more than six feet apart in the throng, I didn't see or hear her for over three hours. As we left Kingston and wound our way up the twisty mountain roads, the crowd pitching and heaving, I hung on to an overhead rail for dear life, straddling our luggage and constantly on the alert for teefs. The ride to the north coast seemed to take forever. The stifling air smelled of sweat, and I could barely think over the din of the patois exchanges among the hundred-or-so passengers.

As we neared our destination, people began to disembark as we stopped in the villages along the way. My body ran with sweat and both arms ached from holding on to the safety rails. I finally saw Maria, who'd just gotten a seat up near the driver. When, at last, we arrived in Port Antonio,

I felt vastly relieved that we'd gotten there with our luggage intact—if not my sunglasses.

Maria and I climbed out of the bus exhausted, happy simply to be able to move freely. We made our way through the now-familiar streets to the Holiday Home, a guesthouse where Jennifer had reserved a room for us, and checked in. Our expected three hour trip had taken us over six hours and we'd arrived just in time for the festivities. We freshened up and headed to a previously-designated jerk restaurant on the coastal road in the dusk. Others had begun to congregate, to eat in preparation for the pub crawl. Rick had asked me to be sure and wear my "Onward Through the Fog" tee shirt for the occasion and crowed when he saw me arrive wearing it.

Jennifer had joined the Jamaican staff behind the bar, handing out beers and plates of food. She and Rick had worked out a standard fare for supper, and we all dined on jerk chicken and bread. Complementary fish soup was provided by the establishment's proprietors, who were thankful for all the business. Rick explained that their landlord owned not only the restaurant, but also the mountain property that we'd be going to for a cookout the next day.

About thirty people had made it to the event. Most were PCVs, with a few Jamaicans and sundry expatriate Americans thrown-in to spice the mix. Among the celebrants were Marty, one of the Jesuit seminarians who'd soon be moving in next door to us, and Frank, a D.E.A. agent assigned to the embassy. We were all primed to party. Rick took the floor to explain the origin and rules of the crawl.

"Welcome one and all to the First Annual Port Antonio Pub Crawl. This event was modelled after a Peace Corps pub crawl attended by Bob's sister when she was a Volunteer in Africa. Very strict rules were observed on that historical occasion. In line with this proud tradition, we've tried to set this thing up *correctly*, first consulting the Oxford English Dictionary to define our terms.

"There, we found 'pub' defined as a colloquial noun, an abbreviation for 'public house,' or 'tavern.' For our purposes, we've decided that, to qualify as a pub, an establishment must meet the following minimum criteria. It must have at least two stools. It must serve white overproof rum as well as dark rum. It must include in its bill of fare *both* Red Stripe and either Dragon or Guiness Stout—preferably both."

The crowd cheered.

"As to the 'crawl' part, the O.E.D. definitions are, 'to advance on the hands and knees or on the belly,' 'to sneak about,' 'to be alive with insects,' and 'to feel creepy.' As not all participants may wish to be alive with insects, to feel creepy, or to sneak about, we've decided to adopt the first definition, with some latitude given to those who might wish to advance from pub to pub in an upright position, as long as they are able to do so. We would hope that none of you upstanding members of our expatriate community will feel *obligated* to advance on your bellies—but who are we to quibble with Oxford?

"I'd be remiss not to point out that, while the consumption of alcoholic beverages is not a *requirement* for participation, it is certainly recommended. The *only* requirement, in the spirit of our collective commitment to supporting the local economy, is that each participant consume *at least* one beverage of his or her own choice at each establishment which meets the strict criteria qualifying it for our patronage.

"We welcome you to this pioneering endeavor to find the *true meaning* of a Jamaican pub crawl and invite you to explore new dimensions of slackness, setting the standard for future Volunteers to follow. Thank you."

And we were off with a rousing cheer, into the Jamaican night. We started out by visiting three hole-in-the-wall rum bars, whose proprietors received the sudden crowd with delight. We filled the bars and spilled out onto the sidewalk. I'd get beers for Maria and myself, then move among the clusters of pubcrawlers, never staying with any conversation for very long, just taking it all in. Maria pursued her own course through the sea of chatter.

Having fed the coffers of some of the humbler drinking establishments in Port Antonio, we went on to a tourist bar built on a pier in the harbor. Besides the main saloon, it had upper and lower decks. I'd splurged and bought myself a few high-quality Jamaica Boy cigars for the occasion, and lit one up when I joined a circle of revelers on the upper deck. Several people wanted to sample a good Jamaican cigar, so it got passed around the circle as if it were a joint.

From the harbor we proceded to the relatively large Square View Bar, on the village square. There I found myself in a circumstance I could never have predicted, standing at a bar in the Tropics, drinking beer and talking with a Jesuit priest and a DEA agent. Some local fellow in the crowd behind me identified a tall blonde at the other end of the bar as Errol Flynn's daughter. I remembered that Errol Flynn had once owned an estate in Port Antonio. I felt like Graham Greene.

Some of our party had gotten fairly looped by this point, while others had just gotten started. I'd nearly reached my limit and Maria had already switched to soft drinks. We decided to go along for one last round before we retired for the night. We all left the square and headed down a side street to yet another modest rum bar.

As we approached, one of the vanguard waved us back, saying, "It just closed." Then someone shouted, "It just re-opened!" and we piled into the empty pub. Reggae music poured from a boombox behind the bar. The proprietor beamed at us, saying that he'd decided to stay open as soon as he'd seen all of us "thirsty cowboys." As we hung out, a few Jamaicans joined us, including a gray-bearded old Rasta who made speeches about Jah and world brotherhood. I bought him a Red Stripe and we toasted Jah's bounty.

When Rick and I got to talking, nothing in the difference between our ages ever got in the way of our rapport. We shared an enthusiasm for Jack Kerouac and Bob Dylan, in particular. When the music stopped and the barmaid started fiddling with the dials on the boombox, I broke into a loud rendition of "Like a Rolling Stone." Rick had joined-in by the first *DIDN'T YOU?*, and by the time we got to *HOW DOES IT FEEL?*, three or four others were singing along. When we'd finished the chorus and stopped singing, we got cheers and applause from the easy-to-please crowd. Nancy threw me a coin. I caught it and called over to her, "Hey! That makes me a *professional!*"

Soon afterward, Maria and I said our goodnights and walked back to the Holiday Home, as the rest of the group crawled on to the next pub. We got back to our room before midnight, joking about the capacity of some of the younger folks and glad we'd stopped drinking when we had.

The next day we learned that the hard core crawlers had gone on to close down several bars. Rick told me about the "mystic vibes" at the last club, which had run out of beer around sunrise. He described a somehow-weird, dimly-lit scene, with roots reggae playing continuously. There were no slack yout's (i.e. youths, pronounced "yoots") on the scene, but rather a number of older Rastas who'd engaged in deep conversations with him and the other Volunteers. He concluded with his favorite descriptor: it had been *awesome*.

Neither Maria nor I had drunk enough to suffer a hangover, but when we arrived at Rick and Jennifer's house around ten, we saw an open bottle of aspirin on the kitchen table right next to the coffee pot. Several of the people who'd spent the night there still slept on the living room floor; others were awake, but groggy from too much beer and too little sleep.

I got directions to the house, up on a nearby mountaintop, that a PCV named Neil rented from Rick and Jennifer's landlord. We'd all be meeting there for a barbeque in the afternoon. Maria and I went back to the guest house, grateful for the respite of the shaded porch after our walk in the scorching heat. We'd arranged to get a ride up to Neil's place with Johnathan, a former PCV who'd stayed on to work on the Peace Corps staff and had a car. He and his lovely Jamaican girlfriend, Sondra, had also stayed at the Holiday Home.

Neil's house stood on the inland slope of a mountain ridge. His yard afforded a panoramic view of the Rio Grande river, snaking through the lush valley below, and of the Blue Mountains. When the clouds lifted, you could even see Blue Mountain Peak. We'd all chipped in for food and drink and, as the veterans of the pub crawl began to trickle in, we set about preparing the barbeque. We soon had jerk chicken cooking in a typical Jamaican grill, made from a fifty gallon drum, and had breadfruits roasting in a firepit.

I saw Johnathan open a beer and pour a tiny bit on the ground before taking his first drink. When I asked him about it, he told me of the Jamaican custom of giving the first sip "to the duppy." Apparently it's a good idea to keep them placated.

Our plan for the next day was to hang out with our friends for a few hours at the Dragon Bay beach, then catch a country bus home. We took a taxi to the beach, but halfway there it got a flat tire. The car had no spare. My immediate thought when the driver slowed to a stop in the middle of nowhere was, *does he really have a flat, or are we about to get teefed?* I got out and was actually *relieved* to see the deflated tire. As luck would have it, Johnathan and Sondra drove up within five minutes and gave us a ride the rest of the way.

We'd brought along our snorkeling gear and swam out to the reef together. The water was clear. I got carried away by the beauty of the coral and the irridescent fish and swam out farther than Maria. By the time we headed back toward shore, I felt dangerously fatigued and had to work at keeping my breaths slow and regular, fighting back panic. I started panting in spite of myself, but had the presence of mind to flip over on my back and float while I caught my breath.

When I finally made it to an submerged rock ledge where I could stand and rest, it was already occupied by three American swimmers— two men and a woman—who talked investments. They eyed me suspiciously and stopped talking, then swam to shore. I think I may have interrupted a secret real estate deal. Maybe they thought I was a spy for their competitors.

Back on shore, we ran into Frank, the DEA agent we'd met at the pub crawl. We learned that he came to the north coast almost every weekend to scuba dive and that he'd just harvested seventeen lobsters. To our delight, he offered us a ride back to Kingston in his air-conditioned BMW. Not only that, but we stopped at the Boston Bay jerk center on the way home, where he paid to have some of the lobsters cooked and treated us to our first taste of jerk lobster—two apiece!

True to the stereotype of hard-drinking DEA agents, he had a cooler full of beer in the car and drank one after another as he drove. It didn't seem to affect his driving. We traveled along the scenic coastal highway, talking, and listening to Jimmy Buffet tapes.

Although curious, I hesitated to bring up his job; but he soon waxed effusive on the subject. He joked about the popular rumor that the DEA had two hundred agents on the island, saying that he was one of only three stationed in Jamaica. He'd been at the drug symposium I'd recently attended and laughed at Dr. G's claim that crack cocaine abuse had been reduced by ten percent as a result of the demand reduction program. He dropped us off at our house around five.

The crime situation only got worse the longer we stayed. An article about deportees returning to Jamaica appeared in the *Gleaner.* It stated that in the past five years over 3,300 Jamaicans had been deported from the U.S., England and Canada—most of them from the U.S. Many had been served time in prison and most had been deported for drug offenses or for violent crimes. A so-called rude boy interviewed for the article bragged that he'd "licked down" (i.e. killed) several Yankees. He'd been deported several times, he said, and had never had any trouble going back. He bragged that once he got back so quickly he found his car right where he'd parked it, his ganja stash still in the glove compartment. He had every intention of returning to New York.

I read somewhere that returning rude boys often expected to regain their former positions in Kingston gangs, only to be told by their successors, "You nah rohn t'ings now, me rohn t'ings!" As a result, there were many loose cannons on the streets—violent men who'd become used to having a lot of money while living abroad.

In late October all the Volunteers on the island got summoned to Kingston for a mandatory safety conference held at the Courtley Hotel. I didn't expect much from the sessions, but attending meant hot showers, air conditioning, and comeraderie, so I didn't complain.

In a group exercise we were asked to cluster around signs with the names of various kitchen appliances on them, choosing the one that we felt best represented how we saw ourselves. I decided to join the can openers. When asked why I chose this appliance, I replied that I felt like I was opening a can of worms at my work site. The leaders gave us a problem to discuss and asked us to come up with proposed solutions.

We can openers talked about the problem but generated no solutions in the allotted time, and none of us took notes. When the leaders asked for group reports, I was delegated to speak for the can openers. I went to the mike and said, "We can openers are, of course, on the cutting edge. However, I'm afraid we just went around and around and didn't even make a dent in the problem."

After the laughter died down, one of the leaders deftly segued back to the topic. He said that I'd illustrated a good point, that having a sense of humor helps in dealing with stress.

During a break I got to talk with Michael, the Volunteer who'd been caught in the crossfire dungtung. Since then, he'd been detained by the police for two hours while a whole busload of passengers was searched for weapons. He told me that both he and his boss, the Don, had received death threats after the Don had switched party affiliations.

"Mine came by phone," he told me. "The caller said, 'I wan' tahk to de white man.' I got on the phone. The caller asked, 'Who dis?', and I asked

'Who are *you?* 'You de white mon wha' work deahso?' I said yes. He said, 'You gwan die!' I hung up."

Michael had been immediately reassigned after reporting this at the Peace Corps office. He told me he'd been having a recurring dream in which a gunman broke into his flat and shot him. He said he expected that his former boss would be killed before the year was out.

Rory showed me a badly scraped forearm. He told of being on a country bus when a fight broke out in the back. He had the misfortune to be down in the doorwell with the door open, and got shoved out of the moving bus, landing on the pavement at around twenty miles per hour. He'd been fortunate not to sustain a serious injury.

To our sorrow, Les told us that he'd soon be ETing. "Some days I love Jamaica," he told us, "other days I'm just scared."

That night after dinner, we hooked up with our friend Sherrie and her gregarious Jamaican boyfriend, Jimmy. They ended up joining us in our room for a drink, the bar being too expensive on our Peace Corps budgets.

I never knew how seriously to take Jimmy, but he was always entertaining. His latest scheme to make money involved setting up a paramilitary camp and teaching survival skills: getaway driving, firearms training, dirty fighting techniques, and so forth. He claimed to know some of the world's best mercenaries and told of being jailed on another Caribbean island for just *being with* one of them. He swore the two of them hadn't been up to anything, but evidently the local government had felt skittish about the possibility of a coup d'etat.

He also told about riding in a super powerboat with some friends. They were going full-throttle and bouncing high in the air like a skipping stone, just offshore from a dense mangrove swamp. The captain lost control and the boat got lodged high in the mangrove canopy. Some "chinamen" later came through the swamp in a boat and when the captain tried to hail them, they first thought it was a talking parrot up in the trees. Or so Jimmy said.

By November we felt like we were over the hump. Not only had we completed our first year of service, but we'd made plans to fly to Charleston and visit my parents for two weeks in December. The prospect of our mid-term visit Stateside excited us. We found out we could get a cheaper round trip fare from Montego Bay than from Kingston, so we arranged for a shuttle flight across the island.

I always felt secure in our house, although I worried when I got there before Maria and she didn't get home until nearly sunset. I felt helpless at times without a car or a phone and was sometimes within minutes of setting out to look for her when she arrived. We had power blackouts with increasing frequency, and would sit and read, write, or play backgammon by the light of our hurricane lantern, while lizards croaked outside.

Two of Miss Kitty's litter had been given away, so we were down to her, Hopeful, and Miss McGillicuddy—who was always underfoot when we cooked or washed clothes. We took to calling her The Divine Miss M, or Miss M for short.

One Saturday Maria was doing the laundry and I heard her cry out. I ran to her and found her examinining her hand. "I just got stung by a scorpion, " she calmly informed me. "It was in one of the sinks."

It scared her worse than it hurt her. She showed me what looked like a bee sting on her palm and the stomped remains of the scorpion. The wound stung for a few hours but healed quickly. We were a little more careful after that.

Maria continued to expand her cooking repertoire, learning how to roast breadfruit in the oven and trying out new varieties of yams. She'd bought a Jamaican cookbook and learned to prepare Jamaican specialties like ackee and saltfish. Sometimes we'd cook jerk chicken out back on a grill improvised from an old tire rim.

Maria's job remained frustrating. Not only did she have classes to teach, student nurses to supervise, student logs to read over, and tests to grade; she sometimes got handed special assignments. One evening she complained that she and Jackie not only had to prepare a meal for a staff luncheon, but that they had to buy the food on a very limited budget. She asked if I had any suggestions for feeding thirty people for practically nothing. I suggested loaves and fishes.

Maria took Rainuke under her wing, helping her to apply for the School of Nursing, going shopping with her, and talking to her when she got homesick. We'd gotten a Scrabble game in a care package from a friend, and we took to playing with Vasanth and Rainuke and lending the set to them. Sometimes they beat us.

I'd also gotten some cassette tapes of classical music that I'd left with my parents to mail to me, and shared them with Vasanth, who'd expressed an interest in Western classical music. He, in turn, introduced me to Indian classical and popular music. I didn't tell him, but some of the female vocals I heard sounded to me like Minnie Mouse yodeling.

One day at the beginning of a new treatment cycle on the ward, while we screened new admissions, an intense young man intercepted me just outside the ward. He'd been hanging around for several days, demanding admission. The day before he'd managed to enter the ward and had been yelling: why wouldn't we admit him? who's the program for, anyhow? he could pay for his treatment! He had to be escorted off the premises by security and I heard him threaten to kill one of the guards.

He'd calmed down by the next day, but remained insistent that he be admitted. I told him that if he were to have any chance at all, he'd best listen to me.

"You're going about this the wrong way, mon. You're not going to demand your way into the program. The only way you're going to be admitted is to show the ward resident that you're someone who's likely to benefit from what we have to offer. And, yesterday, you blew it."

"Me was ahngry. Me mentahl state—"

"And maybe you'll be in a mental state where we can help you sometime, but you have no more *right* to be admitted than thousands of other Jamaicans who need treatment. I know that you were given an appointment for evaluation at the Psychiatric Ward, which you didn't keep. If you can't comply with treatment recommendations, you're not going to benefit from treatment. And, frankly, you don't look like you're likely to accept *anyone's* authority. It's up to you to show us you're a good candidate for admission."

This gave him pause. He said he'd comply with treatment and asked me to put in a good word for him. We rapped knuckles and said, "Respect."

Then I went on the ward. There I interviewed an attractive young woman who wanted to be in the program. She told me her story of increasing dependence on cocaine and the lengths she'd gone to to get it. When she could no longer feed her habit with the money she made at her job, she'd started having sex for money. She'd never considered herself a prostitute, she said, because she only had sex with men she knew and liked. When she found herself in bed with a stranger, she knew she needed help.

I also interviewed Alfonso, who had many a hard luck story to tell about his years of alcoholism. He told me he'd never known his parents and had started drinking at age ten. He said he'd never had a lasting relationship with a woman. Unasked, he showed me scars on his chest, arms, and head, from fights and drunken suicide attempts. He related breakups with girlfriends, betrayals by drinking buddies he'd thought were friends, drunken robbery attempts, and various other humiliations he'd endured. He concluded, "Me don' own a pin." He knew he'd die young if he didn't stay in recovery, but he admitted he still wanted to drink.

The newest absurdity on the job was the proposal that we start an occupational therapy program for the Detox Ward. One morning a financial honcho from the Drug Abuse Secretariat met with Sister M and me to discuss it. He'd secured a $J20,000 grant to repair a small OT building on the grounds that hadn't been used in years and to set up a program. It soon became clear that he didn't know occupational therapy from rocket science. According to his plan, the program would not only teach patients occupational skills but would be self-sustaining in a short time. He seemed to have some picture in his head of birdhouses or potholders or something being churned out by patients from the Detox ward and making a profit.

His plan had several major flaws. It seemed to take for granted that all or most patients would require occupational training whereas, in fact, many of our patients already had job skills. It specified no saleable product for the workers to manufacture and no means of marketing any which might be produced. It didn't take into account how much work time would be required for a successful, profitable operation, or how that might impact on other treatment priorities. The biggest flaw, however, was that it contained no mention of an occupational therapist.

"How can we have an OT program without an occupational therapist?" I asked. The money man didn't appear to have thought of that. He'd secured the grant by promising concrete results, but had no idea of what would need to be done to set up a training program that could be a meaningful component in the overall program. It all seemed an attempt to get free money—yet another instance of Alice in Wonderland logic. *Anything I say three times is true.*

The thing I felt best about on the job was my growing rapport with the ward nurses. As an American and the only male assigned full-time to the ward on the day shift, I was still an outsider to some degree; but as the nurses got to know me and to rely on me, they gradually took me into their confidence. I enjoyed our banter in the nurses station and their good humor made even the most trying times bearable.

June had resolved the conflict arising from her informal role as Sister M's deputy the only way she could, by resigning. She looked sad when she announced her impending departure and I was sorry to see her go.

Sandra continued to serve as the informal leader on the staff. Her warmth, wit, and tact enabled her to soothe hurt feelings and resolve conflicts among the other nurses. Inez was cheerful and optimistic, a true believer in the teachings of Science of Mind, but not at all preachy. Francine, quiet and maternal, avoided conflict wherever possible and had a kind heart. Still something of an outsider, Ann was perceived as being in Sister M's camp. She kept her true feelings hidden until they leaked out into her demeanor, and in things implied but not stated.

Martha, fiftyish and overweight, had a great sense of humor that sometimes had an edge to it. Although she came across as an upright, matronly Christian on the surface, she had a ribald streak and would regale us with stories about Jamaican men and their legendary propensity for philandering. I remember her telling of an acquaintance who came home to find her man in bed with another woman. He leapt out of bed and made for his trousers when he saw her standing in the doorway, but she just waved him back, saying, "Finish!" and walked away. The other nurses dissolved in laughter. One choked out, "Me gon' wet me foot!"

At a staff meeting in late October, knowing I was halfway through my term of service, I finally asked for feedback on my role in the program. Only the ward resident, Sandra, Martha and Inez made it to the meeting, and I saw it as a good opportunity to put myself on the agenda. After we'd discussed some program and policy issues, the others turned to me.

I briefly explained the Peace Corps' goals, referenced the program's lack of structure and supervision relative to my years of practice in the U.S., and asked how I was doing. Was I doing what they expected of me? Would they like me to do more or less of anything? I mentioned that I'd hoped staff nurses would co-lead my groups with me, repeating my invitation.

The others assured me that I was a valued team member and that I was performing the role expected of me. Sandra asked if I had a job description, saying that she'd never seen one and therefore had no basis for knowing what was expected of me. I told her that Sister M had never developed one as far as I knew.

Sandra said we were all in the same boat regarding lack of supervision and explicit deliniation of job responsibilities. We'd all, she said, had to invent our own jobs and guess about how well we were doing them. Nobody mentioned anything about my request that someone co-lead group with me. The meeting affirmed what I'd sensed about my acceptance as a team member and my job performance, but still left me guessing about what my role might be in improving the program.

We only had four patients on the ward when I started my groups, and three of them smoked cigarettes. One day as the time for group neared, one of the smokers, Gerald, begged me to escort him outside for a smoke before we started. Martin joined in the pleading. I should have known better, but I decided that since we had so few patients, we could hold an "informal" group session outside, under a tree near my office. Alfonso, the alcoholic I'd recently interviewed, joined us. The fourth patient had a medical appointment. As we left the ward, I told the three men in my charge that this was an experiment, advising them to stay in my presence and not to test my limits.

Gerald had assured me that he could easily get a cigarette from ward orderlies, but he seemed to be hanging back, while the others charged ahead. When Alfonso disappeared from sight, I ran after him and told him to come back and stay with the rest of the group. He seemed to be complying but, by the time I got back to Gerald, he was off again. I'd been set up.

I tried to get Gerald and Martin to return to the ward with me, so I could look for Alfonso; but Gerald had just gotten his cigarette and lit up. He wouldn't budge. I eventually made sure that everyone returned to the ward, resolving never to try another outdoors group.

That afternoon, even though I'd told the nurses about the incident, when I came back from lunch I saw Gerald and Martin smoking on the breezeway outside the ER. They told me that Sandra had given them permission to leave the ward. I asked if she'd given them a time limit and they said she hadn't.

When I asked Sandra, she said she'd told them to be back in five minutes. They'd been gone for over an hour. I expressed my surprise and dismay that they'd been allowed off the ward unsupervised so soon after taking advantage of me, adding that I thought it made me look foolish for trying to enforce the rules.

The next day things got even worse. My heart sank when I heard Gerald and Martin get permission to leave the ward for a ten minute smoke break, but I decided to ignore it and went into the counseling office to write-up clinical notes. When I checked at the nurses station an hour later, they still hadn't returned. In that time they could have easily bought and used any drug they'd wanted. Martha and Francine looked chagrined, but both protested that they weren't going to go looking for them.

I realized then just how low staff morale had sunk. Most of the nurses had already given up on this batch—they just didn't care anymore *what* the patients did. Martha shrugged and said, "We cahn't discharge them. We ohnly hahve four in this batch ahs it is."

I went back to the counseling office but was too angry to focus on my paperwork. When I returned to the nurses station, Martha saw how upset I was and asked if I needed to talk. I really wanted to ask, *is this a Detox Ward or a hotel for addicts?* I managed, however, to express my dismay more tactfully. I said that I was hard-pressed at times like this to believe that my presence made any difference at all in the program. Francine echoed my feelings of helplessness and near-despair.

Martha patted my shoulder and expressed her sympathy, saying, "Dohn't let it get to you. We dohn't, anymore."

Then Howard came in, expecting to lead a movement therapy session. He listened to the expressions of doom and gloom, then gave me his own take on Jamaica.

"Jamaica is like nowhere else in the world. Jamaicans have a genius for getting around things, for finding and exploiting any weakness in any system. You can't change anything or anyone. You don't come here to teach, you come to learn."

Later in the week I ran into Tim and Teresa at the Peace Corps office. They told me they'd decided to E.T. They'd already been thinking about leaving, but when they'd gotten back to MoBay from the recent safety conference to find that their apartment had been ransacked, it had been the last straw.

Teresa said, "I've heard too many Volunteers in their second year complain that they're not making any headway in their jobs. When I ask why they're still here despite their discouragement, I keep hearing, 'Well, I've only got six months to go.' I decided some time ago that I'd never resign myself to hanging tough just so I could say I stayed for the whole two years. I've had it. I'm ready to go home."

Kai Meng came through for us again, inviting us to join him on a weekend "birding" expedition in the north coast parish of Trelawny. The trek had been organized by the Gosse Bird Club, so we'd be following an itinerary and not just walking around in the bush with our landlord. One of our destinations was a part of the island known as Cockpit Country, an especially wild and impenetrable region of hills, where runaway slaves—called Maroons—had fled during Jamaica's plantation era and had successfully defied British attempts to round them up. They'd established their own tribal society up in the hills, and eventually the British had signed a peace treaty with them, granting them autonomy.

You could get your passport stamped as a visitor to the Maroon nation, if you could find your way to Maroon Town. Some maps still carried an inscription in the center of Cockpit Country, "Me no sen', you no com." We wouldn't be going all the way into Maroon country, however; we'd just be looking for birds on the northern rim of the hilly region.

Kai Meng picked us, and Rainuke, up at six on Saturday morning. We proceeded down the now-familiar highway through Spanish Town to May Pen in his new pickup truck, then turned north and headed up into bush country that foreigners seldom see. As we passed through mountain hamlets we drew a lot of stares and, time and again, heard the cry, "Whitey!" from children who seldom saw white people. In fact, we were even more exotic than they thought: a Maylaysian, an Indian, and two North Americans!

We had our gear stashed in the bed of the pickup, so when we rode through crowded market squares in the larger towns, I kept an eye out for teefs who might try to snatch it. As we drove through such out-of-the-way places as Chapelton, Crooked River, Christiana, Wait-a-Bit, and The Alps, we passed countless goats, donkeys laden for market, men carrying machetes, and women and children with loads balanced on their heads. We stopped to take pictures from time to time and had a lunch of deviled chicken and macaroni salad on the roadside around noon.

We arrived in the coastal town of Falmouth by mid-afternoon. There we met the rest of the bird club and two PCVs who worked in local environmental projects. By the time the last person arrived, we numbered eighteen. We discussed plans then set out for a nearby fish farm.

The farm consisted of a network of levees and man-made ponds next to a salt marsh. The ponds held tropical fish, small feeder fish, and catfish. Todd, one of the two other Volunteers on the expedition, showed us one of his projects. He pointed out a pond in which marlin hatchlings were being raised as breeding stock, to be released in the ocean.

We set out along the levees, finally ready to start birding. The seasoned birders came equipped with binoculars, tripod-mounted telescopes, and reference books. I even saw a copy of the classic **Birds of the Caribbean**, by James Bond, whose name Ian Fleming had borrowed for his fictional super-spy. I had my camera and my telescopic zoom lens, and the birders were generous in sharing their optical devices, so I quickly got into the spirit of things. As the club members identified birds, they would "tick them off" on checklists they carried.

We saw egrets, sandpipers, herons, stilts, moorhens, teals, and kingfishers, among other wild fowl. I followed first this group, then that one, taking photos, watching, and listening. I found the birders as interesting to observe as the birds—a singular species, viewed in its natural habitat.

The more experienced members helped newer members to identify whether they had just seen a greater tufted snit or a lesser tufted snit, and other such fine distinctions. Sometimes I heard them debating among themselves, referring to coloration; shape; size of beak, breast, or bird; length of throat or legs; posture; movement; and so forth. They also discussed preservation of nesting grounds and habitat, and speculated as to whether species thought extinct just hadn't been spotted in recent years.

The real enthusiasts were not at all like any wimp stereotype of bird-watchers, but seemed as hardy and dedicated as Marines. True birders have patience, stamina, eagle vision, rock-steady motor coordination, and finely-honed deductive abilities. They will rise at three in the morning, eager to be on their way to a site where they hope they might just see a black-billed parrot. It's impossible to get them to move in a straight line from Point A to Point B on anyone else's schedule once one of them says he *thinks* he saw a rare bird somewhere off to the left. They can give precise descriptions of both birds and landscape.

"See that white stump on the waterline? Now see those three trees to the left, behind the stump? There's a bush near the base of the middle tree. The bird is just to the right of the bush. Can you see it now? You can tell it's a *lesser* tufted snit by the size of the tuft."

We got back to the vehicles before dusk and loaded up to go on to our second site—a marsh on the other side of Falmouth where we hoped we'd see and hear some whistling ducks. We parked on the side of the coastal highway and walked down a dirt road until we got a good view of the marsh. Mosquitoes ate us alive. We stood there until dark looking, listening, slapping. No whistling, no ducks.

We drove back toward town, stopping at an open air bar and restaurant where the Trelawny Environmental Protection Association had arranged a reception. A recent invention in Jamaica, local EPAs were Non-Government Organizations. NGOs are common in developing countries, doing needed things the governments can't afford to do. PCVs often work for such organizations and this was no exception. Todd had helped to start TEPA.

We ordered drinks and pushed three tables together. Our hosts provided hors d'ouvres, and we ate, drank, and got to know each other. After we'd each introduced ourselves, representatives from TEPA and the Gosse

Bird Club spoke about current and upcoming projects: advocacy, educating schoolers about ecology, and promoting environmental awareness. As the evening went on, the discourse broke up into conversational clusters.

Maria and I got got into a conversation with Kai Meng and a handsome, confident Jamaican "yout'" named David, who wore a khaki uniform and affected a military bearing. He told us that he hoped to become a Jamaica Defense Force pilot, preparatory to being a commercial airline pilot.

Kai Meng said that he loved military strategy, although he hated war. The only way he'd serve in the armed forces, he said, was if he could be a general. Four stars.

We left around ten, winding up a mountain road to the house Todd shared with a young Canadian man. We'd thought we'd be spending the night outdoors, but Todd had offered the use of his living room floor for as many as could fit. About eight of us had taken him up on his offer. Exhausted, Maria lay down under a blanket on the sofa and tried to sleep. Rainuke also retired. As we waited our turns for the bathroom, Kai Meng, Todd, his housemate, a woman named Katherine, two Jamaicans, and I sat around the dining room table and talked about Eastern religions.

Actually, Kai Meng did most of the talking. He spoke about buddhism, chi (i.e. life force), chanting, acupuncture, and "polishing your karma." When Katherine mentioned she had a headache, he offered to rid her of it, telling her that he did acupuncture in his medical practice. He used a pen tip, rotating it on a spot between her thumb and index finger. He did it on both hands, explaining that each hand only worked on one hemisphere of the brain. Within thirty seconds she pronounced that her head no longer hurt.

We broke up around midnight, claiming spots on the living room floor and curling up in our sleeping bags and blankets. Maria hadn't been able to fall asleep for the conversation in the next room and the loud music outside. It had been a long day and I fell asleep quickly.

Someone turned on the lights and woke us all around three thirty. I sat up, groggy, and put on my boots. The smell of coffee filled the air. As the others took turns in the bathroom, I poured myself a cup of the strong brew and ate a ginger bun and cheese—a Jamaican staple. Maria had only slept fitfully and was on automatic pilot. When Kai Meng said that he hadn't slept at all, Maria contradicted him. She'd heard him snoring.

We set out at four, Katherine crowding in with us in the cab of Kai Meng's truck. The rest of the group from the day before, who'd overnighted in Falmouth, rendezvoused with us at Todd's house and we convoyed up the road in the pitch dark, the headlights making a tunnel in the gloom.

As we wound our way up through the jungle, we passed occasional clusters of houses and shacks beside the dirt road. At one such place, we came across a JDF raid in progress. Our convoy was halted by an armed guard. A truckload of soldiers carrying sidearms and M-16s had deployed around a concrete block house whose entrance was illuminated by the truck's headlights. Two soldiers herded a shirtless yout' into the back of the truck. When the suspect protested, one of them hit him on his back, just below the neck, with his gun butt.

The driver of the lead car got most of the questioning, but a sergeant stuck his head in Kai Meng's window, asking who we were and what we were doing there. Kai Meng told him we were birders, going birding. The sergeant grunted and waved us on.

Kai Meng speculated that we'd come upon a drug raid. I'd been shocked by the sight of the yout' being struck and felt helpless, knowing there was nothing we could have done. Such things went on every day on the island. I'd heard enough stories about the deplorable conditions in Jamaican jails and prisons to feel sorry for the young man, regardless of what he may have done. It was a sobering start to an otherwise carefree day.

Up and up we went, the sky lightening in the east. The jungle around us began to take on definition in silhouette, although the sun hadn't yet appeared. We arrived at our destination and parked. The world took shape around us as we prepared to set out on foot, and we found ourselves surrounded by beauty.

I've never seen another place quite like the Cockpit Country. Geologically, it resembles an irregular egg carton of hills and valleys, with trees and undergrowth in innumerable shades of green. While most of the limestone hills were clad in jungle and scrub, some displayed expanses of vertical rock face, bright in the early morning light. As the sun rose over distant hills, burning away patches of fog in the valleys, the scene reminded me of stylized Japanese prints I've seen depicting cloudy mountain vistas.

Some of the fertile, silted valleys were farmed—mostly sugar cane, banana palms, and rows of trellised yam vines, looking like ranks of kudzu soldiers. Bird cries filled the air in every direction and mosquitoes buzzed all around us. The hot sunlight burned off my grogginess along with the fog.

Maria and I got our cameras from our packs and started taking photos: misty landscape shots; close-ups of spiderwebs and colorful blossoms, jeweled with dewdrops; golden sunbeams filtered through tree branches. It was a gorgeous morning, a world all new again.

As we all set off up the road, I lit a cigar. We walked and looked and listened, snapping photos and slapping mosquitoes. Small flocks of yellow parrots flew overhead and a lone kestrel hunted in the sky. We both saw and heard black birds called "chatty crows," for their busy cries—much more complex than mere caws. Someone pointed out a Jamaican oriole perched on a branch, and hummingbirds hovered here and there, drinking nectar from flowers. I even saw wild parakeets for the first time.

By ten the sun was high and hot, and the best time for birding had passed. We returned to where we'd parked the cars and started back down from the Cockpit Country. David rode in the back of the pickup, jumping out and running ahead at times to cut plants, which he stashed in the truck bed. Once he ran ahead to a shack by the road and quickly procured some yams and bananas from its inhabitants. I overheard a brief exchange between him and another yout'.

"Wha' unu doin'?"

"Lookin' for birds."

"Lookin' for *birds!?*" The country yout' looked at David like it was the strangest thing he'd ever heard.

Although the bird club outing had officially ended, Kai Meng had planned a side trip to a place called Windsor Cave, where he said we'd have lunch. I expected a restaurant next to a tourist attraction. The site turned out to be on the edge of the Cockpit Country, well off the beaten path. We turned off the public road onto a private drive leading in to what had once been a plantation. When we stopped at the estate house, I saw no indication that we were anywhere near a cave entrance. The cave, I later learned, attracted occasional parties of naturalists, but few tourists.

The estate custodian, an Englishman named Mike Schwarz, invited us into the house. Although he'd spoken to Kai Meng and had known we were coming, he hadn't understood we'd be expecting lunch. No problem, he assured us, Sugar could easily throw together a soup. Sugar was the name of the Jamaican man who helped him manage the estate.

Mike was blue-eyed, bearded and balding, almost a caricature of the colonial planter in his wide-brimmed hat. An expatriate jack-of-all-trades who'd lived abroad for years, he made his living doing maintainance at a nearby resort on the coast and managing the guesthouse at the Windsor Estate. He grew coffee on the estate and had coffee beans drying in the sun on tarps in front of the house. I guessed he was about my age, partly from the music playing on his stereo system: Arlo Guthrie and Peter, Paul, and Mary.

He told us where to find the cave entrance, explaining that the cave extended for over thirteen miles, with openings at either end. A few parties of spelunkers and naturalists would come every year to explore it, but few had traversed its entire length, as you had to do some rope-climbing and cross an underground lake to get to the other end.

Maria and I set out along the forest trail that led to the cave entrance. We barely entered the cave, as we only had one flashlight and the rocks were slippery with bat guano; but even in the first chamber we could see a forest of stalactites and stalagmites in the gloom. I decided not to venture any further without a seasoned guide and adequate equipment.

On our way back to the estate house, Maria said she wanted to look around. I was too hot and thirsty to explore, and went back to the house in search of shade and water. But when she hadn't returned twenty minutes later, I set out to find her. I soon came upon her, just down the road. She was talking to a middle-aged Rasta straddling a bicycle when I found her.

The Rasta held a machete in one hand, an unlit spliff between two fingers in his other. At first he was apologetic, upon learning I was Maria's husband. "Me was jos tahlkin' wid you wife, mon."

"No problem, mon."

He introduced himself as Franklin, telling us that although he'd been a cave guide for fourteen years, he'd never gone the whole length. He'd been interviewed for international television broadcasts about the cave. He invited us to come back sometime for a tour of Underground Jamaica.

We returned to the house for a lunch of pepperpot soup, bread, and delicious estate-grown coffee. Pepperpot soup is a Caribbean perennial, a spicy concoction of whatever ingredients you have at hand to throw in the pot. What's left becomes stock for the next pepperpot.

After we ate, we paid for our meal and bid goodbye to Mike and Sugar. On our way back to Kingston, Maria, Rainuke, and I took turns dozing and keeping company with Kai Meng—who showed no signs of fatigue. We thanked him heartily when he dropped us off at home. He drove away, smiling and waving over his shoulder.

The next day on the ward, I learned that two women—Sally, an alcoholic, and Vera, a crack addict—had joined the new batch. The fourth man in the program, George, had recovered from an illness that had kept him from being in on my disastrous attempt to hold group outdoors. Alfonso remained sad and withdrawn, saying little in group meetings. Nobody had really opened up in our first two sessions, although Gerald and Martin both enjoyed the spotlight and talked a lot. Early in our third meeting, Gerald pronounced that group was boring.

"You know," I said. "I agree. So what are you gonna *do* about that? I can't make you guys get real with each other. And until you do, we're just gonna hear more of the same old war stories and Twelve Step mottos."

"Wahr stahries? Wha you mean, wahr stahries?"

"War stories are stories about using. What it was like that time, who you were with, how you scored. You know, like veteran to veteran. Addicts tell war stories to pass the time and to avoid taking risks in group."

"You nah wan' we tahlk about *usin'* in group?" Gerald challenged.

"That's not what I said, Gerald. See, war stories don't include the downside—the consequences of using. They can trigger what's called "euphoric recall," memories of the *good* times you've had when you were using. We all know you had some good times using drugs before you got addicted to them. Reminiscing about the good times isn't going to help you stay in recovery. We don't need to hear any of you telling us about your best high, or how you and your friend used to smoke ganja and skip school to hang out on the riverbank.

"No risk, no gain, friends. Those of you who play it safe here aren't going to get nearly as much from the program as those who're here to really *work*. And what we need now is for one of you to take the lead and take some risks. Then, I guarantee nobody will be bored."

Alfonso broke the silence. "Wan time, when me was dronk, me bite off a constable's finga."

That got everyone's attention.

"Noht de 'ole finga, unnastan'. Jos de tip. Im wag im finga in me face an' lectcha me. Me get vex wid im an bite im. Dem t'row me in jail tree week."

When it was clear to me he'd finished, I asked, " How do you feel about that, Alfonso?"

"Was bahd. Me no should ha' dohn it, bot likka mek me wicked."

"I don't mean what you *think* about it. Do you have any *feelings* about what you did?"

"Ya, mon. Me hembahrrass to t'ink me dohn soch a t'ing. De constable im jos doin' im job, im try to 'elp me, an' me bite im...like me a hahnimal."

"Thank you for sharing that, Alphonso." I addressed the group. "That took some courage for him to admit. But lest you think I'm suggesting that you need to spill out your deepest, darkest secrets in group, I'm not. You all have valuable things to share with the rest of us—some of them moderately risky for you, others very scary even to *think* about sharing with people you're just getting to know. But now that Alphonso has made an honest self-disclosure, who'll go next?"

George spoke up, telling us about how he'd lost his career in the JDF because of his crack habit. He'd been a corporal, a specialist in gun maintainance. After his discharge his skills had earned him a niche in a gang, but he'd loved soldiering. He didn't take any major risks in group that day; but he told us his story, including the price he'd paid for his addiction. Group had started to pick up momentum.

The following week I learned from the nurses that Alfonso had confessed to having drunk "a beer" (six, probably) on the day I'd tried to hold group outdoors. Sandra wanted me to get a consensus of what the patients thought should be done before the ward resident decided on a consequence.

I assembled the patients in the group room and used the issue at hand as an exercise in group process. I started by stating what we all already knew and asking for group feedback on what the consequence should be—even though the final decision was out of their hands. I introduced a technique called "doing the rounds," where we'd go around the circle, letting each group member have his or her say on the matter. I suggested that they avoid second- and third-person statements, and judgements of Alfonso (i.e. "you shouldn't," " he shouldn't have"), and stick to "I-statements," starting with "I think," "I feel," "I want," "I'm upset that," and so forth. Statements could be directed to the group or to Alfonso, but any criticisms or confrontations should be constructive, I told them.

The first round went fairly well, although some group members hadn't yet caught on to making clean I-statements, saying things like, " I feel you shouldn't have done that." But the group members came down unanimously against dismissal from the program and were supportive of Alfonso's recovery.

Having heard them out, I then made the same points about the risks of tolerating drug use in a residential treatment program as I'd made in previous groups. I told them about enabling.

"Every behavior communicates something, and Alfonso's behavior might communicate that he isn't ready for this program. Of course, I could be wrong about that. What speaks in his favor is that he admitted his relapse to all of you. He took responsibility for it.

"I'll be frank with you. If I ran this program, discharge would be the automatic consequence for using. No appeals or exceptions. This isn't a hotel for addicts, folks. But it's not my decision to make."

Vera said, "Bot rohm 'is prohblem. Is only beer im drink den."

"That's a good example of addicts' rationalization. Alcohol is alcohol, and a relapse is a relapse. Vera, do you think it would be less risky for you to sniff powdered cocaine than to smoke crack?"

She got my point. I talked about the difference between a full-blown relapse and a slip—defined as a single-episode relapse—then we did the rounds again, on the subject of Alfonso's ability to benefit from the program. This time they did a better job of making clean I-statements.

Alfonso stayed in the program and nobody in the batch ever complained of boring groups again.

During an individual session with Gerald, he admitted that he avoided talking about important things in group, saying that he still thought I might be a DEA agent. Despite his suspicions he opened up to me, telling me about the abuse and neglect he'd experienced as a child. He expressed very mixed feelings about his parents. He said he felt guilty about not loving them, as a son should, and said he waged a constant battle with his own accumulated anger.

I told him what I've told many people who suffered abuse from their parents. "There's no way you're *supposed* to feel. You feel what you feel. You may not like it, but you can't force yourself to love someone. Look, maybe someday you'll be able to forgive your parents, maybe you won't. The important things to realize are that you didn't *deserve* the abuse and that you're not the person they told you you are. Now *you* get to define just who Gerald is."

In group Gerald and Martin continued to engage in one-upmanship and to tell war stories. The Romance of Drugs, I labeled it: gold chains, guns, double-crossed drug deals, you-think-*you've*-seen-large-quantities-of-cocaine!

I called them on their game and asked them to cease and desist. However, they persisted to the point where I had to announc that this was no longer group therapy. I said I couldn't in good conscience continue to preside over a war stories contest. I dismissed the group.

Gerald stormed out of the room and Martin, stunned, got quiet. I waited a few minutes and re-convened group, at the request of the remaining members. It was just the reaction I'd hoped for. Gerald returned, angry, saying that I just didn't like having *him* talk at all in group. Martin seemed to have gotten the point of my intervention, but Gerald's simmering anger required a target that wasn't moving.

He verbally attacked the alcoholics in the group, trying to deflect attention from himself. He talked about them as if they were one person, with one personality. They always talked about the same things, they were superficial. Only he and Martin *really* told it like it was.

I described Gerald's tactic to the group. They got it. He shut up.

I went on to say that they all stood to benefit more if they took risks, and I challenged them to take advantage of the few sessions remaining in the treatment cycle. When I was confident that some kind of equilibrium had been restored, we ended group by holding hands in a circle and reciting the Serenity Prayer.

That night I wrote in my journal, "I'm feeling better about my job this week, as I know I'm doing what I can to improve things. I'm fully cognizant that I may just be feeling better because I'm creating a temporary illusion that my being here will make a difference, but for now that's enough—just knowing I'm doing my best."

In late November I got a message on the ward to call a sales representative from the CIBA-GEIGY drug company. He introduced himself as David and told me he'd like to take me to lunch, to discuss my request for nicotine patches.

He picked me up at the hospital the next day at noon. We ate lunch at Mee Mee's, a Chinese restaurant in Liguanie. We chose chicken and shrimp dishes, and shared. The power went out shortly after we ordered, but the restaurant had a generator. We ate by dim light, the thrum of the generator in the background.

David assured me that the donation of the nicotine patches had already been approved. Apparently the lunch was just a corporate ritual to seal the deal. He said would deliver the Habitrol patches to the hospital himself and do a presentation for the staff, at our convenience. Business completed, we went on to talk about other things: crime, capital punishment, and our respective travels.

It was a pleasant lunch and a departure from the routine. Normally, I'd have spent the hour reading and eating a sandwich and a banana in my little office. When David dropped me back off at the hospital, I felt like a true international development worker.

The day of our Stateside vacation finally arrived. We took a taxi out to the airport, where we caught a shuttle flight to Montego Bay. We'd reserved a room at the Wexford Hotel, downtown by the bay, our flight to Savannah booked for the next morning. The hotel was more expensive than we'd been led to believe. Rationalizing that the air conditioning and the satellite TV would help in our re-entry process, we cashed our last traveler's check.

We had all afternoon to explore downtown MoBay. Most of the prices in stores near the bay and the town square were listed in U.S. dollars, and familiar items cost many times what we paid for them in Kingston. Rum that I bought for $J 90 (less than $4) a bottle cost $10. Maria proclaimed the mangos she found *obscenely* expensive!

We knew that if we walked far enough and found a neighborhood grocery store, we could save some money. But we were on vacation, American money burning holes in our wallets, so we paid tourist prices—actually quite reasonable by U.S. standards. Maria had roasted a breadfruit to take to the folks back home, and we bought some spices, bottled jerk sauce, a bottle of spicy fish paste called Solomon Gundy, and a few other local delicacies. I also bought a bag of stacked bullas, fat ginger cookies you could buy at any snack shack on the island.

Then we hit the tourist shops, looking for cheap trinkets to give as Christmas gifts. We grumbled about some of the prices, but bought some good representative Jamaican craftwork without breaking our budget. Shopped-out and sweaty, we made our way back to the hotel and went for a swim in the pool. After hot showers and Headline News, we ate supper in the hotel restaurant, joking about how we weren't *really* tourists.

The next day, after an uneventful flight, we landed at the Savannah airport in the late afternoon. While we'd been waved through Jamaican customs without having our bags searched, it took us hours to get through U.S. Customs. They searched *everything*, leaving no sock unturned. They examined our craft purchases carefully. They even lanced the bag of bullas down the middle with something resembling an icepick. Maria said she doubted it was sterile.

Our dear friend Dennis awaited us outside customs and there were hugs all around. He helped us carry our luggage to his car. I wore a jacket, but started shivering as soon as we set foot outside. It must have been forty to fifty degrees colder than in MoBay. When we got on the road, the first things I noticed were the lack of potholes and the winter landscapes, brown and barren in contrast to the year-round lush greens of Jamaica.

Dennis drove us to the home of Ted and Ruth, some of our other best friends from the years we'd lived in Beaufort. We planned to spend a day and two nights with them on St. Helena Island before going on to Charleston. Ted was a notary, ancillary to owning and running a marine construction company. He'd built their house on a beautiful piece of wooded, marsh-front property on a bluff with a panoramic view of the marshlands. He'd also built a pier that extended out over the reedy mud flats to a floating dock on the creek.

By the powers invested in him by the State of South Carolina, he'd married us out on that dock in 1990, in a small ceremony attended by about thirty family members and friends. He'd said we could even choose our own diety, in whose name our union would be blessed, or we could keep it secular.

Ted and Ruth's place has always felt like home to us and, more than that, a source of spiritual nourishment, with its Spanish Moss-draped oaks, wild minks swimming in the waters of the high tide, and ospreys nesting on top of a pole high above the salt marsh. Supper awaited us when we arrived. When we'd finished eating, Maria and I broke out gifts and photos, and we spent the rest of the evening catching up and regaling our friends with stories of Jamaica. Dennis stayed until after two.

The next day we ventured into Beaufort to do some shopping. The first real culture shock we experienced was seeing white people all around us, everywhere we looked. When we went to the supermarket and to a discount department store, we were both amazed by the sheer volume and the variety of merchandise on display. We had some major re-supplying to do while back in the States, but felt too overwhelmed to buy any more than the bare neccessities on this first outing.

My old friend Don arrived from Alabama the following day and drove us to my parents home in Mount Pleasant, across the Cooper River from

Charleston. There was much hugging and kissing before we sat down around the kitchen table to swap stories. I withheld some details of life in Kingston, as my mother is a chronic worrier. I'd decided to wait to tell *all* the stories until we'd come back for good.

The next two weeks went by in a blur, and I got behind in my journal writing. I know that Don left the day after he dropped us off and that Maria's father arrived a day or two later. I remember walks on the beach and an overnight trip to Columbia, where we stayed with Pamela—who'd visited us with Ben. Several local friends joined us at her house for supper. We'd brought photos with us, and our stories had become refined from the re-tellings by then.

And we shopped. I bought clothes, a new watch, sunglasses, cigars and pipe tobacco, books, cassette tapes, and various small tools that we'd often wished we'd had at hand. I ate apples, pears, and old familiar snack foods, having had to make due with plantain chips and bullas for the past year. Just as I was starting to get accustomed to the American way of life again, the time came for us to return to the Tropics.

My brother drove us to the Savannah airport and saw us off. When we landed at the MoBay airport we only had to endure a cursory inspection of our luggage, but we discovered that one of each of our two suitcases hadn't been loaded on our plane. The shuttle flight over the mountains to Kingston took less than twenty minutes. At the Kingston airport we filled out forms on our lost luggage during our long wait in line for customs. Once we'd been cleared, we lugged our two remaining suitcases out to the curb and caught a cab home.

Back at the house it was almost like returning to family. Vasanth had not only plugged in our fridge, but had stocked it with milk and other basics. Rainuke (who'd been accepted at the School of Nursing) joined us out on the patio, where we'd been telling Vasanth about our trip—he and I both puffing on cheap American cigars. Our stove had just run out of gas, so Vasanth and Rainuke invited us to eat with them. We had a hot, spicy rice and beans dish, plain rice with yogurt, and some of the peppery, pickled limes we'd had before. Maria and I joined them in eating Indian-style, using the right hand to convey food from plate to mouth. The four of us played a game of Scrabble after supper, which Vasanth won. Then Maria and I retired to our house, exhausted from our travels.

The sights and sounds and smells of Jamaica took a little getting used to on the first day back, but after several bus rides and some shopping at an outdoor market, things started looking familiar again. As the days went by, our two weeks in the U.S. seemed like something I'd dreamed.

Out on Ted's floating dock I'd heard Ted and Don commiserating, singing the prosperity blues. Ted felt nailed down by his ownership of a successful and growing marine construction business. He owned boats, barges, cranes, and piledrivers and always paid his workers and his bills on time. Don ran a thriving private counseling practice and employed several people. Money wasn't a problem for either of them at this juncture in their lives, but both wished they had more time. Time to be creative, time to travel.

"Be careful what you wish for," I'd said. "I'm living on a tropical island and sometimes I find myself with time on my hands, but *I* don't have any *money!*"

Part IV

December 1992–October 1993

Our next shared ordeal involved finding and reclaiming our lost luggage at the airport. I got off work after lunch on Thursday, having been notified that the suitcases had arrived. Maria and I took a taxi, arriving at three thirty, requisite forms in hand.

The arrival terminal in Hell can't be much worse than the Norman Manley Airport on the week before Christmas. Many Jamaicans have kin in North America and Christmas is a favorite time for reunions. A lot of prosperous Jamaicans who don't go "afahren" for the holidays make shopping trips to Miami to buy gifts. Although December is relatively temperate in Jamaica, the main terminal wasn't air-conditioned and was packed to the rafters with sweating travellers. Long lines waited to depart and to clear Customs. A river of people eddied and swirled around fixed structures and waiting lines, everyone intent on getting somewhere. Porters called out, offering to carry bags. Freelance currency exchangers quietly plied their trade in the crowd. Arriving passengers lugged not only suitcases stuffed to overflowing, but also boxes tied with string, bulging beach bags, and shopping bags full of consumer goods. People were impatient and tempers flared.

I just wanted to get our stuff and go. Fat chance.

The woman Maria had called at the lost luggage office had been rude over the phone and Maria had told her so. On her advice, we first went to the Air Jamaica baggage office on the arrivals side of the terminal. We waited. The woman we eventually spoke to went off to seek answers and returned with directions to the office of the transport service that served Air Jamaica, on the departures side. We waded into the press of moving bodies again. We found the office and the woman Maria had spoken to on the phone.

When we showed her our papers, she scolded us like we were children. "I *told* you to go to Air Jamaica!"

We tried to explain that we already had and that they'd sent us here, but she wasn't listening. Maria again confronted her about her rudeness. When she continued to ignore us, Maria got angry and made to leave, but someone had locked the door behind us.

"Let me *out* of here!" Maria demanded. An office worker unlocked the door. "You need to get a new job!" Maria called over her shoulder to the sullen clerk.

We proceeded to the main Air Jamaica office and waited some more. We finally got the attention of a helpful young woman, but she was a ticket clerk and not really familiar with baggage problems. She suggested that we go back to the Air Jamaica baggage office and ask to speak to a supervisor. This we did, traversing the airport for the third time. After waiting to see a supervisor, we finally got our papers stamped to get us past security, into the baggage pick-up/customs area—a vast, high-ceilinged room filled with hordes of incoming passengers and their piles of luggage, packages and bags. Just crossing the room to what we thought was the right counter was an ordeal.

We had no luck tracing our baggage at the first desk, but at the second one we tried we gained admittance to a baggage loading bay, where I soon found my suitcase. We couldn't find Maria's, though, so we split up. I lugged my suitcase across the hellish arrivals room to stand in line at the customs desk. I explained that we were there to claim lost luggage and that we'd filled out declarations both in MoBay and in Kingston. Did I need a third to clear customs now? Nobody had given me one. I was directed back across The Pit, to the counter behind which I'd found my own bag, and told to ask for Form PD 38 or somesuch piece of colored paper.

I went and got the form and, standing at the counter, just happened to look down. There, not two feet away, sat Maria's suitcase, with its distinctive rainbow strap. So I had the luggage and the customs form, but Maria was still off somewhere looking for her bag. She had the lost luggage form—and my glasses! I felt generally irritated and increasingly bewildered.

I got into one of the lines for customs and for the next half hour inched my way toward the inspection counters, frantically scanning the mob for Maria. Without my glasses, I couldn't even read the customs form, let alone fill it out. I felt like I'd explode if I didn't get out of there soon.

Finally I saw my wife, her white face standing out in the sea of brown faces. I called out to her and she joined me in line. When we got to the inspection counter, the Customs officer scanned our papers, stamped them, glanced at the contents of the opened suitcases, and let us pass. We went out into the dusk and caught a cab home.

Some days after work, rather than waiting for a 22-A bus at Papene, I'd take another bus that only went as far as Liguanie and walk the mile-or-so down Mountain View Road to Olympia. Shortly before Christmas, as I walked past the National Stadium, I spotted an entrepreneur selling "Christmas trees." Actually, they were three foot tall shrubs with gnarly little branches, painted silver. I bought one and carried it home, where Maria trimmed it with a string of tiny colored lights and improvised ornaments. She'd bought some dried sorrel leaves at the market, which she brewed to make a popular seasonal drink—red and tangy. We'd bought each other gifts and made other preparations for our second Christmas in Jamaica.

On Christmas day, after exchanging gifts, we managed to catch one of the few buses running and rode up to Liguanie to have dinner with our friends who'd rented the big house near Bamboo Pen. Sadly, it would be our last chance to see Jackie and Paul, who'd be returning to the States due to a medical condition Jackie had contracted. Also present were Celine and the other Volunteers who lived there, and a few other guests, including a young German woman and a seminary student from Surinam.

After a dip in the pool—the only time I've ever had a swim on Christmas—I dressed and joined the others on the veranda for drinks and chat. Late in the afternoon we feasted on roast chicken and stuffing, mashed potatos, gravy, green beans, and salad, with lemon and pecan pies for dessert.

I got to talking to the seminary student. He told me he planned to return home soon to do some graduate studies on a Maroon tribe known as "bush negroes," who professed Christianity but had incorporated elements of African polytheism into their religion. He said that they couldn't *really* be Christians if they believed in more than one god and practiced obeah. He told me that one of their gods was a river god and that if someone was drowning, they'd make no attempt to rescue the person. The river god apparently expected everyone to know how to swim and would claim anyone who hadn't learned to travel safely in his domain.

It didn't really seem like Christmas to me until I set out for Hope Road with Celine, who'd prepared dinners on foil-wrapped paper plates to deliver to Liguanie's two perennial street people—one of whom I've described as The Watcher. The only time I'd ever seen him interacting with another person at his adopted bus shelter, he'd been raving; but when we greeted him, he displayed a gentle demeanor and gratefully accepted Celine's gift. Barefoot and dressed in filthy rags, as always, his dreadlocks wild and matted with dirt, he betrayed no trace of madness.

We then took the other dinner to an old raggedy-man who hung out on the corner of Hope Road and Old Hope Road. He, too, politely expressed his gratitude. I felt moved by Celine's kindness, happy to be a witness. I was reminded of a prayer written by Mother Teresa about serving God, "in His distressing disguise."

On Boxing Day, the day after Christmas, we caught a bus for Spanish Town and went to Alvira's for dinner, picking up three cold Red Stripes at Mr. Mirage's shop for old times' sake. At our request, she'd prepared an appetizer of "mannish water," a traditional Jamaican soup made with goat innards. She told us she hadn't acceded to our request during training because she was afraid we'd tell the Peace Corps she'd fed us nasty stuff. Actually, it was quite…interesting. Pungent. An acquired taste I decided I had no wish to acquire.

After a second "hoppitizer"—Chivas Regal this time—we sat down to dinner. We ate roast beef, ham, fried chicken, macaroni salad, and vegetables. After supper we chatted with Alvira on the porch for an hour or two, then left to catch a bus back to Kingston.

Vasanth invited us to a big New Year's party he was hosting. He also invited Rory and Rachael, our most frequent houseguests. They arrived on their motorcycles in the late afternoon on New Year's Eve Day and we all pitched in to help set up for the party. Other than the four of us Americans and a few Jamaican spouses, all the guests would be Indian.

We'd decorated the front of Vasanth's house with streamers and a Happy New Year banner, as the party would be an indoor/outdoor affair—weather permitting. We set out tables and chairs on the patio, savory smells already emanating from Vasanth's kitchen. Knowing that our Indian friends tended to eat late in the evening, I prepared a snack tray— cheese, and Solomon Gundy on crackers—to tide us over. As guests began to arrive, Vasanth made sure everyone had a drink. As usual, he considered an empty glass an automatic invitation for a refill, so I nursed my drink, knowing that the party would go on for hours.

Several of the men at the party were doctors. Most had Indian wives, but a few had married Jamaicans. Those couples with children had brought them along. The conversation was almost exclusively in English—probably for our benefit. Maria disappeared for a while and returned with Rainuke, both of them in traditional Indian dress, complete with the red dots on their foreheads. Rainuke had wrapped her in a long, colorful, silk sari and both of them looked lovely.

Vasanth and Rainuke served dinner around ten, setting the food out on the tables outside for the guests to help themselves. We had lamb and chicken, two kinds of rice, a spicy salad with yogurt dressing that could also be used with the plain rice, and pan-fried bread. Everyone but Rory and Rachael ate with their fingers—right hand only, if you please.

The sounds of reggae and American pop filled the air for most of the evening and, as the rum continued to flow, the generally-reserved Indian men began to loosen up. I switched to coffee after dinner, knowing we'd soon be drinking champagne. Vasanth looked pained when I refused his offer of a refill of rum. People started to dance and everyone seemed to be having a good time.

As midnight approached, several of the men got boyishly silly, dancing wildly, throwing firecrackers, shaking up the bubbly and spraying it over the people around them. We celebrated the arrival of 1993 with the familiar, tipsy fervor of American New Year's parties—shouts, hugs and kisses (between spouses *only*), hearty handshakes, and dancing.

The frenzy lasted the usual fifteen or twenty minutes, then the guests began to depart. Those remaining helped our host and hostess to get the leftover food inside, and we cleared the patio of all but a few chairs. Vasanth handed me another rum, unasked. By one the party had become small and sedate, with sitar ragas for background music. Maria and Rainuke each said their goodnights and retired. I broke out cigars for the few remaining men and we sat around in the warm night, talking, drinking, and smoking.

Our first outing with Linda, to Hellshire Beach, had led to her invitation to join the turtle watch. We shared a common interest in World Music and African culture. The more we hung around with her, the more we liked her. A feisty, independent, divorcee, she was fiercely committed to the cause of racial equality. Anything smacking of racism or sexism lit her fuse.

She worked in a dungtung community development project. As women involved in the project got to know her, some approached her and asked why white people were so much better at managing than black people. Linda said she'd stifled her spontaneous response until she'd had a chance to run it by her Jamaican supervisor, who gave her the go-ahead. Instead of telling the women, "Well, that's just not the case...", she said something like, "Stop believing that bullshit! You don't need white people to make this project work!"

In traveling by bus around the eastern tip of the island, Linda had fallen in love at a glance with the seacoast community of Long Bay and had resolved to come back someday and explore it. When she saw that someday coming, she asked us if we'd like to join her.

We met her on a Friday noon at Halfway Tree. The three of us took a bus down to the dungtung terminus and only had to wait forty five minutes for our bus—named "Eastern Queen"—to arrive. We actually got seats, but had to wait another half hour for the bus to fill up. Shortly after we got on the road, a tire went flat. Something had apparently come loose on the undercarriage and we had to stop at a mechanic's shop for a quick welding job. It was two-thirty before we left the city.

The ride seemed interminable, as we stopped every few miles to drop and add passengers. By the time we got to Long Bay the sun had already set. We'd seen no hotels or guest houses on our way into the tiny coastal settlement. We asked the bus driver to drop us off in the middle of town, but when we got out we saw only scattered houses and a few small shops beside the highway. No village square, no village.

Linda had spoken to somebody who knew somebody and *thought* she had a contact for lodging, but we had no idea where we'd be spending the night. We briefly considered re-boarding the bus and going on to Port Antonio, but opted instead for the adventure at hand.

An almost-full moon had just risen above the shimmering sea, framed by the silhouettes of tall coconut palms between the highway and the beach. We could hear the pounding of the surf and smell the salty ocean breeze. We hefted our packs and set out to explore.

Linda found the man she'd been told about, at a small roadside grocery store. He told her that all of Sister Precious' guest rooms were taken, but that a man down the road had a room free. We found the house and the caretaker—who acted drunk—agreed on a price for lodging. Thinking we'd solved the problem of where we'd stay, we stashed our packs in the room, headed back up the road to a cookhouse on the beach side of the road, and ordered supper.

We ate a Jamaican version of chop suey, with sides of rice-and-peas and slaw. The young woman who served as both cook and waitress introduced herself as Lolita. She proved to be quite a talker, entertaining us with stories about crazy tourists she'd met, as she prepared and served our food. She told us that few tourists came to Long Bay and that most who do are Europeans. She said that some people called it German Bay, as it seemed to attract mostly Germans.

By the time we got back to the guest house, the drunken caretaker had changed his mind about our staying. We took our packs out of the room, returned the key he'd given us, and went back to the cookhouse to ask Lolita if she knew of any place we could stay.

She was just closing up when we arrived. "No prohblem, mon. Me t'ink se Sistah Precious got wan room. Com, me tek you deahso."

She turned off the lights in the cookhouse and escorted us across the highway and up a private driveway, telling us about Sister Precious as we walked. "She a good Christian lady. She keep me sohn fi me when me wohrkin'. If she nah 'ave a bedroom, she let you stay in de pahlah ."

Sure enough, Sister Precious proved to be a warm, gracious hostess, renting us her parlor for the night. The sofa bed was only big enough for two, so I ceded my place by Maria's side to Linda and made up a pallet on the floor. Maria warned Linda that I snore.

We stayed up for over two hours, sitting on the front porch with Sister Precious and Lolita, listening to Lolita's stories. She said that she still corresponded with several German and Italian tourists who'd come to Long Bay. She kept referring to "you people"—clearly referring to white people—and our strange ways.

"You nevah see a Jamaican nekked ahn de beach. No, mon. Bot *you people*, you com an' de women-dem, dey go ahn de beach wit' dem breas' hahngin' out. Ahn de mon-dem, sohmma dem tek ahff ebryt'ing! Wan time me go to see dis faht Itahlian mon wha' jos' stay in im room ahtfa im girlfrien' leave im, ahll hupset an' depress'. Me knock ahn im door ahn im say com in.

"So me go in de room ahn see im sit ahn de bed, nekkid—noht a stitch! No shame 'bout im faht body. Im jos' drink rohm, play im guitar, ahn cry ahll day! Me tell im get op ahn put ahn im pahnts, ahn im ak like *me* de strange wan. Me tell im to get out in de sohn, eat som food. Im ahn *vacation*, me tell im.

"You people!" She shook her head, remembering.

The next morning we got up around eight and headed to the seaside cookhouse for breakfast: eggs, toast and coffee, all prepared over a wood fire. Lolita, it seemed, was always on duty.

Then we took a long walk up into the hills, chatting with people we met along the way. By the time we got back to Sister Precious' home, a couple had moved out of the back bedroom and we moved in. Again, the bed was only big enough for two, so I'd have to sleep on a pallet for the second night. We changed into our bathing suits and walked down to the beach.

When we checked-in with Lolita on the way, she told us she'd just baked a loaf of banana bread. That and some fruit turned out to be our lunch. We hit the beach, quickly discovering that the pounding, treacherous surf precluded swimming. Even wading got us drenched with spray.

The three of us spent the afternoon sunning ourselves, reading, and talking to a dreadlocked beachcomber who introduced himself as Rainbow. He asked us about life in America, then told us about life in Long Bay, living up to his colorful name in the process. He just enjoyed talking to foreigners and never asked us for money, as had been our experience with such encounters in the tourist towns of the north coast.

That evening we had drinks in a thatch-roofed open air bar, then found a restaurant. After a meal of chicken, fries, and slaw, we returned to the rooming house. Linda, Maria, and I played gin rummy on the dimly-lit porch until almost midnight, securing the card piles with rocks to keep them from blowing away in the brisk sea breeze.

I awoke the next morning remembering a dream in which I'd met Bob Marley. Somehow sensing that I might not be welcome in the house where I met him, I asked him if I could stay a while. Without any animosity, he said I'd better leave. But he took the time to show me his guitars and some mementos, and shook my hand warmly before I left him and woke up.

Maria, Linda, and I bid goodbye to Sister Precious and stood waiting for the bus in front of the cookhouse by nine. I had a cup of coffee and some bullas for breakfast. A light rain—known on the island as a "woman rain"—began to fall. We took out our umbrellas and stood by the roadside swapping stories under their shelter until the rain gave out. Then we sought out shade, as the road began to steam in the sunlight.

We got seats on the bus. Throughout the trip back to Kingston we saw people walking beside the road, dressed in their brightly-colored Sunday clothes, on their way to or from church. The bus made it to the dungtung terminus without incident in about three hours. Maria and I hugged Linda and thanked her for asking us along on her latest adventure.

The new batch of patients on the ward consisted of the usual mix of male alcoholics and crack addicts. Alcoholics tended to be less volatile than than cocaine users, and this group was no exception. Early on in the groups I could see a split between the two factions.

Two crack addicts initially vied for group leadership. Colin looked like a powderkeg about to blow—edgy, and angry at the world. Samuel came from an upper-class family, had spent much of his life in Los Angeles, loved attention, and expected privileged treatment. Sometimes they allied themselves to attack someone in group, but mostly they competed.

In our first group meeting Colin and Samuel revealed their contempt for alcoholics—they were just drunks, rummies. They slurred and staggered and vomited and fell down in public. They passed out in doorways and pissed themselves. They had no class.

An alcoholic named Norman counterattacked, saying that crack turned men into violent criminals and women into prostitutes. At least *he* could afford his drug of choice without resorting to crime, and *his* drug was legal. Cocaine cowboys were the scum of the earth.

I'd seen it all before and waded into the fray. "Gentlemen. This is not a contest. Addiction is addiction, and it is *not* pretty.

"Look…users of Drug A tend to feel superior to users of Drug B, and vice versa. Most addicts tend to romanticize their drug of choice. Crack addicts think they're hip, using a popular, imported, *exotic*, drug. They come to know this shadowy, criminal world, because cocaine is illegal and a daily crack habit is expensive. Dealers wear gold chains and drive slick cars.

"Alcoholics, on the other hand, minimize the damage they're doing. Their drug is *legal*, so it can't be *that* bad, right? They're *real men*, who just can't seem to hold their liquor like they used to. They're not really like those *addicts,* who smoke crack. And so forth and so on."

Looking around the room, I could see both alcoholics and crack addicts nodding in agreement. I went on.

"Guys, you might be real different as individuals, and the *kinds* of losses and humiliations you've suffered might vary considerably, but each of you is here today because you've finally had the courage to admit that you're an addict. *All* of you have that common bond. And whether you're addicted to alcohol, or crack, or heroin, or tranquilizers, or glue—the point is, you're addicted. You can't stop, even though you want to. And in that regard you're all brothers.

"It's not us or them. You don't climb to recovery over the bodies of your brothers, you become their allies in recovery. You don't look for the differences between people who share your drug of choice and those who use other drugs; you try to learn from your allies in this struggle. When you learn something about what *each one of you* has *in common* with everyone else who shares this problem of addiction, you'll understand your own problem better. Now, what do y'all think about what I've just said?"

We discussed universal aspects of addiction, then went on to do personal introductions. Samuel, who'd been in group therapy in an addictions program in the States, went on at some length about his life in the fast lane in L.A. He said he knew he had to give up cocaine, but didn't want to give up ganja and alcohol. The other group members kept their introductions short.

When we got around to Merle, a sullen teenager and the youngest in the circle, he tried to decline, saying, "Me nah like to cohnfess. Me here to lahrn, noht to tahlk." I cajoled him into at least telling us who he was and where he came from, and naming his drug of choice. (Crack.) After everyone had spoken, we ended the meeting with the Serenity Prayer.

Inevitably, the same old problems of living on a locked ward arose. The nursing staff now routinely gave the patients permission to leave the ward to smoke, and this privilege got abused from day one. I recommended, as a consequence for staying off the ward beyond the allotted time, that each man get the same number of minutes off the ward weekly, and that violators be docked one minute for every minute they were late getting back. When they'd used up all their weekly time, they'd just have to stay inside when the others went out for a smoke—of *whatever*.

The nurses agreed in principle, but subsequently failed to strictly enforce the rules consistently over the three shifts.

Other than that, things started out fairly smoothly with the new batch. Samuel acted like he should be treated differently than the commoners but, a group veteran, he actually helped model some positive group behaviors and sometimes backed me up in my interventions. In one particular morning meeting, however, it became clear that he and Colin had fallen out. He taunted his rival, who rose to the bait and looked like he was about to go off.

After I'd pointed out Samual's tactic and calmed Colin down, I went on to talk about anger management. I shut up when the building began to shake. I faced a roomful of shocked expressions. I'd never been in an earthquake before, but the sensations were unmistakable. The rumbling and quaking only lasted a few seconds. Plaster dust fell from the ceiling. Nobody spoke. Then everyone started talking and we all rose to our feet.

The quaking had stopped. Nothing had fallen in. My first thought was that we needed to get out of the building, before an aftershock hit. My next thought was, *Maria's down at Belleview today! What if there's a tidal wave?* I remembered the earthquake that had plunged Port Royal into the sea. I remembered Atlantis.

I told the group we needed to get outdoors. Some ran for their cigarettes and the others headed straight for the exit with me. The nurses appeared from the nurses' station and one said she thought we should stay put. I quickly persuaded her otherwise and we all evacuated the building.

The earthquake hadn't caused any obvious structural damage to the hospital. Whole clinics and ambulatory wards emptied out onto the grounds between buildings. Everyone milled around and a holiday excitement filled the air. When a half hour passed without discernable aftershocks, the crowds dispersed and people began to trickle back into the hospital. Within an hour things were back to normal.

At home that evening I learned that Maria hadn't been at Belleview after all, but *had* been down near the harbor, in a classroom with other nurses. She told of the same kind of stunned reactions I'd seen, and described a roomful of nurses diving for cover under desks. We learned on the evening news broadcast that the quake's epicenter had been near Kingston and that it had registered five point six on the Richter Scale. Only a few concrete block buildings not reinforced with steel rods had suffered damage and there had only been one fatality on the whole island.

Samuel continued to speak freely in our group sessions, serving as a good role model for honest self-disclosure, if not for prosocial values. He spoke without shame about how he'd skimmed money from his family's business, rationalizing that he'd been treated unfairly and was just taking what was rightfully his, anyway.

He told us of his "turning point" as an addict in L.A., when he'd decided he'd had enough of living in the streets, neglecting his health and appearance. His solution? He'd made an abrupt transition to an upscale lifestyle by becoming a coke dealer himself. Not only had he been able to support his own habit, he'd started living in swank hotels and spending thousands on shopping sprees. He had no qualms about having been a pusher—if he hadn't sold the cocaine, somebody else would have.

On the positive side, he confessed to having brought a spliff on the ward with him when he'd been admitted to the program, and having learned that he needed to give up ganja, too, as it had triggered a strong craving for crack. Had he not learned this in the program, he said, the first thing he would have done upon leaving would have been to smoke ganja.

Group went relatively well for the rest of the four weeks, without much tension between the crack addicts and the alcoholics. Colin stopped being so angry and provocative, and he and Samuel gradually resolved their power struggle. During the final group meeting, we did the rounds regarding prospects of lasting recovery. I heard the usual spectrum of predictions, ranging from expressions of complete confidence to confessions of fear and doubt about the possibility of relapse. Everyone agreed that group had been a positive experience.

In my continuing effort to improve treatment, I submitted my program assessment—titled "Observations, Reflections, and Suggestions"—to Sister M, Dr. S, and the ward staff for their consideration. In it I proposed that we form an interdisciplinary committee to select a treatment model and to work on policies and procedures. I outlined a levels system, where patients earned privileges by complying with ward rules.

Howard, our Guyanese movement therapist, also had an agenda. In line with his New Age beliefs, he thought that both staff and patients should be taught about the effects of drugs on the subtle body, the astral body, the chakras, and the aura. He offered to do inservice training. Our respective proposals seemed to be received with equal approval by the staff.

At home I got another taste of contemporary Indian culture when I looked at a magazine that Rainuke had loaned Maria. It looked to me like the Indian version of *Cosmopolitan*, without the cleavage on the cover. The advertisments included clothing ads featuring light-skinned models in both Western high-fashion dresses and in saris, as well as ads for cosmetics and Barbie dolls. Several of the full-page clothing ads, with their doe-eyed models, had copy combining Western "literary" paraphrases and adspeak:

"Her eyes hold laughter, her smile holds a promise…in cool white and warm rust. The hand-worked design on the yoke evokes the romance of a bygone era."

"Stopping by the woods one summer evening…in festive Khari printed two-tone cotton with richly contrasting Dupatta."

"He loves me, he loves me not…the richly beaded Khurta front works well with the busy print."

I read a mercenary, mean-spirited article, couched in pseudo-feminist jargon, about how to tame a spoiled Indian male, in service of one's long-term goals. "It's up to you to…spirit yourself into his heart—if he has one—and capture his soul mind or whatever…. (Spoiled wimps) can be taught to come to table and can even perform in front of guests.…They have never known what it is to have a bit in the mouth and a filly on their back, cracking the whip…. You must help yourself liberally to his cash and other movable goods—excluding yourself—to provide for the day when you may have to…stand on your cute little hennaed-and-silver-ankled feet in pelting rain."

On the ward we'd started the practice of setting aside a "fifth week" between our four-week treatment cycles, for staff meetings and training. I'd made copies of my program critique to distribute to the staff and had asked for a meeting during the fifth week to discuss its proposals. I gave an advance copy to Dr. S prior to the final ward rounds for the current batch, as I knew he'd be off the island the following week and hoped for some kind of endorsement before he left.

Sure enough, after we'd finished the final staffing of the departing patients at ward rounds, Dr. S made summary comments about how the program was going. He mentioned some of my proposals favorably, specifically endorsing the idea of forming a committee to look into treatment models and to formulate policies and procedures.

The meeting the following week went well. The nurses had had time to read and discuss among themselves what I'd written, and I found them guardedly receptive. Some feared that a strict levels system would wash *everyone* out of the program, but liked the idea of getting more systematic about enforcing ward rules. I made it clear that I didn't expect all of my proposals to be implemented, just discussed.

We agreed to form a committee to work on policies and procedures. To their surprise, I declined to chair the committee, as I thought that position should be held by one of them. "Not exactly a mandate," I wrote in my journal, "but at least a foot in the door."

One day when she was supervising student nurses at Belleview, Maria witnessed a shooting on the grounds just outside the locked ward where she was working. She heard a commotion and looked out the window just in time to see a policemen shoot a "madman" in the groin. Several constables stood watching as the man fell to the ground. One of them kicked him, ordering him to get up.

Nobody else seemed to be doing anything to help the shooting victim, so Maria tried to go help, only to find the door locked. She called out for the orderly with the key and, after an agonizing wait, he appeared and let her out.

The victim was bleeding profusely from his gunshot, moaning and pleading for help. Maria demanded that the policeman stop ordering him to get up, and quickly examined him. Hospital nurses stood among the growing knot of spectators, but none of them helped her. Although Maria—a psychiatric nurse—had little experience with trauma care, she ran to the nearest ward and asked for a pressure dressing to stanch the flow of blood. When the ward orderly said they had no pressure dressings or bandages in the supply room, Maria persuaded him to give her a clean sheet, which they quickly cut into strips.

By the time she got back outside with her makeshift supplies, the policemen had the man on his feet and were trying to get him to walk with them to the emergency room. One of them told her that they'd been assisting in the man's involuntary admission, when he'd tried to grab a gun from one of the officers and had been shot in the ensuing scuffle.

The constables apparently didn't want to get blood on their uniforms, but Maria demanded that the wounded man be carried. Two of the policemen took hold of the man's torso and began to drag him. With the help of one of her students, Maria managed to lift and support his legs, using the cloth strips as a sling.

By the time they got the man to a doctor on a nearby ward, he'd lost a lot of blood. A crowd gathered at the door as the doctor cut the man's pants off and began to clean the wound, with Maria's help. The bullet had entered the man's groin and exited from his buttock. Once the bleeding was controlled and the doctor started an IV, Maria noticed the crowd and told the student nurse to close the door. When that was done, however, the crowd of gawkers simply regrouped outside the window.

After the man was medically stabilized and the crowd had dispersed, both the attending doctor and the chief constable thanked Maria for her prompt intervention. She felt drained afterward, she told me. She'd been going on adrenaline and reflexes, afraid the man would bleed to death before her eyes.

A few days later, a homeowner shot a teef to death just two blocks from our house. We walked past a crowd of gawkers outside the house on our way to work, but didn't know what had happened until we read about it in the *Star* that evening.

February 6th, Bob Marley's birthday, is a national day of celebration in Jamaica. To understand his role in Jamaican culture, take the Elvis phenomenon in the U.S. and multiply it by five or ten. Most Jamaicans enjoy his music and revere his memory. Along with his group, The Wailers, he did more than any other individual to popularize "roots" reggae—an outgrowth of styles known as rocksteady and ska. In his short life he became an international star and cultural ambassador to the world, promoted social justice and pride in African heritage, and helped to bring about a mainstream acceptance of Rastafarianism as a part of the Jamaican culture. During a particularly bloody time in Jamaican politics, he got rival party chiefs Edward Seaga and Michael Manley to shake hands in a ceremony at the National Stadium.

Bob Marley left a musical legacy that will surely endure, writing lyrics that matched the power of the reggae rhythms behind them. "Emancipate yourselves from mental slavery," he wrote, "none but yourself can free your mind." His songs dealt with life's pleasures and heartbreaks, as well as with social themes. "Lively up yourself!" he exhorted his listeners. He claimed that Jah wrote his music and said, "People tend fi undahestimate music. Music is nex' wan to watah ahn food ahn dem t'ing deah."

After Marley died of cancer, a friend described the artist's songs as "light like a feather, but heavy like lead."

Not long after Bob Marley's birthday I attended a free memorial concert at the Cultural Arts Center on the university campus. One of his sons, Julian, was to perform. I entered the stifling auditorium for the afternoon performance, noticing that there were only two or three other white people in attendance. As the hall filled with people, a mobile mountain of a woman made her way to where I sat and wedged herself into the seat next to me. She wore traditional West African garb: a colorful dress that covered her like a tent, and a pillbox hat. She introduced herself, saying she was from Nigeria.

Most people I'd been around in Jamaica, even on the crammed buses, had good personal hygeine; but this woman reeked of body odor and her breath stank. While most Nigerians I've met have been clean and well-mannered, this woman had the social skills of a drunken vagrant. She wouldn't let me ignore her, but kept up a steady stream of chatter as the auditorium filled. I tried to be polite, but prayed for the performance to start, thinking *why me?*

She asked if I lived in Olympia and I said I did. She said she'd seen me and my wife from a passing bus. She asked if she could tag along with me after the concert, meet my wife, and hang out with us that evening. I said no, I didn't even know her. Unfazed, she asked me to lend her $J20. When I said no again, she asked me for $J10, saying she was hot and needed a drink. She promised to pay me back. When I refused her again she started hitting up others in our vicinity for money.

A woman appeared on stage and explained that the performance was delayed due to technical difficulties. She asked us to be patient and I resolved to try my best. At this point Ms. Nigeria departed—in search of liquid refreshment, I presumed. Unfortunately, she returned just as the lights went down. The seat beside me barely contained her bulk. I considered moving, but feared it might bring even more unwanted attention to me.

The first act was a lovely solo dance performed to Marley's "Time Will Tell." My unwanted companion promptly dozed off, slumping over in my direction. The applause woke her up.

Then a performer named Mutabaruka took the stage—a "dub poet." Dub is an African style of oral poetry, and this man was probably it's best known practitioner in Jamaica. He recited poems and presented comedic diatribes, in eloquent patois, about the Babylon System and the corruption of traditional African values by American-style capitalism.

He spoke bitingly about American culture, from his own visits to the U. S. "You go to MacDohnalds ahn you see 'chicken noggats' ahn de menu. Me been round chicken-dem me 'ole life, ahn me nevah 'eard dat dem got a part call a noggat." He spoke of the negative denotations and connotations of the word "black" in the English language and remarked that Black History Month in the U. S. is the shortest month of the year. He was especially critical of the influence of Christian colonialism on African culture. He joked about having gone to a Catholic mass, conducted in Latin. "Fahr ahll me know, dem be sayin'"—and at this point he began to sing a parody of a liturgical chant, stretching each word out into melodic multisyllables—" kill de niggahs!"

The woman sitting beside me continued to call attention to herself whenever she woke from her stupor, making loud comments on what she'd just heard Mutabaruka say from the stage. Heads turned in the surrounding audience; people laughed at her openly. And there I was, Mr. Whiteman, right next to her. For all these folks knew I was her husband.

A steel band took the stage next and played such Bob Marley favorites as "Three Little Birds" and "No woman, No Cry." When roused from slumber by the lively music, the Nigerian woman joined in with off-key, out-of-synch lyrics, sung loudly. I'd had enough. I got up and moved to another seat.

She managed to stay awake long enough to mar the closing number, "Redemption Song," sung by Julian Marley. She not only sang along loudly and off-key, she stood up, swaying to the music and waving her arms. People all over the auditorium turned and looked at her, laughing at her clownish behavior.

Seeing that the concert was about to end, I made for an exit. I stepped out into the sun's glare, shaking my head in disbelief at the Nigerian woman's rude and shameless antics. I wondered if other Nigerians understood something about her behavior that I couldn't—some cultural context—or if they just viewed her as a clown who happened to come from their country.

Was she high on something, or just socially retarded? Why did she attend the concert in the first place, when what she obviously needed was a good, long nap?

The next batch of patients on the ward was probably the most volatile and certainly the shortest lived. It consisted of four men and three women, all but two of them crack addicts. From the outset there were allegations and rumors about sexual activity and drug use on the ward.

Group never really got off the ground. Sessions quickly deteriorated into shouting matches between two of the women. One would accuse the other of hitting on her and the other would scream back that she was a lying bitch. While I could usually intervene in disputes between male patients, I didn't enjoy the same success rate with histrionic women when they fought.

"Whore!"

"Sodomite!"

"Ladies! One at a time, *please!*" They ignored me and kept on yelling at each other. "This is *not* communication!"

Later in the day I'd see the two laughing and talking, as if nothing had happened; but in the next group session the catfight would begin anew. I didn't feel like I was getting anywhere with this group.

I came in one morning to find that five of the seven had tested positive for cocaine in a urine screen. They'd taken full advantage of their freedom to leave the ward and had used on the premises. All five were discharged from the program. Some claimed to see the error of their ways and begged to be given another chance, others tried to bully the staff into letting them stay. But they were all off the ward by the end of the day.

Having procured funds to repair the Occupational Therapy building on the grounds, Sister M had gone on to pronounce an artisan she'd hired our occupational therapist and to put occupational therapy sessions on the weekly schedule. She'd even bumped Celine out of her usual Monday art therapy slot, in favor of this new program, although Celine was a trained therapist and the artisan wasn't. Although I'd seen no signs of problems between Sister M and Celine up until this point, tensions erupted in a staff meeting chaired by Dr.S.

When Celine—who also worked on other wards—complained about her schedule being changed, Sister M lashed out at her.

"You hahve *no right* to bring this op here. It was *my* decision! You should hahve brought it op with *me!*"

"Oh no, Sister," Dr. S responded in his Jamaican-flavored Oxford English. "This is certainly an appropriate forum to bring up the issue. I don't understahnd why you're so opset."

Sister M fumed, barely keeping her composure as she glared at Celine. "*She* knows why I'm opset!"

"No, Sister, I have no idea," Celine responded calmly.

Sister mumbled something about outsiders condescending to people they saw as Third Worlders, asserting that *she* was no fool.

It was then I knew that Dr. S was onto the problems Sister M caused the staff. An astute psychiatrist, his eagle eyes missed nothing in terms of interpersonal dynamics in a conflictual situation, and he handled things deftly. He again called Sister M's attention to her demeanor, then explicitly said that he didn't understand her comment about the Third World.

Confronted about her own behavior in front of her staff, Sister M left shortly afterward, angry and humiliated. When she and Dr. S had left, Sandra reassured us that nobody had ever complained to her about either Celine or myself displaying a condescending attitude toward anybody.

I felt bad about the position Sister M found herself in. I'd come to understand something about hospital politics and had repeatedly been told that nurses, not doctors, ran the wards. As an Administrative Sister assigned to a pilot program, she had a lot of pressure on her to show results in the short-term. The Detox Ward had its enemies.

Given her boundaries, Sister M had for the most part dealt with me warmly and courteously. She'd often addressed me as *my dear*. She just didn't know if I was an ally or an adversary, because I was so outspoken in my criticisms of the program. I think she took them personally and, over time, came to see me as being in the enemy camp. I saw no way to extricate myself from the power struggle if I wanted to be effective in helping to shape the program.

The ward committee I'd proposed started meeting every few weeks to discuss policies and procedures. I gave recommendations for establishing a levels system, with patients earning privileges instead of being granted them regardless of their compliance with rules. I suggested that some infractions be regarded as intolerable—automatic grounds for discharge—and that others be treated as unacceptable, resulting in specific conse-quences. My ideas met with general approval, but implementing them would prove to be a continuing challenge.

One day I ran across Dr. Frank Knight in the men's room on the Psychiatric Ward. Frank was a recently retired staff psychiatrist with whom I'd had some brief but stimulating conversations. One of Jamaica's leading psychiatrists, he'd taught psychiatry at the University Hospital. I'd sat in on some of his "grand rounds" with psychiatry residents, where he'd clini-cally interviewed mentally ill patients behind a one-way mirror, then processed the interviews with the medical students, asking them questions that tested their knowledge.

When I saw him in the men's room that day, however, he was scrubbing out the commode. He smiled at me and said, "They've found a way to keep me on the payroll."

Officially retired, Frank still worked on the Psychiatric Ward, on con-tract. But despite his erudition, his years in London, and his professional status, he was a humble man who didn't see himself as above doing menial work. This toilet seldom got cleaned, so he'd just taken it upon himself to do it. We conversed as I used the urinal and continued as I washed my hands. He'd talked before about inviting Maria and me to his country home some weekend, and on this occasion he let me know he was serious about the invitation. We discussed the details.

Frank picked us up on a Saturday morning and drove us north across the island to his farm at Green Park, up in the hills of St. Ann parish. The cool air was a refreshing change from Kingston's heat and humidity. Frank's wife Susan—a Masters-level psychologist, like myself—had commitments and wasn't able to join us for the weekend, but we met their son and daughter, as well as a visiting friend from England. Nigel was a London policeman—a bobby who walked his beat armed only with a nightstick.

The renovated wooden farmhouse had been built in the middle of the last century, its rustic charm accentuated by family pictures and a simple, homey decor. It stood on a hilltop overlooking a vista of rolling, fenced-in farm fields. Johncrows rode the constant breezes.

Frank was something of a gentleman farmer, with a few pigs and cows, and plans to grow a citrus orchard. A" helper" (i.e. maid) maintained the house, and a farmhand kept up the grounds and cared for the animals. The helper prepared and served most meals. On Saturday afternoon Maria and I got out and explored. Then Nigel and I helped Frank to assemble a picnic table in the back yard. That evening we grilled fish and chicken on a makeshift grill for supper.

The night was cool enough that Maria and I snuggled under a blanket in our small bed. We awoke to a breakfast of eggs and toast, served by the helper on the wide front porch. Frank had to run some errands, so I wrote in my journal out on the porch, while Maria played Boggle with the children. I had to wear a jacket until late morning, to keep from shivering

Later I got to talking to Nigel about his life as a London bobby. He told me that while all policemen are trained in the use of firearms, the knowledge that most routinely carry only nightsticks tends to de-escalate violence in the commission of crimes—especially the use of guns by criminals. The violent crime rate was much lower in London than in any major American city, he said. Nigel had applied for service in an elite special weapons unit, however. One of his hobbies was skydiving. He liked to take risks.

We returned to Kingston on Monday morning, refreshed from our weekend up in the cool hill country. When Frank let us off at our house, we thanked him for his generous hospitality and for an opportunity to spend a weekend in a part of the interior we hadn't seen before.

The fierce rivalry between the Peoples National Party and the Jamaican Labour Party frequently results in bloodshed in the streets of dungtung Kingston. Wearing the wrong color shirt in the wrong neighborhood can get you killed on any day of the year, but the political climate *really* heats up as elections approach. Past elections have been accompanied by blood feuds and riots. Ballot boxes have been stolen, voting stations have been mobbed, and campaign offices firebombed. So as the election for a successor to Michael Manly drew near, tensions rose.

In Jamaica the leader of the party in power serves as Prime Minister. If the PNP maintained its majority of seats in the Parliament in the election, Manley's successor, P. J Patterson, would head the government. If the JLP were to gain the majority, its perennial Don, Edward Seaga, would again serve as Prime Minister, after many years of PNP rule.

One morning on the ward I heard a commotion outside and saw people gathering in the road on the far side of the wall that enclosed the hospital. By the time I left the ward for lunch, the crowd had swollen, and I saw riot police armed with M-16s patrolling the shanty town across the road. I asked someone what had happened and was told that a man had been shot to death within the maze of zinc-roofed shacks. The killer had been seen running away through the hospital grounds. I later read in *The Gleaner* that a JLP assassin had gunned down a PNP neighborhood organizer who was on his way to the privy, then escaped. The campaign of violence had begun.

Isolated incidents of politically-motivated violence were reported during the week before the election. The Peace Corps office put out the word that we were to stay home, or close to home, on election day and the day afterward, as there might be riots. We'd become used to seeing JDF helicopters passing overhead, on their way to patrol in the skies above the dungtung neighborhoods; but on election day they were out in force.

News reports told of scattered roadblocks and a low voter turnout, but no riots.

When Edward Seaga showed up at a rural polling place—supposedly to investigate reports of stolen ballot boxes—an angry PNP crowd gathered outside, forcing him to stay put until PNP stalwart Portia Simpson arrived and persuaded the mob to disperse.

The PNP won the election handily, gaining seats in the Parliament. The Manley era had ended and P.J. Patterson was hailed as the next Prime Minister. There having been only twelve homicides officially designated as politically-motivated, down from fourteen in the '88 election, the campaign was declared by the press to have been relatively bloodless.

One of my long-term clients on the ward, a recovering alcoholic whom I saw as an outpatient, regularly attended AA meetings in Kingston. He told me that in the local Twelve Step jargon non-addicts were often referred to as "civilians" or "earthlings."

The new batch on the ward had quickly split into factions. Two crack addicts, Simon and Barry, used group sessions to strut and fret before a captive audience, vying with me for control of the proceedings. Some mornings I went into the group room feeling like a gladiator entering the arena. One day I got tired of trying to maintain control of the chaos—the shouting, the histrionics, the constant interruptions of anything resembling group process. I again played my trump card.

" I am feeling *extremely* discouraged!" I said, making no effort to conceal my anger. "This is a *therapy group*, not a *stage* for you to perform on! *I give up!*" And I walked out of the room.

I waited a few beats and walked back in, surveying the group members wordlessly. Nobody had moved. Barry waved for me to sit back down, silent for once. I had their attention.

I said my say and we began to discuss what had been going on in group. As we got on track and things began to lighten up, Simon tried yet again to deflect group discussion away from the topic at hand, suggesting that I shouldn't have gotten angry.

"Why the hell not?" I replied. "I'm not some therapy robot. I reserve the right to be fully human as a group leader, just as I respect your right to be fully human as addicts."

I addressed the group. "Did I dis anyone here? Do I owe anyone an apology?"

Heads shook. Simon backed off.

In a later session I called Barry on his continuing "I'm always in control" act in group and, this time, I reached him where he lived. Feeling exposed in public, he got a scared, "lost" look in his eyes. He no longer had an act to fall back on. Seeing his sudden vulnerability, I turned from confrontation to validation—he had his reasons for covering up his true feelings. It can be scary to get real in group.

I made sure that Barry had saved face before ending the session, but noted that he seemed unusually subdued. When we broke for lunch the group members talked and joked with him as usual. He appeared to have learned one of those lessons that groups provide—that you can be exposed in front of a group of your peers and survive. You can know that people have seen something about you that you habitually hide, or even lie to yourself about, and that they can still accept you for who you are.

After lunch I saw him for an individual session.

"You got confronted and you survived. Are you okay, or have we got some unfinished business?"

"No mon. Me respeck what you hahd to say."

I grinned. "You know, when I pinned you down in there I could almost *hear* the gears turning in your brain as you tried to figure out what you were *supposed* to say. What would please me, or impress the group. I think you learned something in there today—something you can only learn when you're on the hotseat.

"You're not in group to please me or to score points. You're there to talk about yourself and learn about yourself, and to learn from others. I know there's a good person buried under all the bullshit. You've piled it up for years and only you can dig your way out. But if you can stay clean and sober, and stop bullshitting *yourself* first, you can do it."

One morning when Dorothy drove in early with Maria and I had to take the bus to work during the morning crush hour, I found myself captive audience to a tandem team of matronly gospel shouters. They'd found their vocation in bus preaching—a different route every day, apparently, to make sure the word got spread out evenly. The rest of us rode to work on the bus; they worked buses.

Dressed in their bright, frilly Sunday finery, each clutched a Bible. Between the two of them, they kept up a non-stop delivery. I guessed that one of them was still in training, as she kept repeating certain phrases a lot. The senior member of the team had memorized reams of holy scripture and improvised, mixing biblical text with seemingly spontaneous expressions of praise and admonitions to heed the word of the Lord. She had her sing-song cadence down pat. When she paused in her delivery, her companion would let out an *Amen!* or a *Hallelujah!*

A few passengers responded with half-hearted affirmations, but most of us just tried to ignore the dynamic duo. I wanted them to go away, but their mission extended to the end of the line.

When the senior gospel shouter started to get hoarse, she stopped preaching, her face sweaty and flushed from hyperventilation. Scarcely pausing to catch her breath, she introduced her buddy—as if we'd *asked* for them to preach to us—who took over without missing a beat. We were all sinners, she shouted, but God loved us anyway. *Hallelujah!*

Back in the States I might have raised my own voice in protest of their obnoxious tactics, but I decided to be a good PCV and kept my mouth shut. I managed to keep it shut until I got off at the route terminus, thinking *Jesus would have blushed.*

We'd gotten used to the limited programming offered by the island's only television station, the Jamaica Broadcasting Company. Other than the news and some cultural shows, we watched little TV. Sunday mornings there was usually an old movie, sometimes one worth watching, like *The Maltese Falcon* or *The Razor's Edge*. We joked about only getting to watch Cinemascope movies in "inemascop" on our tiny black-and-white set.

In March the unthinkable happened and Jamaica's second TV station, CVN, went on the air, giving the JBC some serious competition. Overnight, Jamaicans had 24-hour programming available for the first time. The new station had satellite feeds to ABC, NBC, and even HBO. At first the programming varied from day to day, served up in seemingly random chunks. Programs from the U.S. broadcast networks aired complete with the American ads, and CVN took some time to start doing local programming and running local ads.

While I enjoyed getting to watch ABC News right after the JBC news and liked having more choices, I didn't like the deluge of advertising—another infusion of American consumerism and pop culture—into Jamaica. Now Jamaicans, too, could dial-a-psychic, or call toll-free to order the latest plastic gizmo. CVN even aired a religious infomercial by some American scam artist who claimed that God wants you to be rich.

April brought our second Carnival, and this time Maria attended with me. The Saturday of the big parade we took a bus to the Devon House and had joined the crowds lining Hope Road before the first band of revellers passed. This year's band themes were different—more nautical, as I recall—but the cavalcade hadn't changed in its sensual extravagance. Exposed skin, most of it in shades of brown, glistened with sweat and glitter. Sailors, pirates, mermaids, and ancient Egyptians in gaudy, skimpy costumes shimmied and swayed and bumped and ground their way past us, first to the hot salsa rhythms of Soca music, then to the ringing beat of steel drums.

Move over Dolla' Wine, Bogle, and Butterfly—the new dirty dance craze was The Donkey. Some women did The Donkey while riding on their partner's shoulders, writhing ecstatically, waving their arms, and calling out, "Whoa, Donkey!" Others did it in the more traditional humping conga line fashion. Whether in or out of costume, nobody need be a mere spectator. Children did The Donkey on the sidewalks and higglers boogied away next to their carts. Maria and I took pictures, danced along, and drank in the spectacle.

After the parade we headed for the Peace Corps office to get some water and cool down. By the time we left for home a band of marchers called the Dirty Rats was cooling off with hoses and a keg in an empty lot across from the office. Most still wore their rat ears and tails, and lived up to their name, smearing themselves and each other with mud, and doing some *truly* dirty dancing.

On our way to the bus stop I noticed that Maria and I each wore a few pieces of glitter that we'd picked up from our contact with other dancers. They sparkled in the bright sunlight—red, green, silver—like pixie dust, like we got to take a little bit of the magic home with us.

The two big events on the home front in late April were the arrival, one Sunday morning, of Miss M's four kittens in our unused second shower stall, and the impending arrival of Maria's father, for a week's visit. Miss M had replaced Miss Kitty as Hopeful's mate and had transformed from a rambunctious kitten to an attentive mother during the weeks she'd carried her litter. I'd rigged up the fortress/nursery under the laundry sinks, where Miss M had been born; but she'd had plans of her own. I watched her lying there, smiling, suckling four generic mammalian quadrupeds that might as well have been rat puppies. Cleaning up the back bathroom in honor of our new guests, I spotted and crushed a scorpion, feeling almost paternally protective.

I looked forward to Joe Madeo's arrival. Although he's as politically conservative as I am progressive, we like and respect each other. We've crossed swords from time to time, but both enjoy the game of verbal thrust, parry, and riposte. He'd carefully taken my measure during my courtship of his eldest daughter and found me worthy.

After a career as a Navy officer—a specialist in salvage operations, who still got hired from time to time as an on-site consultant in interesting locations around the world—he'd retired in Tennessee to take up the full-time role of *padron* of his extended family. Ruth, his wife and the mother of his seven children, had died a few years before. He was no stranger to the Caribbean and had been to Jamaica on shore leave many years before.

Maria and I took the week off from work, made reservations at Dragon Bay for three nights, and rented a car. It was the first time I'd driven on the island, and I had to adjust to driving in the left lane and to constantly dodging potholes. We set out for the airport at seven in the evening, arriving only minutes before Joe emerged from customs with his luggage.

On the way back into the city, Maria kept saying that I was too far over to the left. Driving up through a rough neighborhood on Mountain View Road, I hit a pothole and blew a tire. A friendly young man offered to change it for us and had us back on the road within ten minutes, for which service Joe gave him three American dollars.

Then, as we neared Olympia, I drove too close to a bus parked at a bus stop, breaking off the left mirror on the car and scraping the left side against the bus. A 'ductor leapt out of the bus and I could see him gesturing at me in the rear view mirror as I passed. I pulled over to the curb, parked, got out, and walked back to the bus. The 'ductor and I looked at the side of the battered old bus and he quickly decided that no significant damage had been done.

I think the 'ductor had been taken by surprise that a white driver would even stop in this part of town after dark and deal with him man-to-man. He shook my hand and said, "No prohblem. Me respeck you prograhm." I went back to my wife and father-in-law in the car, and drove us the rest of the way home without further incident. Joe had the good grace not to rib me *too much* about my driving, and later commented on the difficulty of adjusting to driving in the left lane.

Joe told us the next morning over coffee that he'd gotten up at six, but had been driven back to the protection of his mosquito-netted bed by the swarm he'd encountered. A veteran of the Tropics, he didn't complain about the stifling heat. Maria had studying to do, so after lunch I took Joe touring in the car. First I drove him up to the University and gave him the grand tour. Then we drove down Hope Road, through Liguanie, to the Devon House. There we turned onto Trafalgar Road, which took us past the New Kingston business district on our way back to the house. Having a car gave me a whole different perspective on Kingston.

After Joe took a nap, Maria drove him up to the new mall in Liguanie to buy some shorts. The mall was air conditioned, had a two screen cineplex, and was one of the few places in Kingston you could go and imagine yourself back in the States—if you didn't look too closely. Few of even the most upscale Jamaican stores have anything near the inventory and selection that we take for granted in the States. In the food court you could get jerk pork and goat rotis, as well as burgers and pizza.

That night Maria baked banana bread and I fixed a Jamaican supper of Bangamary fish, rice and gunga peas, and callaloo. I'd tried to get Joe a bottle of his favorite rum, Mount Gay, only to discover that Jamaica doesn't import rum—coals to Newcastle. So I'd bought him Appleton Estate aged rum, some of Jamaica's finest, and he liked it. Years before he'd introduced me to rum and bitters on the rocks, and I'd found a supermarket that carried Angostura Bitters, so I often drank rum and bitters. But on this night I drank some of the bourbon he'd brought me, while he sipped his rum and bitters and griped about how strong I'd made it. As usual, he later asked for a refill.

Joe can be a charming raconteur, but he can also gripe. He has an eagle eye for detail—probably a result of his years as a Navy skipper. No perceived flaw in a plan or a project under his scrutiny can pass without comment. If he *doesn't* comment on something, you can assume it meets his approval. He also likes to rag me about my political opinions, knowing well that I can rag him right back. But he also enjoys the social equivalent of pushing me in the pool.

I remember a cosmopolitan Thanksgiving dinner one year at Joe's farm. Among the guests was a cultured, elderly couple, who spoke with thick accents. Deposed Hungarian royalty, they'd fled their homeland during the Communist takeover in the last days of World War II, carrying (one imagines) only the gold and jewels they could sew into the lining of their clothes. The old gentleman, now retired, had taught at a private boarding school in the area.

Shortly after the blessing, as we sat eating at the long table the Madeos rig up for such occasions, Joe announced from his seat at the head of the table that I was the family socialist. The elderly couple looked shocked and I had to explain that, having lived in socialist democracies (Austria and Germany) for seven years, I favored a theoretical balance between socialism and laissez faire capitalism. The old folks relaxed visibly once they knew I wasn't a Marxist. Joe grinned his "gotcha" grin at me.

We left for the north coast in the mid-morning. After remarks from both Joe and Maria, over breakfast, about my driving mishaps on the way home from the airport, I suggested that one of them take the wheel. They insisted that I drive. It was a set-up.

We'd decided to take the scenic coastal road rather than the shorter cross-country route. Technically a highway but too narrow to truly deserve the title, the road is heavily potholed in even its best stretches. It winds up and down and around jungled hills, then hugs the coast, passing through rural sugar cane communities and fishing villages. Sometimes the road washes out from mountain streams that become raging torrents after a heavy rain. Even when the streambed is dry, there is no road—just rocks.

It's a challenging road, but I'm a good driver, and on the better stretches I averaged forty or forty-five. I'd begun to adjust my reflexes to driving on the left, but it still took all my concentration to stay centered in my narrow lane while dodging potholes. Not that I avoided them *all*, but I missed all the big ones. The whole time I drove I heard a running critique of my performance from my two passengers.

"You're too far left!"

"You hit that last pothole!"

"You barely missed that truck!"

"Why don't you slow down?"

Despite their criticisms, neither father nor daughter offered to take over driving. I got us to Dragon Bay without mishap, both the car and ourselves intact; but that didn't save me from a chorus of retroactive carping after we checked in, as we carried our luggage to our suite and let ourselves in.

"Fine," I said, holding out the car keys to Maria. "You drive from here on out."

I gave her the keys without rancor, relieved to be rid of the responsibility. It had felt like a no-win situation. She drove more slowly than I, and everyone was happy. At least Maria only had her father's comments to deal with, and she'd had years of practice.

For the equivalent of about fifty dollars a day we got a two-bedroom suite with a living room and a kitchenette. No frills by Joe's standards, but the prospect of three days and nights at the beach, with hot water, air conditioning, and satellite TV sounded heavenly to Maria and me. We unpacked, changed into swimsuits, and hit the beach.

When I returned to the beach later in the afternoon, after exploring a trail, I found Joe standing on the shoreline, looking out to sea. With his hands clasped behind his back, he could have been posing for a Norman Rockwell painting. *The Old Salt Remembers.*

"Maria went back to the room," he said, giving the "r" in Maria its proper Italian roll.

I stood beside him and we looked out to sea together, content just to listen to the surf. If I had clasped my hands behind *my* back too, the painting would have been called *The Old Salt and His Son-In-Law.* The silence was interrupted by a chorus of giggles coming from behind us.

Four young American women in bikinis walked down to the tideline, right beside where Joe and I stood. One of them carried a camera. She remained on the shore while the other three waded out into the waves. When they got about knee-deep, they turned and faced landward then shed their tops and posed, giggling. Joe and I just stood and watched, no longer in Norman Rockwell's world.

"Well," said Joe, after the women had returned to shore.

"Wait 'til you tell them about this back home, Joe. Not something you see every day in Bell Buckle."

Later, having a drink at the Tom Cruise Bar on the beach, I got to talking to some U. S. Coast Guard sailors who were on shore leave. They'd assumed I was a tourist until I told them I was a Peace Corps Volunteer.

"I thought the Peace Corps Volunteers only served in Third World countries," one of them said.

Not bothering to correct his neo-colonial jargon, I told him that if he wanted to see the grinding poverty of a developing country, all he had to do was cross the coastal highway and walk a little way inland to see the *real* Jamaica.

After three days at Dragon Bay we headed back to Kingston. Maria drove, averaging about thirty mph where I'd have averaged forty. We took the overland route and Joe seemed to prefer his daughter's driving to mine, which was fine with me. I relaxed, took in the scenery, and listened to Joe's stories.

Joe is truly a man of the world. He told of living in Egypt for several months while working on a salvage operation in the Suez Canal. His Muslim driver often invited him home for meals with his family and, in return for the hospitality, Joe gave his wife a small refrigerator when he was about to depart. She was so overcome with emotion, she impulsively kissed him—a very immodest act for a Muslim wife. Nonplussed and striving to find a way to save face, the husband said, " This is wonderful.

My wife has kissed her father, she has kissed me, and now she has kissed *you*, too!"

It rained during much of the ride back from the north coast, but Maria skillfully avoided the potholes on the narrow mountain roads and got us home safely. We called Alvira from a pay phone and got ourselves invited to visit her the next day. That night we had curried goat for supper and drove to a downtown theater to see a performance of the annual "national pantomime."

Jamaican "panto" is an ethnic derivation of an English music hall tradition known as a pantomime show—nothing to do with mime. The national pantomime script is chosen in an annual competition and performed by a professional troupe. Pantos are upbeat musicals that invariably feature a boy-meets-girl theme, broad comedy, and political satire. The dialogue is in *deep* patois, but the physical acting conveys the essence of the story even if you can't understand the words. This year's panto was titled "Reggae Son" and had to do with a struggling young singer trying to win first prize in a talent contest that would lead to a recording contract and, presumably, international fame.

The evening got off to a bad start. When we got to the theater parking lot, Maria locked the keys in the car. I went inside the theater to get tickets, only to be told that the show was already sold out. The parking lot was so tightly packed that it looked like someone (i.e. me) would have to stay until the end of the show just to get the car out. Once we got a key.

The theater manager quickly resolved our problems. He told us he just happened to have three tickets left and promised to call the car rental company while we watched the show. We paid him and got to our seats just as the lights went down. The show featured broad slapstick humor, a love story, and an all-singing, all-dancing cast of dozens, in colorful costumes. The onstage action and banter kept the audience in the aisles with laughter.

During the intermission the manager personally brought me the car keys. In the third act the guy got the girl and the recording contract, and everyone danced the *lambada* together as the curtain fell. The three of us thoroughly enjoyed the show. We drove home without any further hassles.

The next afternoon, a Sunday, we drove out to Greendale to visit Alvira. She and Joe hit it off right away. We started out drinking Red Stripes on the porch then moved to the parlor and had a hoppitizer of good Scotch before having a snack of ackee and saltfish and breadfruit, at the dining room table. Alvira took Joe on a tour of her garden shortly before we left. She told him the secret of her success as a gardener: she talked to her plants.

Back at home Joe and I spent our last evening together arguing politics, neither of us gaining any concessions from the other. It had become a ritual.

After I drove Joe out to the airport the next day, I took the car back to the rental agency. We lost our entire deposit due to the scratch I'd put on the car and the broken mirror, and it took all of my logic and patient persistence to make them acknowledge a "mistake" in their billing that would have cost us another $150. I took the bus home, feeling like a PCV again.

The composition of the Peace Corps community in any country of service is constantly changing as new Trainees arrive and as Volunteers either ET or reach their Completion Of Service (COS) dates and depart. Another couple from our training group, Bill and Laurie, had decided to ET. So had Nancy and another friend, the other Bill from Group 58, who had been a frequent overnight guest. He stayed with us his last night on the island and gave me a tee shirt that read BIG UP (i.e. promote, brag about) JAMAICA—*The Next World Power*. He expressed mixed feelings about leaving early, but said he mainly felt burned-out and was relieved to know he was going home. He asked if we ever thought about early termination. We admitted we'd felt discouraged sometimes in our jobs and had questioned whether we'd made a difference. But Group 61 had just arrived to begin training and we were now seen as old-timers. We'd made it this far and had every intention of staying the course through our COS.

Maria had more work than she could manage. Between her teaching, her supervision of student nurses, and her other duties, she hovered on the edge of burnout. She often studied for her lectures evenings and weekends, and had to read her students' log books at home. One night as I was reading for pleasure and she was studying at the table in the next room, I heard her call out, " There are *too many things* in the human body!"

When the Peace Corps training director asked her if she could serve as a training assistant to the new group of trainees and told her that she'd already cleared it with Maria's supervisor at the School of Nursing, she jumped at the chance. She started planning how to wind up at the school and get closure with her students.

We hadn't used much of our vacation time, other than our two weeks Stateside. So we made plans with groupmates Linda and Shirley to rent a car for three days and explore the western tip of the island. We grew worried as the day of the trip neared, because it rained daily, often heavily. The day before we were to leave, torrential rains caused extensive flooding west of Kingston.

By the time we'd packed, rendezvoused with our companions, and rented the car, it was almost two o'clock. We set out, with our spirits high. On the now-familiar stretch of highway between Spanish Town and Old Harbour, we saw an eatery whose sign proclaimed it "The Original Nyam Nyam"—nyam being the patois term for "eat." Then we passed through a low area called Sandy Bay and saw for ourselves some of the destruction wrought by the flood waters.

We saw clothing, boards, boxes, and bedding hanging in trees or tangled in shrubs, where they'd been snagged by branches during the flooding. While the road had been mostly cleared of debris, the surrounding land was covered with fallen limbs and foliage, and ruined shacks. The concrete block buildings wore coats of mud, sometimes chest-high. The locals had already started trying to restore order to their lives, laying waterlogged items out to dry in the sunlight and rigging-up temporary shelters. Some women and children stood by the roadside, holding out hats or empty cans, gesticulating dramatically and begging passing motorists for donations.

We drove up the winding road to Mandeville, a city built on a mountain ridge affording a panoramic view of the emerald countryside surrounding it. Then we drove back down switchbacks to the village of Santa Cruz and the coast. We arrived at our first day's destination, Black River, an hour before sunset. Linda had made reservations at a small hotel called the Bridge House, just over the bridge from the town center—the point at which the coastal highway turns sharply to the north.

We turned off of the highway onto the main street of the small coastal town that stands where the Black River empties into the sea. We passed the usual open-air markets and the brightly-painted facades of shops and rum bars. It was late afternoon on a Saturday—market day—and the pace of commerce had slowed to a trickle of higglers and shoppers on the sidewalks and in the street. Approaching the bridge, we saw a giant sound system being set up inside a fenced commercial park at the edge of town and saw signs proclaiming a night of dancehall music by the riverside.

When we found the Bridge House and Linda went to the registration desk to confirm our reservations, the desk clerk quoted a price considerably higher than what she'd been told over the phone. Linda told her the price she'd been given. The clerk replied that she'd have to talk to her boss to get such a rate reduction authorized, adding that the boss had gone out somewhere. We conferred and decided to check out other available options for lodging.

We left, but it didn't take us long to find out that the few other hotels in town charged even higher prices. We returned to the Bridge House to find a different lady at the registration desk. She gave us a more reasonable offer for two rooms, saying in an amused tone, " We knew dot you would cohm bahck."

After checking into our rooms, we met on the rocky shoreline to watch the sunset. The salt breeze leached the afternoon heat from the air and the western sky took on hues of purple and pink, as the sun sank over distant marshlands. We could hear deejay music across the river.

After dark we set off in the direction of town, in search of supper. On the hotel side of the bridge, the pungent smell of jerk seasoning drew us to a cooking tent in a clearing just off the road. The sign in front of the tent read "St. Beth Jerks." (Black River is in the parish of Saint Elizabeth.) We vowed to return in the daylight to photograph ourselves standing by the sign.

The cook tent had apparently been set up to raise money for some local charity. It offered fried fish, and jerk pork and chicken. Not much else— just bread and beverages. The only thing resembling a vegetable was a hot onion relish. We took seats at the counter and ordered Red Stripes, a pound of pork, and a half chicken. The friendly proprietor talked with us as he hacked up and served our pork and chicken.

"Mos' time, deah be nottin' to do in Block Ribbah ahfta dark—even ahn Sahtaday night. Boht tonight we got a Clash ovah deahso." He pointed in the direction of town.

We could already hear the party cranking up across the mouth of the river from us. A Clash was a contest of sorts between rival dancehall sound systems. On this night Black River had been favored with a major Clash, the five competing sound systems including Inner City and Stone Love— two of the best-known in Kingston. There would be no live singers, only deejays dubbing and scratching and adding their own grunts and words and sound effects to the musical mix. Sometime before dawn, one of the systems would be declared the winner by popular acclaim. Things wouldn't really get hot until sometime after midnight.

Dancehall music filled the night air with its insistent rhythms as we ate our supper by lanternlight, under canvas. This could be nowhere else but Jamaica.

After eating, we walked across the rusty steel bridge into town. For $J50—less than $2—you could enter the arena and dance with the crowd, or you could hang out on the bridge or the street and catch all the sounds for free. We walked up the main street. Most shops had closed, but the rum bars seemed to be doing good business. We wound up back at the bridge, where we listened to the music and watched local boys, armed with flashlights and burlap bags, searching the riverbanks for land crabs.

We met a young man named Tyrone, who asked us within minutes of our acquaintance if one of us could sponsor him for a U.S. visa. He told us he crewed on a fishing boat that worked the waters between Jamaica and the Cayman Islands. Mostly, we talked seafood. He told us that he loved sea turtle soup and turtle eggs. Even though he commented on the declining population of sea turtles, our attempts to educate him about ecology and species extinction fell on deaf ears. All he seemed to care about was the taste.

None of us cared to pay admission to the Clash and dance the night away, so we crossed the bridge back to the hotel, the sounds of dancehall music still loud, but fading in the distance as we walked. We all decided to turn in early and went to our rooms well before midnight.

The next morning we met in the small dining room for a breakfast of bacon, eggs, and toast before getting back on the road. On our way out of town, we stopped by the "St. Beth Jerks" sign to pose for one another's cameras. We got back on the highway and headed north to a beach called Bluefields, where we tried to secure lodging.

While making enquiries near the beach, we met a yout' around ten or eleven years old who told us about a lodge up in the hills and offered to serve as our guide. Maria drove and I rode shotgun as we left the coastal highway and started winding our way up dirt roads into the jungled hills. The boy sat in the back seat with Shirley and Linda, giving directions. As we drove, I heard Linda sharply say "No!" then, shortly afterward, "Stop that!"; but I was too preoccupied, worrying about the deteriorating road conditions, to check out what had happened. We got to a point where the rutted, fissured dirt road became impassable for a two-wheel drive vehicle,; so we gave up and Maria started slowly backing downhill, until we came to a place where we could turn around. When we dropped the boy off at the place we'd met him, to nobody's surprise, he asked us for a tip. The vehemence of Linda's refusal surprised me.

"That *kid* kept trying to put his hand on my thigh!" she said angrily, once we were back on the road. "The first time, I just moved it away and glared at him, but he kept trying. If he'd been any older, I would've slapped him!"

We drove on through the town of Savannah La Mar and on up the coast to Negril. We got a favorable rate at a motel called the Tigress II, after showing our Peace Corps IDs to the desk clerk to prove we weren't tourists. After we went to our rooms and unpacked, Maria and Shirley changed into their bathing suits and went to the swimming pool. When Linda and I joined them shortly afterward to give them the room keys before going for a walk, we found the poolside bartender flirting with them. Maria told me that he didn't believe she was married, as she doesn't wear a wedding ring. When the bartender referred to Linda as my wife, I looked him in the eye and told him, "No, Maria is my wife. Linda's my girlfriend." All four of us kept straight faces. The bartender wore a puzzled frown as Linda and I left for our walk.

In Kingston most Volunteers never got offers of ganja from strangers on the street. In Negril, however, we couldn't walk a block without some dreadlocked yout' offering us ganja, hashish, or psylocybin mushrooms. Some went "Psst" or otherwise tried to get our attention from a distance and mimicked smoking, winding up their pantomimed pitch with an interrogatory shrug. Others just walked right up and asked if we wanted some "herbs," or "indica." We either waved them away or politely declined the offers of those who approached us.

Linda and I talked about "true Rastas" and "false Rastas"—a distinction made by many Jamaicans. Genuine Rastafarians for the most part eshew all drugs other than ganja (and not all Rastas smoke ganja), and are as likely to quote scripture and engage you in a religious discussion as they are to talk about "the wisdom weed." False Rastas wear dreadlocks and may talk the talk, but are really only interested in selling drugs to tourists or picking up foreign women who find them exotic. The north coast, we agreed, abounds in the latter kind.

We returned to the motel, then set out again with Maria and Shirley to watch the sun set over the water and to find a place to eat. We chose a restaurant called "Mr. Natural," which offered mostly fresh fish and vegetables. After we returned to the motel, Shirley went to bed and the rest of us stayed up until almost midnight, playing gin rummy.

The next morning we met at a table on the long porch connecting the rooms for a makeshift breakfast of mangos, papayas, and gingerbread bullas. The sun shone in a cloudless sky. We decided to stay at the Tigress II for another night, notified the manager at the front desk, then piled in the car and headed for the beach.

With its miles of white sand, the Negril beach never gets crowded. Shortly after we'd claimed our little spot on the shore, a group of young German women laid down their gear beside us and proceded to shed their bikini tops. I took in the rays, read, swam in the azure sea, jogged along the shoreline, talked with my wife and my friends, and enjoyed the sights and sounds around me. Sometime around noon I had my first Red Stripe.

My idea of paradise closely resembles the beach at Negril.

After we'd gotten our quota of sun for the day, we headed inland to the craft market. I didn't like enduring the high pressure sales pitches, but the ladies wanted to look around. Because I knew I didn't intend to buy anything, I felt like my presence only served to tease the merchants. In such situations, following someone else's agenda, I tend to fall back into *writer mode*, studying everything around me for future reference.

As I walked within the maze of canopied booths, shopkeepers tried to entice me inside their shops, as if theirs contained something unique. But each one seemed much like the last one when you looked at the merchandise on display: rings; earrings; ganja pipes; buttons made from laquered coconut shells painted in red, green, yellow, and black, bearing such Jamaicanisms as "Irie" (a Rasta greeting meaning something like "good vibes"), "One Blood," and "No Problem"; stylized wood carvings of African design; bamboo trinkets; tee shirts; hats; and Rastafarian icons.

When it became clear that my companions weren't ready to leave yet, I decided to invest myself at a deeper level. Letting the shopkeepers know I was just hanging out while the ladies shopped, I got into conversations that led me behind the outer row of booths into "the other side of the market", where the merchants retreat to smoke and drink and talk when business is slack. A man who had tried earlier to snag me with a hint that I must be racist if I didn't want to "just talk" to him (i.e, about his merchandise) finally heard me: I wasn't in the market to buy anything, but was just waiting for my wife and friends. We got to talking about life in Jamaica, life in the U.S., life in general.

"See, mon," he told me after a while, " me only wahnted to tahlk."

"Yeah, mon, but *here* you know that most times when someone says he just wants to talk to you, he's mainly looking to make some money. Respect, mon. You know what I'm saying."

He smiled and we rapped knuckles. The other people behind the booths caught on that I was a resident, not a tourist, and that they weren't going to make any money from me. Nobody hassled me with sales pitches anymore. The whole pace of commerce seemed to drop away, and I enjoyed myself, no longer impatient to leave.

On our way back to the car, we came across a local talent contest being conducted on an improvised stage in the parking lot. We saw a succession of middle school-aged children dancing The Butterfly—the popular dance that had replaced The Bogle and The Donkey—humping and gyrating up on stage, to the delight of the audience. We waited for the vocal competition to start, but by the time the second moppet in a row started her rendition of "I Will Always Love You", we agreed that we'd heard quite enough, and left.

We returned to Kingston the next day, driving a back route that took us through the isolated inland village of Seaford Town, where we hoped to drop in on our groupmate, Bob. Sure enough, when we got there it turned out that everyone knew him and where he lived.

Bob saw us coming up the drive from the main road and came outside to greet us, surprised to have company. Bob lived in the modest, wooden manor house of a small estate, which he got rent-free in return for acting as caretaker. He invited us inside and introduced us to his Jamaican girl-friend, Elsa.

He told us stories about his life and work in Seaford Town. He loved his assignment in the bush, and had carved his own special niche in the com-munity as a one-man welfare agency. His worst experience had been a short time when Sam—the obnoxious Volunteer described earlier, who treated Peace Corps service as an extended vacation—had been assigned to work with him.

"He finally ET'd last month, just before the Peace Corps was about to terminate him," Bob told us. "While he was assigned here, he'd show up at work maybe two or three days a week and spend the rest of his time party-ing in MoBay. His girlfriend from the States came to visit him here and I couldn't believe the way he treated her. When he introduced her to me, he said,' she did me on our first date!'. She was humiliated and said, 'That's not true,' but he just went on about how great she was in the sack. When he said they were going to get married, it seemed to come as news to her. She seemed to be a decent kid. I hope she has the sense to dump him. What a loser!"

We visited for an hour or two, then got back on the road. It rained most of the way to Mandeville, and we worried that the road through Sandy Bay might be flooded. The rain fell in torrents when we stopped at a roadside eatery to get paper cups of hot corn chowder, which we ate in the car. We sat, sweat-soaked, in the parked car until we'd finished eating, as the vapor from the hot soup kept the windows steamed. The skies cleared after we passed Mandeville, and we drove the rest of the way to Kingston without incident. We dropped Linda and Shirley off at their homes, returned the car to the rental agency, and arrived home before dark.

The rains continued—the wettest rainy season since our arrival. My little collapsible umbrella had wilted with use and I wondered if it would last until our COS. Maria and I each had our days when we wondered if *we* would last.

At work I continued to meet with the staff to work on developing a program model and I started compiling a relapse prevention workbook, to complement my psychoeducational group curriculum. Some days I couldn't see patients for individual sessions in the afternoons, because they had to go to the renovated crafts building to paint floral designs on bottles. They liked it because it gave them a chance to get off the ward and smoke. Sister M called it occupational therapy, but I called it Marlboro Country.

I'd missed the first week with a new batch of patients and hadn't been able to do my usual individual assessments, which I usually hand-wrote in the patients' medical records. I was busy and decided to skip them for this batch, just to see if anyone noticed. Several of the nurses asked why I hadn't done my assessments, making it clear that they valued my input; so I quickly scheduled assessment sessions and caught up.

Although most of the day staff seemed to appreciate my attempts to promote a coherent treatment model, some of the night staff just ignored the rules we were trying to establish. I also encountered some opposition to my efforts from the outside. Some members of the Drug Abuse Rehabilitation Team that met periodically complained that the Detox Ward "wasn't doing what it should." Staff from the outpatient Addiction Alert program and the Patricia House therapeutic community argued that we should shift from our present "closed" program to an "open" program, to better accomodate their needs.

In a closed program, all the patients are admitted at the same time and stay for the duration of the program—in our case, four weeks. The same people attend all the groups and therapeutic alliances form in a certain way, as the group process has a shared beginning, middle, and end. In a program run strictly along these lines—which ours wasn't—there were no newcomers and oldtimers in the group.

An open program continuously admits and discharges patients. Each one may stay for four weeks, but there is a constant flow as newcomers join the group and oldtimers graduate. This makes for a different kind of group process, as oldtimers "see themselves" in the newcomers and form therapeutic alliances with them—for instance, confronting their denial, or modeling self-disclosure.

Each kind of program has its benefits, but I favored continuing with our present model. Addiction Alert and Patricia House thought that a continuous flow of patients through the Detox Ward would better serve *their* treatment models and didn't like having to adapt to ours. We couldn't be all things to all people. If we tried, we'd be stuck in a "model muddle" or, as Dr. S would put it, a "pitchy-patchy" program. So I continued to argue for consistency at the DART meetings.

In addition to my ward duties, I was sometimes asked to teach or to give presentations, in my capacity as an adjunct faculty member at the University Hospital. When I taught my classes on drug abuse and addiction at the School of Nursing, my biggest challenge was keeping all the student nurses awake. Once I was asked to conduct an afternoon workshop on drug abuse interventions to a class of visiting health workers from all over the Caribbean.

An intervention is a technique for confronting an addict in denial and getting him or her into treatment. It has been called a "planned crisis", or "raising the bottom"—referring to the concept that an addict often has to "hit bottom" before coming out of denial. The classic intervention strategy is to ask the addict to come to a meeting. When he arrives he finds family members, friends, and (where appropriate) his boss already assembled. If he threatens to leave, the people in the circle specify consequences should he do so. His wife may say she'll file for legal separation and make him move out of the house; his boss may tell him he'll be fired if he doesn't stay.

Once the addict agrees to stay, the people present express love and support, but confront his addiction and urge him to go into a pre-arranged treatment program. Using the principles of "tough love", they continue to present specific consequences that would result from refusal to enter treatment, including loss of family support and loss of employment. In a successful intervention, the addict breaks down and accepts the option of professional treatment.

For my presentation I'd decided to start out with an orientation on substance abuse, addiction, and treatment, followed by a role-play of an intervention. I would play the alcoholic father, Harry, and had prepared role sheets with identities and suggestions for the participants, who would play the family members, the therapist, and the boss.

I gave my talk, asked for volunteers to play the roles, handed out the role sheets, then announced a break, during which we were to prepare for the role-play. I ended up with a Trinidadean wife, children from Guyana and the Dominican Republic, a Barbadian therapist, and an Antiguan boss. Once confronted, I knew Harry wouldn't walk out, but I made the participants work to keep him in the room.

The exercise went well. Everyone tried their best to stay in character as they confronted Harry with his alcoholic trangressions. He eventually agreed to go into treatment. He got lots of hugs and assurances of support.

In early June Maria and I got invited by Vasanth to join him on a visit to his "uncle." Dr. Vish lived in a town called Southfield on the southern coast, where he ran the St. Elizabeth Parish medical clinic. His home was in walking distance of Lovers' Leap. "Vish" had been a frequent guest at Vasanth's house and we'd gotten to know him, his Jamaican wife Sharon, his son, and other members of his extended family. On weekends we sometimes had curious Indian children hanging around our house, calling us Uncle Jeff and Auntie Maria.

Prakash drove Vasanth, Rainuke, Maria, and me to Vish's home, just landward from cliffs overlooking the sea. There we learned that Indian hospitality rivals, or exceeds, southern hospitality. Maria and I got one of two guest bedrooms, while Vasanth and Prakash slept on couches or pallets in the living room. The cuisine was Indian, not Jamaican—curried meats and rice, cucumber with a minty yogurt dressing, pan-fried bread, and peppery relishes. The women tended to congregate in the kitchen and generally catered to the men. After her initial offers to help were refused, Maria joined in the chat out on the porch.

The satellite TV in the living room stayed on throughout the weekend. There was no point in getting involved in any particular program, however, as someone was always playing with the remote, rotating the dish, checking out alternate satellite feeds and program menus, and selecting some new option. Local people and friends from Kingston came and went throughout our stay. While never the main focus of attention, Maria and I were treated like special guests.

An Indian veterinarian named Vidgian and his wife arrived in time for late afternoon tea on the porch. After the sun had set, Vasanth started taking orders for drinks. Scotch? Would I prefer Pinch or Chevas? People kept on arriving. The men and some of the wives hung out on the porch, drinking and smoking; the children clustered around the TV; and the rest of the women stayed busy in the kitchen. Maria assisted as she could, but on the periphery—a guest, not family.

Dinner was served on the porch around nine o'clock. Sharon handed me a plate filled with curried chicken and pork, rice, and salad. I thanked her, knowing there'd be no point in offering to do the dishes after we ate. Hey! I'm a feminist—but who am I to turn down hospitality or to reject the cultural norms of others?

After dinner the men stayed out on the porch and started telling dirty jokes. The TV was tuned to the Sci Fi Channel—a monster turtle trashing Tokyo, on *Radiation Theater*. As the night went on the crowd diminished. There had been some talk about getting up early to watch the sunrise at Lovers' Leap, but nothing ever came of it. When the party ended around midnight, Maria and I retired to the guest bedroom.

The TV was already on in the living room when I got up the next morning, tuned first to *Meet the Press*, then to the French Open tennis tournament. Around nine-thirty the women served a delicious breakfast of fresh *puri* (round, pan-fried breads, looking like small pita loaves, but lighter); scrambled eggs made with onions, tomatos, and peppers; watermelon sorbet; and strong coffee. Shortly before noon all of us at the house crowded into cars and caravanned down to the beach at Allegator Pond. A Jamaican originally from Puerto Rico arrived from Kingston with four young Filipino women just in time to join us, further adding to the international makeup of our party. We drove down serpentine, potholed back roads through the rainforest.

All along the way, Vidgian kept up a steady stream of jokes—most of them off-color. He told one about the Indian Minister of Defense seeing Indira Ghandi taking a bath. He starts singing the national anthem, so she has to stand up. Another had to do with Nixon, travelling in China and being asked how he thought history would have been different if Krushchev, rather than Kennedy, had been assassinated. He replies, "Well, for one thing, Aristotle Onassis wouldn't have married the widow." After each joke he would laugh heartily, repeat the punchline lest anyone hadn't caught the joke, and look around to make sure we were all laughing.

When we arrived at our destination we saw no pond, no allegators, just a brown-sand beach that seemed a miniature version of Hellshire Beach. There were several cook shacks and round, thatch-roofed bars among the palm trees just landward of the beach, and fishermen sold their catch from their boats on the shoreline. Other than our little UN delegation, everyone else at the beach seemed to be local.

Vish took us to the beach bar he usually patronized. He ordered the first of many "queues" (half-pints) of gin, ice and glasses, and "Ting"—a grapefruit soda. He wouldn't hear of anyone in the party buying his own drink. Throughout the afternoon he made sure his guests had all they wanted to eat and drink. When the bartender introduced himself to Vidgian as "Blackie", Vidgian quipped, "I asked your *name*, not your *color!*" Ha ha ha.

Between the sea breeze, the shade, and the iced drinks, I felt reasonably comfortable even in the mid-day heat. Vidgian continued to hold forth, but we were spread out around the circular bar and I had my choice of several conversations to join in. We, talked, drank, and snacked on fried fish and fresh lobster—officially out-of-season, but available for the asking. There was a running joke about not turning down the offer of a drink, saying "I was raised better (than to refuse hospitality)."

Although we'd been told that the plan was to head back to Vish's around three, around that time Vish dispatched Vasanth to take Sharon and the other women in the extended family—including Rainuke—back to the house to prepare a lunch for us to eat before returning to Kingston. Then he ordered more rounds of drinks for those of us remaining, but I started drinking iced Ting without the gin. We left a little after four, but on the road back to Southfield Vish recognized a friend going the other way and stopped the car to chat with him. This led to a stop at a nearby rum bar and yet another round of drinks.

A meal of curried mutton, rice, and salad awaited us back at Vish's house. Just when I thought we were about to leave, someone proclaimed it "tea time" and we were all offered coffee and tea. Although eager to get home, I surrendered to the situation, knowing I had no control over it. We finally got on the road around six o'clock and arrived home before nine, sated from Sharon and Vish's kind hospitality.

When I returned to the ward and met the new batch of patients, it was clear that I had my work cut out for me. We had a mixed batch of men and women again, which always promised an interesting stew of interpersonal dynamics for group. Most of the group were crack addicts.

Norman had started referring to Dian, whom he'd known to be a prostitute in MoBay, as a "dutty girl." Merline had also rented her body to supply her habit and didn't want to go back to "that dutty road." Hedley had already alienated staff with his constant complaints and his comments about the way the program *should* be run. Evan was trying to blackmail his mother into paying his airfare back to the U.S., where his girlfriend and their child lived, using visitation with the grandchild as his bargaining chip. He used the threat of suicide as his ace-in-the-hole. Norman quickly made it clear that he'd only entered treatment because he had no money and no other options.

The first group meeting got off to a predictably rocky start, with Dian taking stage in her tragic heroine role and Hedley attacking the program. When we did the rounds on the topic of feelings, Evan said that he felt like killing "certain people" who deserved killing. He implied that he'd killed before.

This led us to the topic of violence. I took on Evan, who'd also made histrionic suicidal threats in front of everyone on the ward. I said that I thought he was more likely, in his current mental state, to relapse than to attempt suicide or to kill anyone. (I didn't say that, if he relapsed, I thought that he might kill someone.) I suggested that he had the choice to either feed or not to feed his violent fantasies.

That got us into a discussion of the role of anger in addiction. Group discussion caught fire. Even Hedley, who'd tried to get out of the session by complaining of a migraine, got involved, saying that his headache had eased. We ended—amazingly—on a positive note.

Nobody in this batch complained of getting bored in group. Merline was given to storming out of the room in mid-session. In time, group members confronted Dian's *nothing can get to me anymore* act and Norman started dealing with her as a person, not just a crack whore. Still, she reacted to even gentle feedback as if she were being attacked, betraying her words.

Evan's aggression subsided during his weeks on the ward and he even made positive contributions in group. In one session, trying to get Dian to look at her own defenses, he admitted that he typically put up a front, showing people only what he wanted them to see.

Hedley continued to complain about the program and to avoid dealing with his own issues. One day in group, he asked, "Is dis a 'ospital?" He was just getting started.

I dealt with him as best I could. "Hedley, that's a perfect example of a statement in the form of a question. What is it you want to tell us?"

"Hedley, I'm not going to play your game. You're deflecting again, wanting to talk about anything but yourself."

"Hedley, the world is unfair—that's a given. The question is, what are you going to *do* about that? Are you going to let the world drive you to drink? Again?"

"Hedley, you only seem to know one song, which you sing over and over."

Although I couldn't allow griping about the program's inadequacies to be the central focus of my group sessions, I had to admit that some of Hedley's complaints were valid. Despite my best efforts, we still had no treatment model to guide us and ward rules weren't being consistently enforced. With only three months to go in my term of service, I had faint hopes of making any meaningful difference in the program that would last after my departure. However, I continued to work on my relapse prevention workbook, in the hope that it would help my psychoeducational curriculum take root.

Maria and I had each observed instances of passive aggression often enough in our jobs that we'd begun to see it as a pervasive Jamaican national trait. Sometimes it consisted of failing to follow-through on commitments and subsequently refusing to acknowledge them. It often took the form of withholding any direct feedback, positive or negative, about any potentially-conflictual situation. We agreed that it was probably a holdover from slavery and colonial rule, and that it proceded from a distrust, not of white people, but of authority in general. At times it seemed like nobody was held accountable for anything. Maria told me that when she described "passive aggressive personality" to a class of nursing students, one of them responded, "Miss, dot soun' like mos' Jamaican-dem."

Sunday mornings at home often started with the cry of the newspaper deliveryman, who cruised the neighborhood streets on his motorbike, calling out, "Gleaner...GLEANER!" The first Sunday of every month I'd climb out from under the mosquito netting, pull on some shorts, and run out to meet him and pay for four weeks of Sunday delivery. The other

Sundays I usually got up when the paper was delivered, but took my time going out to get it from the patio.

One morning in late June we awoke to one of the periodic Sunday power shutdowns we'd come to dread. We knew from experience that the electicity would come back on sometime around sundown, but faced a day of relentless heat without fans. It was my weekend to do the laundry. I set about the task before reading the paper, to get it out of the way before it got *really* hot. Miss M and her three kittens played on the concrete patio around the laundry sinks as I scrubbed and rinsed the clothes. They knew that if they hung around long enough, they'd get some milk or table scraps. We'd named the two females Tigger and Carnival, but our favorite was the male, who had a short, deformed crook of a tail. We named him Stump, after the one-armed boy in Fannie Flagg's **Fried Green Tomatoes at the Whistle Stop Cafe**. We liked his bold personality.

We'd tried our best to find good homes for the kittens, but our attempt to place Tigger had been a bust. An eleven year-old named Phillip, who spent weekends with one grandmother, next door to us, and lived with his other grandmother the rest of the week, promised to take good care of Tigger, whom he re-named Cuddles. But in the days after he took possession of her, we saw the poor thing confined in a small wire pen in the yard, filthy and screeching, left alone all day. When we spoke to Phillip, he said that his other grandmother wasn't ready to take the cat yet; so we took her back and cleaned her up. It took her a while to settle down from the shock of her incarceration, and her mother and siblings avoided her at first. But by Sunday things had returned to normal and all the cats had free run of our house and yard.

By the time I'd hung up the last of the laundry on the clotheslines, I was soaked with sweat. I joined Maria inside and read the *Gleaner* while she made corned beef hash and eggs for breakfast, surrounded by mewing cats. Smoke from the mosquito coils hung heavy in the air, without the fan breeze to dissipate it. We read for most of the day to pass the time. I couldn't write in my journal, because my dripping sweat would've made the ink run. We drank a lot of water to compensate for our perspiration.

By noon we'd filled the bathtub, and each of us went back several times during the afternoon and immersed ourselves for a few minutes when the heat became intolerable. Toward late afternoon we felt some blessed breezes blowing up from the harbor. The only music we heard that day was from an ice cream truck that often came through the neighborhood on Sundays, playing the Scott Joplin ragtime theme from *The Sting* over and over and over.

Willard, our Rasta gardener, came by on his rickety bicycle to give us a coconut and to ask if we had any work for him to do that week or any beer bottles he could dispose of for us. I'd been lugging our empties down to a local store in my backpack and collecting the meager return money myself; but now we just gave them to Willard. He needed work, he explained, to pay for repairs on his long-unused Moped.

After he left I used an icepick to puncture holes in the top of the coconut, and drained the milk into a glass. Then I went out on the front patio to crack the coconut the easiest way I knew how. I just threw it straight up in the air. The hull split when it hit the concrete patio in front of me. I pried it apart with my hands as I walked back to the kitchen in search of a knife with which to finish the job.

I sat down at the table, prying the meat from the fragments of husk with a dull blade and popping an occasional piece in my mouth. Sure enough, shortly before sunset we heard the refrigerator thrum back to life. We made exclamations of relief and turned on both of our fans. I remarked to Maria as we luxuriated in the artificial breeze, " I expect the Peace Corps experience tends to be *enjoyed* more in the recollection than in the living of it."

"Well," Maria replied, "I've heard it said that you spend two years serving and the rest of your life figuring it out."

One day while I waited for a bus in front of Olympia School, I chatted briefly with a middle-aged lady higgler who sold sweets to the schoolchildren.

"Wat you doin' heah in Kingston?" she asked. "You a teachah?"

"No," I said,"I'm a psychologist."

"Oh!" She tapped her head and grinned. " Me 'ave to cohm see you sometime!"

I get that all the time, Stateside. Apparently it's a universal joke.

Pushing my way into the next bus to arrive at the stop, I found myself wedged next to a fiftyish woman who wore a heavy cast on her right arm. Having no handhold in reach, she unselfconsciously draped her left arm around my shoulder and held on to me for support as the bus lurched into motion. I was her brother and she knew it. She exited a few stops down the road without a word having passed between us.

One day when he came to collect the rent, Kai Meng asked us if we'd like to come to a lecture on Eastern religions. We said we would and he said he'd pick us up on the appointed evening and take us.

Not until after we arrived at the meeting hall did we learn that Kai Meng was giving the lecture and that it wasn't on Eastern religion in general, but on Nichiren Shoshu Buddhism, the sect that he'd recently joined. A Chinese Maylasian by birth, he joked about how he'd had to come to Jamaica to discover Buddhism. He belonged to the local chapter of Soka Gakkai International, the same organization my German ex-wife had briefly been affiliated with in Stuttgart in the early seventies. I'd even joined in the chanting ritual myself a few times when we'd visited Buddhist friends, kneeling and repeating , "Nam Myoho Renge Kyo."

True believers finger beads as they chant, much like Catholics saying the rosary. It's my understanding that they believe chanting helps to "polish your karma" and to advance you toward your goals. Some people chant *for* some specific thing, although this seems to me to be at odds with the Buddhist principle of engaging in "right action" without being attached to outcomes. Although Kai Meng confirmed my impression that you can chant for, for instance, prosperity; he denied that there was any element of "supernatural" intervention similar to the popular Christian notion of God answering prayers.

After setting up a slide projector and screen, Kai Meng took the podium in front of an audience of perhaps forty people. He proceded to talk animatedly about Buddhism's origin in India and its spread throughout Asia. He spoke of Gautama Buddha and his enlightenment, of the Eightfold Path, of Shakyamuni and the Lotus Sutra. He clarified that Buddhism is a teaching and not a religion. He explained a central precept, revealed by Gautama Buddha: that all suffering comes from attachment. He said that Buddhists share the belief that all sentient beings have the potential of attaining enlightenment.

Then he asked someone to turn off the lights and began his slide presentation. He showed photos he'd taken of temples and shrines in India, Indonesia, Maylaysia, and Japan, and kept up a running commentary on what we were seeing. When the slide show was finished, he turned the lights back on and asked if there were any questions. Maria and I agreed, after he drove us home, that we were glad we'd attended. Even though I didn't hear much new, Kai Meng's lively energy and engaging manner had made for an interesting evening.

When I got to the ward on the first day of the new treatment cycle, I was asked by our new resident—who was seven months pregnant and would be out on maternity leave for much of her six-month rotation—to assess a new admission. Ostensibly "flattened" on neuroleptic medication, he was actually quite psychotic and seemed to be hallucinating. I went into the nurses' station to get him just as he asked Sandra if she loved him and if she'd hug him. He wore pajamas and was barefoot.

I introduced myself and said I'd like to talk to him in the doctor's office.

"Doc," he addressed me, "you a Christian?" I told him I wasn't a doctor, but before I could address his other question he extended his arms and asked for a hug. I declined. He then asked Sandra and me if we'd repeat the words he was about to say. Sandra said no, but we'd listen. The patient launched into a rambling prayer about sin and forgiveness, but quickly lost track of any coherent thread and babbled on in what psychiatrists call a "word salad." Sandra kept urging him to go with me and I reinforced the message.

"We're not here to do what you want us to do. We're here to help you. No, wait, listen to me. If we're going to help you, you need to do what we ask you to do. Now come with me. No, I'm not going to hug you."

By the time we got him out of the nurses' station, I'd done all the assessment I needed to do. He was clearly too psychotic to benefit from our program and I hoped we could persuade the new resident not to admit him. Reason eventually prevailed.

The other new admissions consisted of three men and two women—all crack addicts in their thirties. One of the women, Laurine, was very pregnant and hadn't had any prenatal care. The male patient who would prove to be my biggest challenge in this batch was a dreadlocked Rasta named Cory.

When I convened my first group session, Cory made it clear that he didn't want to attend and said he should be excused. When I asked why, he pointed down to his bare feet.

"Me hembahrress becahs me de only wan barefoot. Me 'ave no slipper. Me sistah, when she pahck me clothes, lef' out me slipper. De Sistahs-dem say me no cahn wear me shoe ahn de ward. Please, Jeff, nah mek me com to group ontil me get sohm slipper."

I knew that Cory was exaggerating for effect, seizing on whatever he could to avoid group. I tried to cajole him into dropping his act, but he continued to wear a hang-dog expression and to plead that I spare him any further humiliation. As this was the first "knot" in group process, the other group members kept out of it, waiting to see what I'd do.

I tried to call him on his game, but he just shrugged and looked at me with feigned incomprehension. I suggested that he had *created* his own embarrassment, that it hadn't just *happened* to him; but I couldn't get him to admit to the game he played. I asked the other group members if Cory's bare feet bothered them in any way or engendered any judgements of him. Most of them seemed amused as they replied that Cory's barefoot condition didn't bother or distract them in any way.

Cory changed his tack. He pointed out that I wore shoes. How could I possibly understand?

I grinned, realizing he'd just given me the solution I'd been seeking. I removed my shoes and socks. I stretched my legs and wiggled my toes, announcing that I wasn't in the least bit embarrassed. I asked Cory if he felt any better now that he wasn't alone. Most of the group members laughed, but Cory just glared at me, his act blown.

I suggested that being barefoot among people wearing shoes was something like baldness: how embarrassed you felt depended entirely upon your attitude. With Cory's diversion behind us, we got down to making introductions and discussing group rules. I left my shoes off for the rest of the session. When I walked into the nurses' station barefoot after group, I had some explaining to do.

Over time, Cory began to get real with me in our individual therapy sessions, admitting soon after our confrontation that he'd learned to cope without slippers until his sister had finally brought him some. He proved to be a sincere Rastafarian. Most "true Rastas" don't use alcohol or any other drug than ganja (if that), and Cory seemed genuinely ashamed of having gotten hooked on crack. When I asked him if he thought he could still smoke ganja "sacramentally," he said he couldn't—it would only lead him back to crack.

He told me that his wife had mostly lived in Canada for the past five years, and I knew it wasn't unusual in Jamaica for a spouse to live "a-fahren." He hoped to join her someday. He said that he'd been faithful to her during most of their time apart, but that he'd recently lost his willpower while high on crack and traded a "rock" for a sexual favor from a prostitute. "Dot's how low me fahllen cohz ah crock."

Six months pregnant, Laurine slipped away from an off-campus Narcotics Anonymous meeting. The van driver, a recovering addict, told the staff that he couldn't account for an hour of her time off the ward. When confronted by two nurses and me, she wept silently and retreated into silence, saying she only wanted to speak to the new ward resident—who, also pregnant, had taken a special interest in her.

"Laurine," I said to her, "all behavior communicates something and what your behavior clearly communicates is that we can't *make* you talk. We already know that, but we wish you'd *choose* to talk to us about this. You seem angry and hurt. Are you feeling ganged-up-on?"

After a long pause she said, "Can I go now?"

Timing is as important in therapy as in standup comedy. I decided to back off for the time being and we ended the interview.

Later in the day, Laurine pantomimed to me through the window of the nurses' station that she wanted to talk, and we went into the empty doctor's office. She poured her heart out to me about her pregnancy, but avoided her disappearance from the meeting the night before. Although she said she had no feelings for her baby and wanted to put it up for adoption, she felt guilty about the effects the cocaine on her pregnancy. She wondered if she might develop feelings for the child once it was born. After we discussed her ambivalent feelings, I brought the focus back to recovery.

Whether or not she could make decisions she could live with, I said, would depend on her ability to stay clean and sober. I asked her if she was willing to talk to the nurses about her disappearance from the NA meeting. Laurine allowed that they'd treated her fairly and that she needed to level with them. She admitted to me that she'd left the meeting to meet her boyfriend, but denied that she'd used. She didn't seem worried at the prospect of a urine drug screen, so I left it at that.

The time finally came for our Close Of Service conference—the last time those of us left from Group 58 would all get together. It had been booked at JAMAICA JAMAICA, an all-inclusive resort in Runaway Bay. Some of our number planned to COS in the weeks following the conference and the other Jeff, who'd ET'd months before, returned to the island just in time to join his groupmates on the north coast. He had a surprise in store for us.

Jeff had proposed to his girlfriend from Group 58, Joanne, and they planned to marry at the conference. The trouble was, Jeff had left the Peace Corps and didn't have a lot of money. At first there was talk of sneaking him in; but wiser heads prevailed and someone was able to help bankroll him as a legitimate guest at the resort for the two nights and three days we'd be there.

The Peace Corps drove the Group 58 Volunteers from Kingston to the north coast in vans. We checked into the resort around noon and had until two o'clock before our first session. It was like abruptly entering another world—a world of cool rooms, hot running water, good service, and well-stocked bars where you didn't even have to run a tab. We suddenly had choices unimaginable the day before. Should we eat lunch at the restaurant in "casually elegant" attire, or in swimsuits at the beach buffet, or just call room service?

We justified three days of getting catered-to as recompense for two years of service and as a step in our re-entry to our lives as professionals back in the U.S. In our meetings we'd be sharing lessons learned at our work sites, continuing the dialogue begun two years before in Miami about what it means to be a development worker, discussing the "disengagement phase" of service, and preparing ourselves for the predictable reverse culture shock we could expect upon re-entering our homeland.

At the resort you always had multiple choices as to cuisine and ambiance. You could order from a menu in the tropical elegance of the restaurant, pick and choose from an amazing variety of dishes at the buffet, or grab a burger or some jerk chicken at the barbeque shack out by the beach. The buffets were a feast for the eyes as well as the palate: rows of banquet tables laden with a variety of meats and vegetables, prepared in both Jamaican and American styles. You could breakfast on ackee and salt-fish with fried plantain slices and fruit; or eat bacon, eggs, and toast, or pancakes. Lunch and dinner buffets featured a little bit of everything. Shrimp, lobster, baked fish, fried fish, shellfish. Ham, roast beef, chicken, mutton, and goat. Caribbean slaw, lettuce salads, fruit salads, pasta salads—even jello salad. Fresh pineapple, grapefruit, and orange slices, fresh coconut and papaya and mango, apples and pears imported from the U.S. Dessert tables held varieties of pies, cakes, puddings, pastries, petit fours, and fruit dishes.

In our meager three days at JAMAICA JAMAICA, we only had limited time to take advantage of what what was at our disposal: sailboarding, snorkelling and scuba; tennis courts and a gymnasium; jaccuzis—including one out on the dunes behind the designated stretch of nude beach; reggae and calypso bands, karioke, a piano bar, and a disco.

Jeff and Joanne had arranged for a simple wedding ceremony on the beach, following the afternoon session on the second day. In addition to any individual gifts, Group 58 bought a set of goblets carved of lignum vitae wood as a group gift. Jennifer served as Matron of Honor and Jeff asked Rick to be his Best Man.

I appointed myself Worst Man, as we men planned Jeff's bachelor party—a running joke. In this capacity, I took it as my responsibility to test his commitment, sauntering up to him at intervals during the evening and saying such things as, "Are you sure you want to go through with this?", "You know, there are other fish in the sea.", and "This is your last night of freedom!"

After all the Group 58 women had gone to bed, the remaining men—including Jeff—headed for the disco for one last drink. As we strode like the Wild Bunch down the cool, carpeted hallway from the lobby bar to the disco, I uttered the obligatory phrase for the final phase of a bachelor party, " Let's go score some chicks!"

I quickly tired of the flashing, colored lights, the blacklights and strobes, the clouds of cigarette smoke, and the insistent beat of the deafening music. I had no interest in finding a dance partner and remembered why I hated the disco scene. Meaningful conversation with my buddies was out of the question, so I bid them goodnight after I finished my Jack Daniels and joined my sleeping lady in the big bed in our cool room.

The next morning at the sumptuous breakfast buffet, Joanne told me she'd heard from Jeff all about my bad boy act the night before. I took that as my cue to tell her my last duty as Worst Man was to hit on the bride. Acknowledging her blush with a grin, I announced that my duties had been discharged and that the last test had been passed. I hugged her and said I was happy for both of them, promising to keep my mouth shut when the preacher asked if there was anyone present who knew of a reason why the couple shouldn't be married.

"Promise me you won't even clear your throat."

"I promise."

Following our afternoon session, we gathered out under the hot sun on the well-tended resort lawn, in sight of the blue Caribbean. Some of the wedding party, including the groom, wore shorts, and some of the guests wore bathing suits. The happy couple stood with the minister—who wore preacher clothes—under a flower-bedecked arch, flanked by the wedding party. Several of us guests took photos throughout the ceremony.

The officiating minister was a retired Salvation Army Major who routinely performed weddings at the resort—sometimes several in a day. He had a folksy delivery and clearly liked his work. He spoke in a rich but cultured Jamaican accent.

"Now Joahnne, you mohst realize you cahn't change Jeff. And Jeff, you're noht going to be able to change Joahnne either....You are cohmitting yourselves to wan another in the bahd times as well as the good times....The wedding bahnd is a symbol of your union—a perfect circle, endless. Ovah time the outside will get nicked and scrahtched, boht ovah that same time, the inside will be worn smooth and flawless."

After the vows had been spoken, the rings exchanged, and the ceremony concluded, the celebration continued with champagne and wedding cake—supplied at no additional charge by the all-inclusive resort—in the shade of palm trees on the shoreline. Among the many toasts, the Reverend Major toasted not only to the fertility of the newlyweds, but also to the fertility of Rick and Jennifer, whom he'd ascertained were thus far "without issue." We dispersed around three-thirty, with the rest of the afternoon free to do what we wanted.

For most of us, that meant either the beach or the swimming pool. The proximity of the bar and the availability of free liquor made the pool the most popular hangout. Maria and I lounged in deck chairs and floated on rubber rafts in the pool, chatting with our groupmates. Jeff and Joanne emerged from their nuptual chambers just before sunset and joined several of us in deck chairs out on the beach.

At dinner I told Jeff about our final wedding gift to them, in addition to our pictures of the ceremony—a honeymoon photo. When I told him what I had in mind, he laughed and told Joanne. That's how Maria and I ended up going to the honeymoon suite with the newlyweds after dinner.

Jeff took off his shirt before getting into bed, and Joanne exposed her shoulders after climbing under the sheets with him. Then they each put on the novelty Groucho schnozz glasses we'd given them, and I handed them each a cigar. Maria had the camera and stood atop the dressing table opposite their bed to get the best frame. Jeff struck the classic Groucho-with-a-cigar pose. When we left them they said they'd be out later to join the rest of us, but nobody saw them until the next day. I joked later in the evening that they must be the kind of couple that's turned-on by rubber novelties.

Maria and I joined the rest of our groupmates, most of whom sat at tables in the lobby bar swapping stories. We still had her camera, as well as four sets of the Groucho glasses. We got our friends to pose for us at the bar, shooting pool, playing cards, and dancing. Then we all got down to some serious partying. Some stayed in the lobby bar, others went to the disco to dance, and a few of us checked out the evening's show in the ballroom—a band playing both reggae and soul music.

Around midnight Maria started yawning and told me she was going to bed. I kissed her and said I'd join her soon. A few of us had decided to go to the piano bar, where they were doing karioke. I ordered a Chevas at the bar and started looking through the play list, waiting for the current singers to shut up and sit down. Neither of the drunken young tourists could carry a tune, but that didn't stop them from singing loudly, as they murdered a perfectly good Almon Brothers song. A few of their inebriated companions cheered and applauded when they left the mike.

Then a Jamaican got up and did a passable Elvis rendition of "Suspicious Minds," while I turned in my first selection. A black woman heated up the room with her performance of "What's Love Got To Do With It." Then it was my turn.

I started out with "House of the Rising Sun," which got a good round of applause—probably because I had friends in the audience. Emboldened, I put in another request. I tried to persuade Rick to do a Dylan song with me, but we later ended up singing "Yellow Submarine."

As I returned to my seat at the bar after my first solo, a forty-ish French woman came over and introduced herself in halting English. A little overweight, but cute, she told me she'd enjoyed my singing. Noticing my wedding ring, she asked me where my wife was. I told her. She asked if I'd be singing again and I said I thought I would. She returned to some friends at her table and I forgot about her, talking to groupmates at the bar.

Shortly after Rick and I had done our Beatles duet, my number came up and I went to the mike for my final song of the evening, "Dancin' in the Street." Polite applause. The French woman intercepted me on my way back to my seat, introducing me to some friends, an English couple from Manchester. She asked if I'd like to join them at their table, but I declined, having decided that she was probably hitting on me. I was flattered, but I didn't want to lead her on. I finished my drink, said goodnight to my Peace Corps friends, and joined Maria in bed.

I awoke groggy, just short of a hangover. At breakfast, some of our groupmates looked like caffeinated zombies on automatic pilot. Then we gathered for our final session—our last chance for group dialogue and closure. We sat at a "U" of linen-draped conference tables in a cool, sunlit room, conference packets in front of us.

We talked about disengagement and re-acculturation and the final goal of Peace Corps service—bringing the wide world back to share with our fellow citizens. The staff nurse gave us details about the delivery of fecal samples to the office in Kingston and another staff member guided us through a checklist in our packets of other things-that-must-be-accomplished-prior-to-COS. After a break we compared experiences at our work sites: small triumphs, tragedies, and bittersweet things in between. Only a few of the group expressed a sense of satisfaction in having accomplished anything specific, or something they thought might survive their tenure. Two or three, including Linda, had asked to extend their tours for up to a year. Nobody said anything profound in the way of summary, but tears were shed and by the end of the meeting everybody got well-hugged.

The session ended around noon. We'd already packed and stashed our luggage in the lobby. We all went to the spacious, sunlit dining hall for a final lavish buffet before we climbed into the air-conditioned vans and rode home to Kingston.

The following Monday found me unmistakably back at ground level, in my neighborhood. Maria had started her new job at Bamboo Pen, so I set off alone for the spot on the Deanery Road sidewalk where we waited for Dorothy to pick us up. Often, as I (or we) walked down the road toward the meeting place, I kept an eye out for packs of guard dogs—the preferred Jamaican burglar alarm—whose owners sometimes let them out of their yards for a while in the mornings. So far neither of us had been attacked, although there had been some close calls. I love dogs, but fear of the unknown pack is rational, not just an atavistic reflex.

Across the street a teenage girl opened the gate to her family's yard and a pack of six dogs, of varyings breeds and sizes, ran out. The lead dog—a mongrel with some German Shepherd blood, but with a coat of long, golden-brown hair—immediately fixed on me and the pack came straight at me, snarling and barking. I instinctively backed up to the fence behind me, unslinging my backpack from my shoulder. Too heavy and slow to sling around as a weapon, I thought it might at least serve as a shield against the snapping dogs. I yelled at the girl to call them off me.

The attack couldn't have lasted a minute before the girl herded the dogs back into the yard and secured the gate, but it seemed a lot longer. For the most part, I'd kept them at bay, but the pack leader had gotten past my defenses and bitten my leg near the knee—barely breaking the skin, but tearing a small rip in my pants. Angry but uninjured, my heart pounding, I decided just to go on to work. If I went home to change pants, I'd miss my ride with Dorothy and would have to take a bus in. I'd deal with the neighbor later, after I calmed down.

I took a 22-A home after work and as I walked down the street toward home, I rehearsed a polite but assertive way of dealing with my neighbor. I fully intended to ask him to pay for a new pair of pants, as well as to demand that he keep his dogs under control in the future. *I won't make a report at the Constabulary Station* this *time.*

Back at the house I changed pants. Then, carrying the ripped pants with me, I set out to talk to the dogs' owner, Mr. Jones. As I approached the fenced yard, I could see that the gate was open, but I saw no sign of the dogs. Mr. Jones was in view on the front porch, talking on a cellular phone. Obviously well-to-do. I hailed him.

I got his attention and he said he'd be right out. Five minutes later, I saw him coming down the driveway to the gate—accompanied by his dogs! The leader came charging at me the instant he saw me, the barking pack right behind him. For the second time that day they tried to encircle me, lunging and snapping, looking for openings. Again, the pack leader got past my awkward, defensive dance and nipped my thigh, again ripping my pants!

I felt furious as my neighbor rounded up his dogs and corralled them in the yard. They lined the fence and bayed as I spoke my piece to their apologetic owner. Gone was my reasoned, neighborly, assertive "I'm not angry" speech.

"This is the SECOND TIME TODAY your dogs have attacked me! I came over here to complain about the attack this morning and to show you my ripped pants—and LOOK!" I pointed to the rip on my trouser leg.

"I'm so sohrry. Of course, I'll make good the dahmage. Ahnd if you—"

"I expect you to pay for two pairs of trousers, but THAT'S NOT THE IMPORTANT THING! Those dogs of yours are DANGEROUS and I want them LOCKED IN and not allowed out on the streets! This had better NEVER happen again!"

"I cahn onderstahnd that you are ahngry—"

"You think THIS is angry? Mr. Jones, you're just fortunate this happened on a day when I was alone. If your dogs ever attacked my WIFE, *then* you'd see just how ANGRY I can get!"

Mr. Jones continued to apologize and to assure me I need never concern myself with his dogs being loose again. As my heartbeat and breathing slowed, I began to regain my composure. He offered to give me cash on the spot, but I told him I'd just bring him the receipts for two new pairs of trousers after I bought them. I warned him that if his dogs ever gave me anymore trouble, I'd make a formal report to the Constabulary. We parted with a final apology and a handshake.

As I turned to leave I noticed a knot of curious neighbors clustered on the sidewalk, and others observing from their porches. The story would be all over the neighborhood in no time. While I hoped I hadn't come across to anyone as an Ugly American, I felt no embarrassment about my behavior. Mr. Jones later reimbursed me for the purchase of new pants, and neither Maria nor I ever got attacked by neighborhood dogs again.

To my surprise, the new ward resident—young and very pregnant—asked if she could sit in on one of my groups. This would be a first and I hoped it might set a precedent. Maria had told me that the psychiatric residents get very little training in group therapy. Sure enough, the doctor made it clear early in the session that she wasn't there as co-leader, but to learn. When group members asked her questions, she generally deferred to me. She seemed more comfortable by the end of the session, however, and contributed some summary comments at my invitation.

I'd wanted staff members to co-lead groups with me all along. Part of the Peace Corps' mission is the transfer of skills to our local national counterparts, and I figured that I could accomplish some of that by role-modeling group leadership skills to co-leaders. So far I'd had no takers. As it turned out, the resident only attended a few of my sessions.

I'd taken a strong stand on another issue involving attendance of group, saying that I only wanted student nurses sitting-in on my weekly psychoeducational session, not the two weekly "process" sessions. Having young women who weren't in the program present was distracting enough to some of the male patients in the teaching sessions, but their presence in the open-ended discussion sessions would have significantly affected group dynamics. At first some of the staff nurses opposed my restriction of student nurse attendance to just the didactic groups: this *was*, after all, a teaching hospital. Over time, however, some of the students were observed to be reacting more like giggling schoolgirls than professionals to things they saw and heard on the ward. The consensus tilted in my favor.

Cory hadn't finished testing my limits yet. One day just prior to the morning devotional, while I poured myself a glass of icewater in the kitchen, he came in and said he didn't want to be late. He showed me several pills he had to take, "asked" me to bring him a glass of water, and left without waiting for a response. He could easily have gotten himself a glass of water and taken his pills in thirty seconds. I went on about my business.

My suspicion that he'd made a polite demand got confirmed later in the morning, when Cory came to me and asked heatedly, "Why you nah bring me de watah?"

"Because it sounded like a demand and not a request, and you didn't even wait for an answer. I generally don't respond favorably to demands. It just encourages the person to make more."

Cory seemed to understand, but he didn't like it. After we later discussed the difference between requests and demands in one of our last individual sessions, he dropped his attitude, saying he'd just needed to know that I hadn't "dissed" him. At the end of the meeting he invoked Jah's blessing on me.

All patients on the ward had to be tested for HIV. In a group session where we'd been discussing HIV and AIDS, Maryanne, the other female crack addict and former prostitute in the batch, shared her fantasy of what she'd do if she ever found out she was HIV-positive.

"Me would dead meself before me get the AIDS bahd. Bot firs' me would go bahck to Mahndeville, where me com frohm, an' 'ave sex wit' ahll de mon-dem me could, spread de HIV aroun'."

Maryanne's HIV test results came back positive.

In mid-July we got invited back to Southfield for another weekend with Vish and Sharon. We drove down on Saturday with Vasanth and Rainuke in Prakash's agency car. As before, the satellite TV in the family room was the modern equivalent of the hearth—the thing that people gathered around when nothing else was going on. We arrived in time for drinks, followed by a supper of chicken soup, slaw, and seafood fried rice. Sharon—one of the few white Jamaicans we ever got to know—came from Southfield. The guests in their home this time consisted mostly of her relatives, both white- and brown-skinned.

In the morning we ate a breakfast of fresh pan-fried rotis; spicy, fried potatoes; a coconut chutney; and coffee. Later we set out for Treasure Beach in a three-vehicle caravan to visit Sharon's father, a commercial fisherman who owned two deep-water fishing boats. Dressed in shorts, a tee shirt, and a baseball cap, he was skinny, with a ruddy complexion. Around his neck was a gold chain with a pendant that read, "Number One Mom." As we exited the vehicles, two children chased a goat out of the family residence. Goats and chickens foraged in the yard Vish, Prakash, Vasanth and I left the women at Sharon's father's home and drove to a nearby beach to buy some fish for lunch. This involved some waiting, so of course drinks were ordered. We sat on crude wooden benches at a table in an arbor of lime trees, within sight of the rocky beach. We could see small fishing boats out on the water and others unloading their catch on the shoreline. As Vish was a prominent figure in the community and a regular customer, we got great service. The Filipino proprietress asked him how many of what kind of fish he wanted. He told her and she sent some-one off to procure the fish for him, then returned with another round of Red Stripes.

A strong fish smell filled the car as we drove back to pick up the women. We all rode back to the beach we'd come to on our first visit and settled-in at the same open-air thatch roofed bar/restaurant as before. Blacky greeted us and took our drink orders: beer or stout for some, gin and Ting for others. We gave him the fresh fish to cook for us.

Some of us stripped down to the bathing suits we'd worn under our street clothes and went for dips in the azure waters beyond the brown sand beach. As we drank and chatted in the restaurant's shade, some Jamaican men played dominos at a nearby table. When Jamaican's play dominos, they often get excited and loud, because they usually play for money. The game play is fast and aggressive. The dominos are slapped down onto the playing surface, so you can tell what's being played in the back of a crowded, noisy bar without even looking. Jamaicans play in rum bars, on the sidewalk, and just about anywhere else that people con-gregate. Wherever two or more Jamaican men gather together and have nothing better to do, they'll scare up some chairs and lay some sheet metal or plywood on top of two wooden crates, and a set of dominos will surely appear.

Blacky served our fish hot, baked in aluminum foil, spiced with onion, okra, and peppers. Along with the fish we got pan-fried cakes of bammy, a bland, white starch made from cassava root (also know as yucca), that tastes somewhat like fried grits. We ate with our fingers. As before, Vish picked up the tab for everyone. We left the beach around three o'clock. After stopping back at the house in Southfield for tea, we headed back to Kingston.

The fact that we only had three months to go in Jamaica was so embedded in my awareness that I dreamed about it. In my dream, Maria and I had returned Stateside and sat visiting with some friends in their home. They asked questions about our Peace Corps experience and I suddenly realized that I couldn't remember anything about the last three months of service. When I checked my back pocket and found no wallet there, I knew I was still in Jamaica. The thought, *I must be dreaming* woke me up.

The newest group of Peace Corps trainees arrived on the island and Maria began her temporary job on the training staff, at Bamboo Pen. Over the six weeks of their training cycle, I also got involved in some training activities. Now an Old Timer, I got asked to take four women who'd be working at the University Hospital—two in their fifties and two in their twenties—on an orientation tour. I met them at Bamboo Pen and we took a bus up to Papine. I walked them through the smelly market to the main gate and then showed them around the hospital grounds while answering their questions.

"Is it always this hot?"

"Can you get by on your living allowance?"

"How do you find a place to live?"

"Are any of the wards air conditioned?"

"Do you like your job?"

"Can you understand patois?"

"How long does it take to get used to this *heat*?"

The PC Training Director had also asked me to reprise a presentation I'd done on stress management at a meeting, for the new trainees. He asked me to "Jamaicanize it" more than my original gig. I came down to Bamboo Pen from work one afternoon and got introduced to the whole training group in the open-air, wood-roofed classroom behind the estate house. After I'd covered the basics of stress and stress management principles, I proceded to relate them to the Jamaican experience: heat, mosquitos, real and imagined dangers, communication problems, the bus system, getting to know a foreign culture. I used as examples things I'd encountered on the ward, dealing with addicts.

Not only did I get a lot of questions and lively applause from the trainees, afterwards several of them came up and spoke with me. Some had questions, others stories of their own.

Two men identified themselves as addicts in recovery. One of them, Danny, asked if he could come up to the ward and sit in on some of my relapse prevention groups. The other, Ralph, who'd been sober for almost fifteen years, had a good recovery story to tell me.

"Back in my drinking days, I used to hang out at Larry's Bar, which was the last stopping-off place between Houston and Hell. Me and the bartender, Craig, went back a long ways. He's been my friend much longer than he was my bartender. Anyway, after I got sober, I finally got around to going to Nepal for two months—something I'd been wanting to do for years. After I got back, I was eating in some diner with Craig when a kind of rough-looking friend of his joined us, somone he knew from his years tending bar at Larry's. He said something like, 'If you're Craig's friend, you must be a drinker.' I told him no, I didn't do that anymore. Said I'd already had more than my share.

"So Craig says, 'You're lucky you didn't know him back in his drinking days. He was an embarrassment even to other drunks.' He was always raggin' me like that. Then the three of us swapped stories about Larry's and some of the hardcases that hung there. Later in the conversation I made a reference to my trip to Nepal, and Craig's buddy looked confused. He held up his hand like to say stop and asked 'How the *hell* do you get from Larry's Bar to Nepal?'"

Danny later contacted me about attending a group session on the ward but, due to a miscommunication, he showed up after the session had ended. When I saw him again he acted miffed, or distrustful. He said that next time he'd call the ward before coming. So I left word with the ward clerk that, if he called, she should let him know he was welcome to join our 1:30 session on Wednesday.

On Wednesday I found him waiting in the hallway when I returned to the ward from lunch. He proved to be an asset in group, role-modelling candid self-disclosure. His account of how he'd happened to come to the meeting had the almost-supernatural quality that I've heard from other Twelve Steppers, talking about the role of their Higher Power in their everyday lives.

He'd been having some cravings and had planned to go to an AA meeting, but other obligations had made that impossible. He knew he needed some kind of meeting, but had forgotten about my invitation until his Higher Power had intervened.

He said he saw another trainee at the Peace Corps office, who owed him money. The other trainee said he'd given the money to my colleague Celine, thinking Danny would see her before he would. Danny didn't even know Celine by sight and asked how to contact her. His groupmate gave him a phone number, which turned out to be the number of the Detox Ward. When he called and identified himself, the ward clerk told him that Celine had just left, but she also remembered to give him my message about the meeting.

"Of all the telephone numbers I could've called in Jamaica today," he told the group, "the number I called provided me with an opportunity to attend a meeting at a time when I really needed one."

I'd heard many complaints from the ward staff about how the program was under-funded. Money had been promised from the National Fund, money raised in two "Crucial Concert" telethons for drug abuse treatment; but we hadn't received any. Howard, our movement therapist, hadn't gotten his modest stipend in months. When I went to the DART meeting—held that month at the Peter's Lane Salvation Army shelter dungtung—I learned more about the situation.

The evening before the meeting, I heard on the news that the next day the police would be cracking down on the army of unlicensed street vendors who sold their wares on the Parade square. Sure enough, when I got off the bus Parade looked like a ghost town, the sidewalks filthy but bare save for pedestrians. The only higglers in sight were afoot, carrying their wares and warily testing the limits of the ban. I'd already gotten the impression that some laws are only enforced one day a year in certain locations, just to show that they *could* be. I had no doubt that everything would be back to normal the next day.

I arrived late, by the clock, but was early by Jamaican time. The Major offered me coffee and pastries, and I joined those already waiting in the meeting room. After a long, boring review of the last meeting's minutes, we got down to business. I could barely hear what people said, because of the trucks in the narrow, stinking alley outside.

It seemed that the Detox Ward wasn't the only program feeling shortchanged by the National Fund; Addiction Alert and the Patricia House also operated on a shoestring. There had been talk since my arrival of establishing a second Detox/Rehab Ward in Montego Bay, but I saw no indications that we were any nearer to attaining that goal than we'd been the previous year. Frustration hung in the air.

The problem, I learned, was that the National Fund responsible for disbursing the money that had been raised had no Director, and hadn't for months. The money was *somewhere* drawing interest, but all we got from the National Counsel was promises. Nobody seemed to be accountable.

The something-must-be-done attitude within the group quickly escalated to the *and-right-now!* stage. An ad hoc committee was formed to draft a document demanding some sort of accountability. Now a shorttimer, I stayed out of it.

I could sense trouble brewing on the ward during our "fifth week" between treatment cycles. When I walked in on the staff meeting, Sister M held the floor and I felt a cool vibe in the room. Dr. Allen, a Trinidadean M.D. who specialized in addictions was present as a consultant, hired by the National Council. Everybody else in the room kept conspicuously silent, and Martha gave me the *Shhh* sign, index finger to lips.

Dr. Allen asked reasonable questions about ward operations which Sister M wasn't able to answer, as she seldom spent time on the ward. Nobody came to her rescue and it became clear to me that the staff nurses were letting her have all the rope she needed to hang herself. As soon as she left with Dr. Allen, after the meeting had ended, the tension broke and the staff nurses told me what had been going on.

Apparently Sister M and the new nurse, Ann, had formally complained to a senior Matron about the performance of the rest of the nursing staff. Nobody else on the staff seemed to trust Ann, but Sister M—in a political maneuver—had nominated her as head nurse and wanted to put Sandra on the night shift. I didn't want to see Ann replace Sandra, but decided not to jump to any conclusions until the dust had settled. I trusted that Dr. Allen had seen behind Sister M's facade of knowing what sort of things routinely happened on the ward.

I'd brought my trusty old Canon 35mm camera with me that day, intending to go on a photo safari to an interesting site near the University after work. Set back from Hope Road, it clearly wasn't just another apartment building: there was too much sculpture in the sprawling yard, including several large works in black wrought-iron. I can best describe it as an artists' colony: a three- story apartment building whose apartments ringed a central, sunlit atrium filled with artworks. The ground floor lobby area contained many works of traditional and abstract sculpture, in stone, plaster, and wood. Paintings in a variety of media hung on the walls ringing the atrium on all three floors.

The place had been endowed by a Jamaican philanthropist and patron of the arts, but had seen better times. Although it contained at least two Edna Manley sculptures and works by other prominent Jamaican artists, it was poorly maintained and had a dusty, junky ambience. The lobby furniture leaked stuffing. An abandoned washing machine stood next to slabs of Roman-style bas-relief plaster castings that leaned up against a section of wall. Fascinated, I shot two rolls of precious, expensive film between the interior and the grounds.

The following weekend, Maria and I joined Linda down by the harbor and caught another bus east to Cable Hut Beach. Hellshire Beach, west of Kingston, is the area's most popular beach; but Cable Hut sometimes draws a good crowd on weekends too. Getting from the shade in the mid-day heat to the cool, wet sand of the rocky shoreline required a sprint across hot, dark sand. Maria and I found many smooth, tide-polished rocks with beautiful patterns, which I lugged home in my backpack. The pounding waves precluded swimming and tidal currents made it hard to keep my footing even in waist-deep water. Getting in and out of the water could be tricky in the heavy surf, and after my last dip in the ocean I jammed my right big toe on a submerged rock and limped for days afterward.

Sunburned and tired, we packed our gear around two o'clock and had a round of cold drinks as we waited for a bus back to the city. When we got to Parade, Maria and Linda set off to shop in the dungtung Coronation Market, while I caught a bus to uptown New Kingston and the Peace Corps office to check for mail before going home.

Although we'd normally have been content to stay at the house on a Saturday night after such a busy day, we had a date with Rick and Jennifer. It was their last night on the island, so we'd agreed to meet at Matilda's

Corner. We joined them in a booth, where they'd already ordered red rum and Ting. We drank some toasts. We talked about strange and wonderful experiences we'd had in Jamaica, about hopes and regrets, about disengagement and closure and culture shock and reverse culture shock and the readjustment blues. We discussed how the Peace Corps experience might have changed us as people, and what we each hoped to go on to do back in the States. It was a good parting.

Sunday we stayed busy all day. Not only did I wash the clothes, I defrosted the refrigerator—something I had to do every two or three weekends—changed the water in our emergency fifteen-gallon water tank for the last time, and shovelled our compost pile onto the garden plot. I carried out these now-familiar tasks with a sense of proactive nostalgia, knowing that I'd soon be returning to a world where it's easy to take the creature comforts for granted, if you make a decent wage.

In the mid-afternoon, while Maria napped, two Jehovah's Witnesses came to our gate and asked if I'd like to talk to them about who really runs the world. I declined, telling them my wife was asleep. Later, Willard came by on his newly-repaired Moped to collect our beer bottles and to ask if we had any work for him.

Maria had found a home for two of the kittens, Tigger and Carnival, with the seamstress who'd sewed her uniforms for her. On Monday morning, before we loaded them into a box for transport in Dorothy's car to their new home, I played with them for the last time, told them that nothing in this life is permanent, and wished them each a good incarnation.

For the first time in many years, the annual REGGAE SUNSPLASH festival was to be held in the Kingston area instead of in Montego Bay. A new concert arena, Jamworld, had been built in Portmore, across the harbor to the west of the city, near Hellshire Beach. SUNSPLASH meant five straight nights of music, each night a different theme. I had every intention of attending at least two of the all-night concerts.

On Thursday I went to International Night by myself, taking a taxi to Jamworld around eleven—just when things would be warming up on stage. I'd stuffed a nylon windbreaker in my back pocket and carried a bota bag full of wine, as well as a few cigars. The taxi fare cost more than the ticket. But it all came to less than $20; so although it was a luxury on my stipend, by American standards it was quite a bargain.

I didn't have to stand in line to buy a ticket. I just paid my money and walked in. The crowd milling around or sitting on blankets on the grassy field between the bleachers and the stage wasn't as big as I'd expected. A group called the Sane Band had taken stage to play backup for the first few acts. As the music started up, people crowded in close to the stage, swaying and dancing. I soon learned that the bleachers were reserved seating, the entrances manned by security guards. Throughout the night I saw only a few dozen people with white skin in the crowd and I never saw a soul I recognized among the thousands in attendance.

As music filled the air, I felt a heady sense of lonewolf anonymity and freedom. I belonged here as surely as anyone else in attendance, and I could let my guard down and share the vibe. I danced without a trace of the self-consciousness I've often felt when dancing at a party. Nothing divided us, not race or culture or class. We were all there for the same thing, all celebrating the happy myth that music will unite the world.

I heard roots reggae, traditional African music, soca, and dancehall rap in French and Spanish. I listened to Universal Youth, Maccaruffin, Crueshal Substance, and Yasus Afari. I paced myself throughout the long night, alternately joining the throng up at the stage to lose myself in dance, walking around the field and watching my brothers and sisters, and sitting on the grass. My energy level waxed and waned. The wine lasted until nearly dawn.

The high point for me came at around four o'clock, when Hugh Maskela took stage for a dynamic performance. Backed up by keyboards, electric guitar and bass, saxophone, and drums, he played his trumpet and sang. The music ranged from jazz to South African tribal music. The audience went wild, crying out for more when the set ended. The crowd thinned after that, but I felt wide awake, determined to stay until the end.

After a seemingly-endless set by a reggae-influenced Argentinian pop band named Los Pericos, I started to fade again. I didn't want to miss the next act, dub poet Mutabaruka, but I lay down on the grass and dozed fitfully while his band set up. Little sips of sweet oblivion. I woke to the amplified sound of Mutabaruka's greeting to the crowd, with dawn's light tinting pink clouds in a sky just turning pale blue.

The unmistakably-Jamaican voice brought me back: where I was and why. Unlike his performance at the Bob Marley tribute, most of his act was musical this time. He interspersed songs with poetry and patois diatribes against the Babylon system. He denounced the "fast food culture" promulgated by the U.S., spoke passionately about re-patriation to Africa, and decried the upcoming visit of the Pope to Jamaica.

As the sky grew lighter I became more alert and decided to stay for the last two groups—a promising, new pop reggae group called Chakula and a solid roots band I'd heard before, Chalice. When I finally left, halfway through the last set, a small crowd still danced in front of the stage; but I'd used up my last moves. The sun burned down on me as I trudged wearily to the nearest bus stop and caught a bus to Halfway Tree. Exhausted and rank from the night of celebration, I joined all the fresh-scrubbed men and women on their way to work. The world was a curbside mural passing through the open underside of the heavily-tinted bus windows as we crowded together like cattle on the way into Kingston.

I caught a 27 at Halfway Tree at seven-thirty, just before the morning crush hour began in earnest. I almost dozed off on my feet, clinging to the chrome rail overhead. I got home just before eight and headed straight for bed, having arranged to take the day off from work. Linda had asked Maria and me earlier in the week if we planned to attend Singers Night that night. I'd told her that two nights in a row would be more fun than I could take at my age. Maria and I planned to attend Reggae Night on Saturday, I told her.

We learned that Marty, the Jesuit next door, also planned to attend, so we agreed to take a taxi in together. We arrived at Jamworld just before eleven and made vague plans to meet Marty at a certain spot at seven the next morning, if we didn't run into him in the meantime and if he hadn't already left. As it turned out, we didn't see him until later the next day at his house. I'd napped during the afternoon and planned to pace myself like a long-distance runner during the long night ahead. We located Rory and Rachael, who'd told us they'd be there. While Maria and I stayed on our feet and mobile most of the time, they stayed camped in one spot all night. The festival had drawn a much bigger crowd than for International Night.

The music consisted of both roots and dancehall reggae. The first performer we saw on stage was a dancehall artist named Shinehead. We wandered around, looking for familiar faces. We found the bleachers again barricaded from us groundlings. You couldn't get in without an ID bracelet, unless you knew someone on the benches who invited you. As it turned out, we did. We spotted Lacy Wright, the embassy Charge d'Affaires, and his wife just as they saw us. Lacy spoke to a security guard and we were allowed to join him and his wife. We made minimal polite conversation for a few minutes, then turned our attention to the music. Not exactly our cup of tea, we all agreed, but not bad for dancehall. Although the Wrights left before midnight, now that the security guard knew us, he continued to admit us to the bleachers. "No prohblem, mon."

We saw a fair amount of whitefolk in the huge crowd, but the tourists were far outnumbered by Jamaicans. Besides Rory and Rachael, we only saw three other PCVs. We listened and danced to such performers and bands as Tiger, Mad Cobra, Junior Tucker, Burning Spear, Culture, Steel Pulse, and The Mystic Revealers. The dancing alternately exhausted and energized us. Tobacco and ganja smoke hung in a pungent cloud over the mass of celebrants. The vibe was unity through music. You felt safe here; you could sleep almost anywhere. In fact, once you got away from the crowd around the stage, you had to walk carefully to avoid stepping on sleepers.

As Richie Stevens prepared for his set, Maria and I retreated to the bleachers and she slept with her head in my lap for almost an hour. She awoke just as the first rosy glow of dawn commenced its raid on the night. The final act, Toots and the Maytals, was just getting started on stage. We got up and walked through the dwindling crowd, joining the celebrants right up next to the stage for a final, long dance to entrancing reggae rhythms.

Agreeing that we'd had enough, we left at seven, having looked unsuccessfully for Marty. We rode into Kingston on a bus, all sweaty amongst the well-dressed churchgoers. We switched to a 27 at Halfway Tree and got seats. Tired as I felt, I noticed a whole different pace than what I'd come to expect on this particular route—a Sunday morning pace. The buses didn't race, and ours even stopped for passengers between stops. Everyone was friendly.

We got home and took showers. Maria made oatmeal, which went down like manna. Then we dragged our weary bodies back to the bedroom to try and sleep through the midday heat, thankful that the electricity hadn't gone out and that our fans worked.

That evening, I wrote in my journal: "SUNSPLASH was another uniquely Jamaican event I'll never forget. I felt plugged-in to a circuit made up of bodies and souls and vibes—a circuit closed in music, droplets in a wave: one blood."

One night after Maria had beat me two-out-of-three games at backgammon, sitting at our little formica-topped dining table, I provoked her with one of my stock teases: "Wanna wrestle?"

It's a metaphor for something having to do with our balance of power, a game we play from time to time. I offer her the experience of being pinned,overpowered, but not hurt or used in any way. It'll be *therapeutic*, I tell her; it's something she *needs* to experience.

Oh no, she says, she'll *really* fight ('tis true!) and someone will get hurt. Maybe me.

Oh no, I reply, hinting that I've had some success providing this experience in prior relationships, and nobody had any regrets or got hurt. I have nothing to prove, I say—we both know I *could* overpower her; but she *needs* the experience of giving up control and learning she can still feel safe.

Never, says she.

There may be a kernel of truth in my banter, but our little sparring game is really an evocation of the spirit of Courtly Love in a new guise: the troubador does nothing without his lady's invitation. In the Kingdom of Love it's the woman who governs. We both know the rules, and one of them is that my lady won't wrestle.

"Oh ye of little faith!" I say, and she rises to the bait.

"You think I don't know what it means to be overpowered? I have two older brothers!"

"Exactly!" I say. "And you're terrified of the prospect of losing control because they were mean to you."

Terrified! Her? No way! She just knows she'd end up getting hurt. Bruised, maybe.

Irrational fear, Q.E.D., says I.

And I continue to play the gestalt guru, always ready to"rassle" my lady into a smile.

The new batch in Detox would be the next-to-last I'd be able to work with for the entire twenty-eight days of the program. The morning after the new patients were admitted, I left my office and showed up on the ward before my schedule required me to, somehow intuiting that I'd be needed. Sure enough, no sooner had I arrived than I heard an altercation starting up in the group room.

"Bombaclaht!"

"Rasclaht!"

I rushed in and intervened, getting between the antagonists and addressing each in turn.

"*Edward*, no need to fight! Andrew, what do you need to do to *chill out?*" By then I had it down to an art.

Once they'd both calmed down I asked them in turn to come into the counseling room with me. I got each of them to take a share of the responsibility for what had happened and asked each to commit to solving problems without resorting to threats or violence. Edward, an alcoholic in his sixties, had allowed Andrew, a mouthy crack addict from the ghettos of Kingston, to get to him. Later in the day I saw them talking together animatedly but not belligerently. I congratulated them.

The next day, I used their conflict and their subsequent reconciliation as the starting point for a session on anger management. Then, in the afternoon, I had my assessment session with Ralph.

Ralph wore his hair in short dreadlocks and came across as mild-mannered. But when I asked him if he'd been having any adjustment problems, he replied, " Yah mon. Me 'av prohblem-dem wid mon-dem wha' act like you frien', boht nah *really* you frien'." He went on to say that this kind of hypocracy upset him so much that he dwelt on thoughts of violent revenge.

"Have you ever acted on such thoughts?" I asked.

"Two, t'ree time me beat sohmwan wha' treat me like dot."

"Is there anyone on the ward you want to hurt?"

"Nah, mon. Me jos' hupset."

We talked about values around violence and the fact that you still have choices when you're angry. When I started talking about how hard recovery can be, I noticed tears welling in his eyes.

"Are you okay?" I asked.

"Yah mon."

I had no subsequent problems with fighting from this all-male batch. My group sessions gradually picked-up steam. One day Edward compared working the Twelve Step program to climbing Mount Everest.

"Yeah," I replied. "Recovery can sure be a slippery slope. But if some psychopath who had a gun on me told me I had to mount an expedition and climb Everest, or die, and I knew he could make good on his threat, I think I'd do my best to get to the top. What other choices do *you* have if you want to live to old age?"

When someone complained about how hard it is to keep from relapsing when you're in crisis, I validated his comment then shared something I'd read in a Narcotics Anonymous publication: "Even if your arse falls off, don't use. Just bring your broken arse with you to a meeting and we'll help you carry it around with dignity."

The city of Kingston throbs with music, from giant sound systems that can turn any block into a dancehall on a given night, to the sounds of loud radios and boomboxes filling the air late at night or on a lazy Sunday afternoon. Maria and I had by now learned to tune out the neighborhood guard dogs baying in cacaphonous counterpoint in the night. We lived close enough to the dungtung area that we often heard the rotors of JDF helicopters overhead on weekends and saw them patrolling the skies, like giant mosquitos passing over the palms and mango trees on our horizon. Our house was directly below the flightpath of certain northbound flights from Norman Manley Airport, so we also became accustomed to the occasional roar of jet engines in the sky.

There is, in Jamaican culture, a median institution between the family dwelling and the neighborhood: the yard. A yard—whether in the city or in the bush—consists of a cluster of houses or shacks sharing a common courtyard. The communal area might be a garden or just a dusty plot of ground. In the city, fences or walls surround most yards. The people who share a yard may or may not be kin, but they are a kind of extended family. Clarence might say, upon meeting a person from the north coast who works in a resort with Sarah, that he grew up in the same yard with her.

In the bush, a yard might be a mini-community that comes together around a standpipe—the only local source of fresh water. Residents not only fill buckets from the standpipe, but also take off their clothes and bathe by the side of the road. In cities, yards exist in both lower and middle-class neighborhoods.

The shanty towns that occupy the barrens of Greater Kingston are also often subdivided into yards. Although a walled compound with only two houses might not strictly meet the definition of a yard, Maria and I learned something of the familial comeraderie of the institution in our friendships with our Indian neighbors.

The yard culture is a theme in Jamaican arts and media. Many of the scenes in the pantomime play we saw with Maria's father were set in a yard. In a classic reggae song from the seventies called "Tenement Yard," Jacob Miller laments the lack of privacy for a Rasta in the yard: "too much watchee, watchee, watchee." *Lime Tree Lane,* a patois sitcom/soap-opera— one of JBC Television's most popular original programs—featured a cast of characters living in and around a yard.

Because Maria worked on the training staff, we both got involved in the swearing-in ceremony for Group 62—the fourth and last group to graduate during our tenure. I set out from the house to join Maria at Bamboo Pen, hoping to get there at least an hour early. I sprinted to catch a bus at Olympia, but it drove off just as I got to the stop. As luck would have it, a private security guard in a company pickup truck drove up to me and threw open the passenger door.

"You wan' cotch de bus?"

"Ya, mon."

I hopped in and he sped off, going through the gears like a racecar driver and passing the bus halfway to the next stop, where he dropped me off. I thanked him and he drove away with a smile and a wave. As I entered the bus, the driver grinned at me, acknowledging that he'd seen what happened. Another small victory in the commuter wars.

Everything seemed to have gone wrong when I got to Bamboo Pen. The photographer who'd agreed to show up an hour before the ceremony to take the traditional group photos of the Trainees posed on the porch steps hadn't appeared. I was conscripted to take all the photographs I could with cameras belonging to the Trainees. Person after person approached me with their high tech, foolproof cameras all set to shoot. At one point I know I had ten cameras hanging around my neck, with more beside me on the gravel walkway. I took shot after shot until the official photographer finally came.

The caterers still hadn't arrived at six-thirty, a half hour before show-time. Neither the Bishop scheduled to give the invocation nor the guest speaker was anywhere in sight.

As seven o'clock approached, most of the Trainees and invitees had already taken their seats in front of the stage. I saw Alvira in the audience and waved to her. The Jamaican choral group that had been called in at the last moment to substitute for the Constabulary Band went into over-time, entertaining the crowd with traditional songs. I greeted latecomers and handed them programs.

Lacy Wright showed up just in time, escorting the guest speaker. Minutes later the Bishop finally appeared from the direction of the park-ing area and took his seat on stage. The ceremony started on time—by Jamaican time. I stuck around to watch the swearing-in, feeling nostalgic. Then I went around behind the massive estate house to the food tent, to see if I could help.

The caterers had just unloaded their pans and trays of food onto the serving tables. I joined Maria and others on the training staff, pulling the plastic wrap off of containers, as the hungry horde began to trickle, then swarm, into the tent. I managed to prepare a plate for Alvira before the crowd at the tables got too thick—a piece of jerk chicken, rice-and-peas, Jamaican slaw, and samples of other side dishes. I delivered it to her where she stood on the lawn next to the tent. She thanked me with the regal grace of someone who had every right to expect such service—as indeed she did. She was, after all, still our Jamaican Mama.

I excused myself and waded back into the throng to fill a plate for myself. If this swearing-in ran true to form, I knew that every morsel laid out on the tables would be quickly consumed.

The Peace Corps provided no alcohol with the meal, but the new Volunteers had a few cases of beer on ice for the informal party to follow. After the official guests had eaten and departed, Maria and I helped to clean up behind the caterers. The former Trainees had gotten to know both of us during training. Some of them brought us cold Red Stripes and pitched in to help. After we'd finished working, we joined the other Volunteers on the broad, well-lit porch of the estate house for toasts and celebration. A boombox filled the air with reggae music and some of the people danced, while others talked excitedly about their assignments and what they hoped to accomplish. Maria and I listened and smiled at one another with the knowing smiles of veterans. Among the last to leave Bamboo Pen, we got a ride home with one of the staff drivers.

We stayed up until past midnight, talking about idealism and reality. Tomorrow the Volunteers of Group 62 would be driven to their new homes all over the island and would begin to grasp the realities of the individual tasks they faced. Some would stay and some would leave early. Few PCVs, we agreed, are starry-eyed idealists bent on saving the world. Most Volunteers we'd met seemed more pragmatic than idealistic—people who seek challenges and face them with both feet firmly planted in reality.

I suppose that—at least in most cases—the successful completion of a Peace Corps tour requires a re-evaluation of one's ideals and a certain amount of re-prioritizing. The realities of living at ground level in a developing country can't be ignored or altered. You either adapt or you leave. I think that most people who make it through the screening process know to expect the unexpected, and have few or no illusions about their motives for volunteering. They go where they go as much to learn as to teach.

Despite the best efforts of DART, the National Fund had continued to stall on delivering promised funds. People weren't getting paid adequately, and some of the members of the team seemed near the point of mutiny. This put Dr. S in the difficult position of having to mediate beween the ward staff and the National Council on Drug Abuse. Even his considerable skills at mending fences and smoothing ruffled feathers failed to assuage the legitimate concerns expressed in a staff meeting. Beneath the surface of the expressed complaints, staff morale was low due to continuing resentment over Ann's promotion by Sister M. Most of the nurses still felt loyal to Sandra. Sister M was noticibly absent from the meeting.

As a short-timer, I tended to stay silent in emotionally-charged meetings; but on this day I joined in the fray. Dr. S had responded to a flood of complaints with a generalism about needing to develop team resources. I couldn't hold my tongue any longer.

"Dr. S, the problem isn't so much with internal resources as with the lack of external resources. In terms of the Serenity Prayer, there is precious little we can change. We *know* what we can and can't change but serenity is in short supply around here lately. We're told we're supposed to be a pilot program that will grow into something bigger and better but, in fact, we seem to have a pretty low priority in the scheme of things."

Dr. S listened without apparent rancor and some of the nurses nodded in agreement, so I went on. "We have no treatment model, no official Ward Sister, no effective means to enforce ward rules. We're under-funded."

I wanted to mention a few other things, like the fact that we ostensibly had an occupational therapy program, with no occupational therapist; but I kept to the short list.

Ann brought the tensions within the staff to the surface, responding to something Martha had said earlier. Without mentioning her favored status with Sister M, she said that she knew she was seen as the outsider. She attributed her exclusion to the other nurses' attitudes.

Dr. S tried his best to get Ann to acknowledge the collusion with Sister M that was so apparent to everyone else in the room, but she continued to evade. At one point she hinted at resigning. To my surprise, Martha, Sandra, and Inez urged her not to quit.

At this point Dr. S rapped his fist on the table and everyone went silent. "I will ahdmit to a reputation of pouring oil over troubled waters rahther than always offering the cohncrete solutions that may be earnestly desired in sohch situations."

He looked around the room as he went on. " I've ahsked for a full-time physician for the ward, as well as a Ward Sister on the premises, and order-lies. Boht I am telling you—there mohst be drahstic changes on the part of the stahff. Or else."

We all knew what the "or else" meant. Years before, I'd been told, he'd closed down the pediatric psychiatry ward, leaving it to be used for storage of the donated Canadian library books. He'd clearly told us to shape up or ship out. I respected that, although I didn't know how much of the solution was in our control.

His threat hung in the air after he departed. Ann excused herself and left when the silence grew too loud. After she left, Martha said something to the effect of, "Well, that's that. Now it's out in the open." She spoke with some satisfaction in her voice, implying that something had been brought to completion.

"It's just *begun!*" Sandra responded ruefully.

The next time I went to the Peace Corps office, Janet, the new Country Director saw me and asked if she could speak to me in her office. One of the new group of Volunteers, she told me, was having adjustment problems complicated by anxiety attacks and insomnia. When she'd asked John if he thought he needed to ET, he'd pondered for a moment, then said that he really wanted to complete his tour of duty. He'd asked if he could meet with me to talk about symptom management, prior to making a decision.

Janet said he'd been impressed by my stress management presentation and thought I might be able to help. I agreed to meet with him, with the understanding that I was just informally consulting as a peer, not work-ing with him as professional counselor. I left a note to this effect in his mailbox, asking him to contact me. When he did, I invited him to join Maria and me for supper the next time he came to Kingston.

He took me up on the invitation the following Friday, showing up at our house shortly before sunset. Not knowing if John wanted her to be involved, Maria withdrew at first. But once he and I had established a relaxed, conversational dialogue, I invited her to join us and took orders for drinks. The three of us sat in chairs out on the patio and talked, as the honey light faded and towering, green palms turned to silhouettes in the obsidian sky.

John genuinely wanted to stay in the Peace Corps. He said that he'd gone through a phase of panic attacks and insomnia in college, but he'd gotten over them—until Jamaica. While he hadn't actually had a full-blown panic attack yet, he constantly worried that he would. The only Volunteer assigned to a rural village, he confessed to feeling isolated and to wrestling with some self-doubts. The insecurity and the daily fear of "losing it" were bad enough, he said, but the insomnia made it a living hell.

"I'm tired all day, every day and when I *try* to sleep, I can't. Sometimes I can feel my heart racing for no reason and I have to fight to keep my breathing under control."

"Sounds like combat fatigue," I replied. "And why not? You just parachuted-in and you're still reeling from culture shock, still trying to figure out what it is you're there to do. That's a stressful adjustment for anyone."

Part of what John needed was a safe space in which to find some respite and, on this night, we were able to provide such a space. We filled him full of fried Bangamary fish and yams and callaloo, and we talked for hours. I encouraged him and gave some suggestions for symptom management, but focused more on choice of attitude, and awareness of mental sets and expectations. *Shoulds* and *musts*, I said, can paint you into a discouraging corner.

When John began to yawn, we invited him to stay overnight and he sleepily accepted. I stayed up late, reading, and was gratified to hear the sound of his snores emanating from the guest bedroom.

The next morning John thanked us for our hospitality and for the best night's sleep he said he'd had in weeks. He left after breakfast, saying he felt much more confident. We scheduled a follow-up session at my office on the ward for the following week.

There, I taught him a muscle relaxation procedure, introduced him to some principles of rational thinking, and gave him some homework exercises designed to help him tell his rational thoughts apart from his irrational thoughts. I suggested that anxiety doesn't simply happen, but that we *create* it to some degree, by thinking in limited ways.

"When things don't go the way I want them to, nobody but I can determine what that *means* in the greater scheme of things. Was it inconvenient, or disappointing, or was it *awful?* Or *terrible?* No matter what happens to you, only you can determine your attitude toward what's happened. Easy to say, huh?"

The last time I saw John was at a Devon House happy hour, shortly before our departure. He thanked me again for my help. He said he really liked his village assignment, his sleep had improved, and he'd stopped worrying about panic attacks. He attributed his progress mainly to what he'd learned about rational thinking. He felt sure he'd be able to complete his service.

On September 15 Maria and I celebrated the second anniversary of our arrival in Jamaica. For the first time it sank in that we were the only couple from Group 58 still on the island.

A lot of my clothing and gear was wearing out: my work pants and shirts, my jeans, most of my socks, my umbrella, and my backpack. The second of my two briar pipes had almost burnt-out, leaving me only a well-used corncob pipe that didn't draw right. My sneakers were held together by Shoe Goo and my Birkenstocks had finally started to deteriorate from repeated exposure to salt water.

Routine events took on special significance, seen as *the last*: the last gas cylinder for the stove, my last quarterly report to the Peace Corps, my last

GG shot, my last batch of new patients on the ward. One day while passing a student dorm on the University campus, I saw a man kick a mongoose off of the second-story porch he'd been sweeping. The varmint survived the fall, apparently unhurt, and ran off into the bushes. I thought, *now that's something I'll probably never see again.*

One of the last patients I worked with intensively, Benton, taught me a lot about what it was like to be a crack addict in Kingston. He knew he'd sold not only all his material possessions, but also most of his dignity, to support his addiction. He made no bones about having done some nasty things to stay alive and to feed his habit, within the dungtung gang culture. His life had been pretty grim even before he'd started using crack.

He described his last residence, his mother's house, as a twelve-by-twelve zinc-roofed shack that she shared with five other people. Everybody in the yard knew he was a crackhead. He said he usually got up at four-thirty to bathe and wash his clothes at the standpipe, staying out of everyone's way.

He knew that if he returned to the neighborhood drug-free, ex-cronies might kill him because they couldn't trust him anymore. If the wrong person suspected you of being a police informant, he told me, you were as good as dead.

Benton had lived in death's shadow for years and knew that his whole future depended on recovery from addiction. He said he owed his life to a lucky accident. Coked-up, he'd walked into the path of a truck, sustaining a head injury that had landed him on the Psychiatric Ward. Ward 21 had transferred him to the Detox Ward. He told me that, compared to where he'd lived, the Detox Ward was like The Pegasus—one of Kingston's best hotels.

Although he cautiously opened up to me in our individual therapy sessions, he never shook my hand and he asked me the first time we met to stop keeping notes. He confessed to being somewhat "para"(noid), as he'd had to deal with informers in the past. I honored his request, but after each session I'd quickly record on my notepad all the detail I could recall.

One day after a session Benton came back into the office and demanded that I give him my notes. I told him he'd have to give me a good reason before I'd do that. He couldn't give me a good reason, but said he wanted to know what I'd written. So I held out my chicken-scratch notes for him to follow and read them verbatim. "Got a problem with any of that?"

"Nah, mon." Benton paused before he left the room and held out his fist to rap knuckles with me. "Respect."

Maria had returned to her uniformed status as a teacher at the School of Nursing and I'd started group therapy with my last batch of patients on the ward. I'd finished my Relapse Prevention Manual and, for the first time, was using it comprehensively as a framework for my psychoeducational sessions.

Things started-off deadly dull in group, with most members trying to avoid any risks, asking me to simply instruct them. I declined, saying that there were better uses for our time.

When patients asked me to talk about some subject or other—self-esteem, or cravings, or whatever—I'd throw the topic back to them: what you you think it means in terms of *your* recovery?

I pointed out how bored everyone was, suggesting that there were all kinds of topics that could engage our emotions as well as our minds. The energy level gradually rose from meeting to meeting, as members became engaged in a dialogue. We started to discuss relevant issues in personal terms and group process eventually kicked into gear.

I'd already tested each of the relapse prevention modules on previous groups—The Disease of Addiction, Relapse Prevention, Stress Management, Anger Management, and an introduction to the Twelve Steps. With this group, I tried to tie everything together. I hoped to leave behind a relapse prevention curriculum that would be incorporated into the program and used after I'd gone. Sustainable development.

"The map is not the territory," as Alfred Korzybski observed. Every model has its strengths and limitations. I cobbled-together my relapse prevention curriculum, freely borrowing from the available literature on rational thinking, cognitive therapy, the disease model of addiction, and the role of self-help groups in recovery. I've attended a few open AA and NA meetings over the years and know enough about Twelve Step recovery programs to respect anyone who strives in good faith to "work the program."

Twelve Step programs are rooted in the disease model of addiction. Newcomers soon hear that they have a chronic, progressive, relapsing disease that can never be cured. In AA and NA closed meetings—for addicts only—members admit their addictions and support one anothers efforts to stay in recovery. If a newly clean-and-sober addict keeps attending the same group, he finds a whole new support system of people who don't drink or use drugs and who try not to judge other addicts. Many of them get together between meetings, and some members who've been sober for a long time become sponsors and make themselves available at all hours to help prevent relapses. It may not be for everyone but, as twelve steppers like to say, "It works if you work it."

That's not to say I necessarily favor the disease model of addiction over other models; but as a PCV I needed to adapt to local standards. Working on a hospital ward, the medical model was a given—although one of the residents who served a six-month rotation handed out fundamentalist Christian literature that attributed crack addiction to demon possession.

Accepting that they have a chronic disease called addiction helps millions of drug abusers who've lost control of their lives to stop using. For years I've encouraged people with drug problems to consider going to Twelve Step meetings, because they help a lot of people. Indeed, joining an AA or NA group seems to be the *only* thing that works for some. Many addicts with years in recovery will tell you that they couldn't have done it without going to meetings and that they'll need to keep on going to meetings for the rest of their lives.

And they're right—for themselves. But others who've been clean and sober for many years have told me that, at some point in their spiritual development, they outgrew the need for support groups and for consciously "working" the Twelve Steps. Personally, I think that there are as many different patterns of drug dependency and abuse as there are drug abusers. And I believe that there's more than one path out of the woods.

Models are just maps, and some seem more helpful than others in guiding drug abusers out of the mazes they've lost themselves in. A model that works for most addicts won't necessarily work for all. I take issue only with those who will tell you that there is only *one way* to a lifetime free of chemical dependency—whether they tout AA, or Jesus Christ, or Dianetics.

I say, *whatever works.*

On the last day before the current batch would be discharged from the ward, I went in to work by bus. I managed to jam my way onto the bottom step of the second bus that stopped to pick up passengers at Olympia. For the first mile I hung out the doorway without even a rail to hold onto, just the open door. At least it was cooler out there in the breeze.

I'd long since mastered the art of conserving grip-strength in crowded, lurching buses—relaxing my hands whenever I felt adequately braced by the warm press of the bodies around me, but always ready to tighten my grip in an instant if I started to lose my footing. Halfway out the door as I was, I knew that the collective inertia of the other commuters could possibly force me off the step, with the bus going up to forty miles-per-hour.

I thought, *I could really be hurt!* But as passengers disembarked at the first two stops, I managed to squeeze my way up to the second step, where I could reach a steel rail. I got to work drenched with perspiration, but safe.

By the time I arrived, the scheduled AA volunteer had called to cancel his morning meeting and the patients had persuaded the nursing staff to let them hold a "concert" in the group room instead. Maria had told me about impromptu ward concerts she'd attended at Belleview. Concerts are a folk tradition where a loquacious master of ceremonies introduces those who volunteer, and each performs in turn for the audience. On hospital wards, concerts are social occasions in which both patients and staff participate. Some sing, others make spontaneous speeches, or recite poetry, or tell stories. Everyone is encouraged to join in and share their talents. Nobody is ridiculed.

The offerings at this concert ranged from a capella reggae songs and interminable hymns sung in ragged harmony, to dramatic recitations of doggerel verse and flowery thank-you speeches from the patients to the staff. Laughter and applause filled the air.

The assembled crowd wouldn't let me off the hook. I did a favorite joke, the one about the peg-legged pig, in Southern dialect. I'd heard Jamaicans trying to imitate a Southern drawl before, but had never heard a good impression. I told the story as if it had really happened to me, to expressions of mirth and delight. Nobody had ever heard me speak that way. The punchline brought an explosion of laughter and subsequent demands that I do something else. I encored with a dramatic recital of Lewis Carrol's "Jabberwocky," delivered in an English accent. This also got an enthusiastic reception. We concluded by holding hands in a circle and singing "Let There Be Peace on Earth."

Maria and I checked-off item after item on our COS lists: physical exams, dental exams, turning in fecal samples, and scheduling exit interviews. We started to consolidate and box non-essential belongings to ship back home. We talked about how our lives would change when we returned to the States.

Maria wanted some time off before she had to return to work and we agreed that I'd try to get a job that would support us both while she got her bearings. She even speculated about living somewhere in Central America and studying Spanish for a few months before returning to the nine-to-five. I joked about becoming a marketable commodity again.

We'd planned to use up our accrued vacation time over the last few weeks, tapering-off the time spent at our worksites and travelling around the island. Although we did cut down our time at work, as it turned out we found quite enough in Kingston to keep us occupied. As the ward nurses kept pointing out, Maria and I had already seen more of Jamaica than most Jamaicans.

We went on photo safaris around the city, starting already to see things through new eyes. I took Maria to the art gallery/artists' colony that I'd explored on my own. We went back to the National Gallery and to other galleries we'd never gotten around to visiting. We finally went to the Bob Marley Museum on Hope Road, which we'd passed hundreds of times and dismissed as merely a tourist shrine. Cashing our few remaining travellers' checks, we started doing some serious shopping for unique Jamaican craftwork.

The Ward Theater, located on the rim of Parade, staged a production of the Stephen Sondheim musical *Sweeny Todd*. The play is set in Victorian-era London. Casting was completely color-blind, with most of the cast being black. Although we'd never attended a performance at The Ward, mainly for reasons of security, we decided we could afford taxis both ways, and I made reservations. Another legacy of the Colonial era, The Ward was an opulent, old-style theater, ornately decorated—more European than Caribbean in its ambiance. We enjoyed an excellent presentation of the bizarre, romantic musical comedy about a bloodthirsty barber. I forgot the Jamaican accents and the multiracial casting as I got lost in the performance. Afterward, we easily caught a taxi at the curb and got home from dungtung without incident.

During the last few weeks, I only went in to work when I knew there was something for me to do on the ward. I attended staff meetings, although I felt like something of a lame duck.

I got the distinct impression that Sister M was avoiding me.

Dr. S surprised me at a staff meeting when he brought up the topic of psychological testing. After I'd refused to administer the MMPI to patients as a research instrument, because the test hadn't been normed on the Jamaican population, he'd delegated the task to an Indian psychologist on the staff of the Psychiatric Ward. He told me that a literature search she'd performed had confirmed my belief that there was no body of research to support the validility of the MMPI as a good test for Jamaicans. He had no obligation to follow-up with me on the subject, and I appreciated the gesture. I took it as a graceful acknowledgement of my professionalism from a psychiatrist I respected.

Sometime that same week Maria shared her nursing students' teacher evaluations with me. Although she'd often wondered if she'd made a difference, some clear themes emerged: *you cared, you listened, you showed us things we didn't know about people with mental illnesses.*

Maria didn't feel she'd been able to leave any lasting imprint on the School of Nursing during her tenure on the faculty. Her legacy was to help shape the professional lives of those she taught. I have no doubt that many acts of compassionate understanding and effective care resulted from her work—acts performed by Jamaican nurses who caught-on to her message that mentally-ill people are our brothers and sisters. Maria touched lives. Her service sent out ripples of influence, the consequences of which she will never know. Such are the intangible rewards of Peace Corps service.

One of the last mornings that Dorothy drove us in to work, she invited me to attend Maria's goodbye party at the School of Nursing the following week. The noontime "fete" started out with a traditional Jamaican meal: akee and saltfish, callaloo, boiled green bananas and dumplings, with bread pudding for dessert. Then Dorothy and others on the teaching staff made speeches praising Maria's contributions to the program. They gave her some hand-embroidered floral doilies as a goodbye gift. We were both invited to speak and had an opportunity to publicly thank Dorothy for all she'd done for us. Much was made over my giving her a hug and a peck on the cheek. Several people took snapshots.

Having been asked to reprise a training session on counseling, I arrived on the ward one morning the following week to find the long table in the group room covered with a linen tablecloth and laden with plates of tiny sandwiches, pastries, banana bread, and cake. A large teapot stood on the shelf by the window. I'd suspected the training might just be a pretext to get me on the ward for my own farewell fete, but I feigned surprise.

Not only were Dr. S and the whole day staff present, but Sisters from other wards and a few other guests. My impending departure had occasioned an official Detox Ward coffee morning, such as we'd had a few times before during a "fifth week" with no patients on the ward. Martha told me she'd invited Maria on the sly, but that Maria had a previous engagement. Sister M was conspicuous by her absence.

Everyone crowded into the group room, leaving the food untouched. Sandra gave the first speech, saying that I'd become a valued member of the treatment team and that I had a way of getting-through to patients as the individuals they are. She also praised my contributions—unspecified—to the program.

Dr. S spoke next and was more specific about my innovative ideas and my initiatives, while acknowledging with some humor that I might not always have *felt* that my suggestions had made a difference in the program. Turning to me, he assured me that my relapse prevention curriculum and other things I'd implemented would remain an integral part of the program long after I'd left.

Martha spoke of the vacuum I'd leave behind as a treatment provider and Francine said she didn't know how the staff would be able to manage without me. Both of them, as well as Inez, told me it had been a pleasure to work with me. Celine referred to my cheerfulness and thanked me for helping her to find her place on the team. She called me a raconteur. A guest from another drug treatment program acknowledged that, while we had not always seen eye-to-eye on issues discussed at DART meetings, I'd made meaningful contributions to drug rehabilitation in Jamaica.

Talk about music to a Peace Corps Volunteer's ears! Finally, I was getting some specific feedback. And it was positive! The apparent warmth and sincerity of the expressions moved me and I felt, for the first time, that I'd successfully completed my assignment.

After the others had finished, I took the floor. "I'm a happy man today, although I'll be sad to leave in many ways. I'm happy to be with you good people in Jamaica today, happy to know I'll be here for another week-or-so, happy at the prospect of going home to rejoin my family and friends, happy to know that before long I'll be making money again."

That got a laugh.

"Some of you here today have joked with me about how I've become a Jamaican. When I got to talking about Jamericans with a taxi driver the other day, I asked him if two years in Jamaica qualified me as a Jamerican. Without hesitating, he said, 'Nah, mon. Four year, meenymum.'"

That also got a laugh.

"I want to thank all of you for your support and your friendship. As you know, I've had my frustrations over the past two years, but working with you has made it all worthwhile. I've learned a lot, both from y'all on the staff and from the patients I've been privileged to work with. I hope that I've had some lasting influence on the program, but only time will tell. My greatest sense of achievement comes from my inclusion in the team here on the ward. "

I looked at the familiar faces around me, one or two with sad expressions, but most of them beaming. "You let me in. You let me know I was one of you. And that made all the difference. Thank you."

The speeches out of the way, we served ourselves from the refreshments table, poured cups of tea or coffee, and chatted. This wasn't, I surmised, the time for hugs. That would come later, as I said my individual good-byes. The fact of my impending departure hadn't yet fully sunk in, but this occasion made it all the more real.

My suspicions that Sister M had been avoiding me proved to be accurate. I never once saw her during my final weeks of service.

Our last week on the island was a blur of activity, as we packed and sorted and finished final tasks, such as closing-out our bank account and saying our goodbyes to Kai Meng Lui and Alvira. Only a few items remained on our COS checklists. Soon we'd pick up our passports at the Peace Corps office and would be given our plane tickets and preliminary checks from our Readjustment Allowances, so we'd have money in our pockets when we arrived Stateside. We'd each accrued around $6,000—$250 per month of service—to see us through until we had an income again. The balance would be mailed to us later.

The day before our departure we went out to Lime Key with Vasanth, Prakash, and Rainuke. Prakash drove us all to Port Royal, where we hired a launch to transport us out to the island. We sunned ourselves, swam, and took turns using the snorkelling gear. We floated and dove amid the coral formations and brightly-colored fish, emerging from each dive to the sight of blue sky and distant green mountains. The launch came back for us in the late afternoon and we returned to Port Royal, then drove around the crescent peninsula back to Kingston.

That night the Catholic service workers from next door joined us and our Indian neighbors for an eclectic potluck dinner: Maria's deviled chicken, a spicy Indian rice dish, cucumber salad with yogurt dressing, and an improvised pizza. Maria and I excused ourselves after supper and returned to our packing and cleaning, which kept us up well past midnight.

Having said our goodbyes to friends, co-workers and Peace Corps staffers, one of our last painful disengagements was with the cats. Miss M and Hopeful had watched our packing with detached, bored looks. Stump, the only remaining kitten (now almost full-grown), had followed us around, sniffing at everything and looking quizzical. Maria and I had talked about the possibility of taking Stump back to the U.S. with us, but had decided not to. I explained to the cats that we still loved them but wouldn't be seeing them anymore. They responded with feline indifference.

I awoke the next morning before the alarm sounded, the sun barely over the horizon. I put water on the stove to boil and took a shower. By the time I'd finished, Maria was up and about. She handed me a cup of coffee when she joined me in the bathroom to take her shower. We had two hours before we were due at the airport and still had a lot to do.

The Peace Corps may coddle Trainees somewhat, providing charter buses and such; but when your COS date comes, you hire your own taxi to the airport. However, in our case, we'd been offered a ride in Prakash's car, so we didn't have to sweat-out the timely arrival of a cab. That doesn't mean we weren't sweating, though.

We'd arrived in Jamaica with twenty-eight other hopeful Trainees, all wanting to be sworn-in as Volunteers and to serve for two years. Only half that number still remained on the island. Most of them would be leaving over the next two weeks. Some would stay for a vacation prior to departing, and two or three others—including Linda—had gotten their tours extended.

Willard showed up on his Moped around 8:30 to bid us goodbye and to see if we had anything to discard that he could use. We thanked him for all his help and his gifts of fresh fruit, and gave him a jar of leftover peanut butter and all the empty beer bottles we had on hand. He drove off, waving with his machete as he disappeared around the corner.

We frantically finished packing. When Vasanth showed up at our door to ask if he could help, he looked mournful. Excited as I felt at the prospect of going home, I shared some of his sadness. We'd become friends. Maria had given him haircuts, the three of us had discussed almost every topic under the sun, and he'd been a very gracious host. We acknowledged that we'd miss one another's company, as he helped us to load our luggage in Prakash's trunk.

We petted the cats one last time and did a final sweep of the house, to make sure we hadn't left anything important behind. Then we locked the door, giving the keys to Vasanth. He accompanied us to the airport, but hardly said a word on the way.

The Kingston I saw on our way out of town was the same Kingston I'd seen on our way in for the first time, two years before; it was I who had changed. I saw the beauty and the squalor through new eyes, trying to memorize all the sights, now so familiar to me, knowing that the details would fade with time. The colors of my own country would seem drab by comparison. I studied the faces of people we passed, their bright clothing, the colorful blossoms, and the vibrant greens of the mountains whose beauty I'd come to take for granted. I vowed that someday I'd return to this lush island to refresh my soul.

Prakash had to get to work, so neither he nor Vasanth accompanied us into the airport terminal. After we'd taken our luggage out of the trunk, I shook hands with Prakash, thanked him for the ride, and wished him well. I expected to hug Vasanth but, when he thrust out his hand, I took his lead and settled for a formal, firm handshake. We promised to stay in touch.

Maria and I lugged our suitcases to the ticket counter and checked in, soaked with sweat. We both had light jackets in our carry-on bags, as we expected the temperature to be at least thirty degrees colder when we landed. We exchanged most of our remaining Jamaican money for American dollars while waiting for our boarding call, keeping one bill of each denomination as mementos.

As the plane taxied toward the runway, I said to Maria that once the wheels left the tarmac, our titles would change; we'd be Returned Peace Corps Volunteers. Like the Marines say, "once a Marine, always a Marine", PCVs remain Volunteers for life, not ex-Volunteers. RPCVs continue to serve in the capacity of working on the fourth goal of Peace Corps service: "bringing the world back home." This is accomplished by way of public speaking, participating in the World Wise Schools program, and other means of educating Americans about the countries we served in and the problems faced by developing nations.

We held hands as the jet came to a stop on the runway. I grinned at Maria. "We *made* it! Now it's back to the land of the big highways."

"The land of the blue light special," Maria countered.

"The land of the tailgate party."

"The land of the chicken nugget."

I laughed and said, "I'm not going to feel like an American until I have my own wheels again."

"All I'm looking forward to now is a hot shower. And a crisp apple."

The plane lurched forward, picking up speed until it rose into the air. It tilted to the right as it climbed and I looked out the window at Kingston, far below, trying to spot our neighborhood. Once we were over the Blue Mountains, the view was often obscured by clouds.

Maria leaned over and looked out as we flew over the north coast, minutes later.

Cuba was already visible to the North. I strained to look backward for a last glimpse of the receding island below us, feeling at home in the world.

Afterword

The first thing we had to get used to upon our return–besides the cold–was the hordes of white people we saw everywhere. It didn't seem natural. We also felt overwhelmed by the vast quantities of merchandise on display in stores. And after two years of being surrounded by the lush colors of a tropical island, the winter landscapes in the U.S. looked pale by comparison. It took us a while to get re-oriented, so that normal American things didn't seem strange. However, perhaps because we're both seasoned travellers, we didn't experience the jarring reverse culture shock that some RPCVs go through.

Maria and I lived a vagabond lifestyle for our first three minths back Stateside. Within a week of our return, I'd bought a used car and was starting to feel like an American again. (Maria's old Pontiac had given up the ghost while we were gone.) My parents' house served as our home base while I looked for work in Columbia, and we visited friends and relatives in Georgia, Alabama, and Tennessee.

In December I got offered a job in Columbia, with a start date in early February. That gave us until Christmas to travel and catch up with loved ones, and a month in which to re-settle.

We drove to upstate New York to visit one of Maria's sisters and her family, staying with relatives in Virginia and Pennsylvania along the way. While in New York we spent two days skiing at a nearby resort. Maria was a novice to the slopes, but I coached her and she learned quickly. By the end of the second day, she was able to ski down her first mountain with me.

Almost everyone we visited asked us about Jamaica and the Peace Corps, but few besides our parents cared to listen to our accounts for more than a few minutes before bringing up more mundane topics. A few stock tales got refined in the telling and re-telling, but hardly anyone seemed to want to know the details. This surprised us, even though we'd been told in our re-entry briefings to expect it.

In January we found a place to live in Columbia, then drove up to Bell Buckle to retrieve our worldly possessions from Joe Madeo's attic. By the middle of the month we'd settled into our new home and Maria had a car. She didn't look for work right away, but started to plan for a several-week stay in Costa Rica, where she'd live with a local family and study Spanish. By this time we both felt thoroughly American again, although we'll never see our homeland in quite the same way as we used to.

So what did we get out of our two years of service in Jamaica? Primarily, I suppose it gave us perspective–on our life choices, on our own culture, and on the world as a global village. I don't think we'll ever take our citizenship for granted. And our sojourn gave each of us a heightened sense that all people of all races in all nations are one family.

Serving in the Peace Corps taught me something I already knew, but at a deeper level: that people are essentially the same everywhere. In Jamaica I stood out as a foreigner on the streets, surrounded by people of color in a sprawling, crime-ridden city. And yet the only times I felt afraid to be where I was were during the robbery attempt on the bus, and the earthquake. I re-learned that all people have the same essential needs and the same existential choices.

As a psychologist, I've done a lot of intelligence testing and have thought a lot about the concept of intelligence–concluding that it is an artificial construct with only limited utility. I'm pretty good at estimating range-of-intelligence from conversation, when I put my mind to it. I believed before I left that, person for person, Jamaicans would be just as intelligent as Americans, although perhaps not as well educated. But now I *know* that.

My early worries about my ability to do good therapy with Jamaicans proved unjustified. Once I got an ear for patois, doing individual and group therapy proved much more similar to than different from my work in the U.S. I had to be very attentive and to fine-tune in some areas, to allow for cultural differences as I understood them; but my clients responded to me in just the ways I'd come to expect in my Stateside practice. The same interventions worked in the same ways. Therapy is always challenging. Doing therapy in Jamaica was just challenging in subtly different ways.

I gained confidence in myself as a result of Peace Corps service, although I like to think I also learned some lessons in humility. The need to adapt to local customs and standards required me to be patient ("soon com!") and to question some of my own assumptions and predispositions. But my inclusion as a colleague on the Detox Ward and the fact that I completed my assignment strengthened my belief in my ability to be flexible and to persist in challenging situations.

Maria and I never regretted our decision to serve, and we remain grateful for our opportunity to live and work on the beautiful island of Jamaica for two years. Although not all PCVs complete their assignments, and some question whether their contibutions made a difference, I believe that the Peace Corps has helped in some small way to make the world a better place. And because Volunteers represent the American people, not the Department of State, they succeed—in a way that other U.S. development agencies cannot—in putting a human face on America for untold thousands in the countries where they serve.

Volunteers may not leave behind monumental achievements when they depart, but they affect peoples' lives, sending out ripples whose effects can't be measured. And regardless of what may or may not have been accomplished in objective terms, the Peace Corps experience has given hundreds of thousands of Americans the opportunity to live in developing nations, to learn and grow, and to return home with a more global perspective. Our shared conclusion about our years of service is so universally expressed by RPCVs that it has become known as the Peace Corps Mantra: "I got more than I gave."

As to the ambiguities about our Peace Corps service, we have the rest of our lives to try and figure them out.

THE END

****

Glossary

A

a—to.

ackee—a starchy fruit with reddish skin and yellow meat, which is poisonous until it blossoms, revealing a large black seed. The meat is boiled, then fried, and resembles scrambled eggs. Traditionally served with onions and saltfish (cod).

a-fahren—in another country, overseas.

B

Babylon—also "Babylon System." A Rastafarian term for systems of authority and "downpression"; the Man; the police.

baggies—panties, knickers.

balmyard—a place consecrated to spiritualistic healing practices, often enclosed by a high fence and festooned with colored banners.

batty—(bohtty) arse. Spandex tights are called batty-riders and gay men are contemptuously referred to as "botty mon." "Bomba" and "ras" also mean arse.

big mon/woman—refers to age, not size. Mature, not old.

big up—to extoll or brag about, as in, "Big up Jamaica!"

blodclaht—"blood cloth", or menstrual rag. A major epithet–fighting words in some situations.

bombaclaht—"arse cloth", or toilet paper. See "blodclaht."

bulla—a fat gingerbread cookie.

bush tea—one of a number of herbal teas, often used as folk remedies.

C

calaloo—a green, leafy vegetable, similar to spinach.

chillum—or chillum pipe. Pipe used to smoke ganja.

coffee morning—a "morning tea." A social get-together with coffe, tea, and finger foods.

C.O.S.—Close of Service, completion of Peace corps commitment.

C.O.W.—Community Orientation Week. The fifth week of Peace Corps training in Jamaica, when Trainees visit the communities to which they will be assigned.

cow cod—bull genitals. A country delicacy, often prepared in a soup.

D

dancehall—a hip-hop style of Jamaican music, also known as deejay reggae. Also, the venue, whether a rented hall or an improvised outdoor gig with a big mobile sound system.

D.A.R.T.—Drug Abuse Rehabilitation Team. A planning committee consisting of representatives from Jamaica's main drug rehabilitayion agencies and treatment facilities.

deah-so—there, over there.

deejay—dancehall reggae. Also, the performers who emcee at dancehall gigs, sampling and scratching at multiple turntables, and vocalizing in counterpoint to the music.

-dem—suffix denoting the plural, as in, "de mon dem."

dis—to disrespect, or insult.

dogheart—a vicious thug.

Don—especially in dungtung Kingston, the neighborhood crime lord.

downpression—oppression. A Rasta term.

dreadlocks—distinctive braids worn by Rastas and others who wish to be seen as Rastas. Also, a Rastafarian may be referred to as a "dreadlocks."

'ductor—a bus conductor.

dungtung—downtown.

E

E.T.—"early termination" of Peace Corps service.

F

festival—corn fritters/ hushpuppies, often served with fish or jerk.

fi—"for to", in order to, or because. "Im go a dungtung fi buy sohm fish."

foot—entire leg and foot.

G

ganja—marijuana. Many Jamaicans who do not smoke ganja will drink ganja tea, believing it to have medicinal value.

H

helper—a maid or domestic worker.

herbs—ganja.

higgler—street vendor.

H.I.M.—His Imperial Majesty, Haile Salassie, regarded by Rastafarians as Jah's earthly incarnation.

I

I-and-I—first-person singular pronoun, used by Rastas. "I-and-I give praise to Jah fahr im bounty."

im—he or she, him or her. The plural is, "dem."

indica—a kind of cannabis, or ganja.

irie—(eyeree) a universal greeting, meaning "good times" or "all is cool." Jamaican *Gemutlichkeit.*

J

Jah—God, according to the Rastafarians. The God of Moses and the House of David, but with an African identity.

JDF—Jamaica Defense Force.

jerk—spicy hot barbeque flavored with Scotch Bonnet peppers, a marinade for chicken, pork, and seafood. Authentic jerk is cooked over pimento wood for the distinctive smoke flavor.

JLP—Jamaican Labour Party

johncrow—a black carrion bird seen all over the island.

K

kumina—ceremonial drumming and dancing practiced by syncretistic cults, said to invoke spirits. Related to the African myal cult.

L

lick on—to take a draw or a hit from a chillum or crack pipe.

M

mannish water—soup made with goat genitals.

mek—to make or to let. "Mek we be t'ankful to Jah fi ahll im blessing."

mince—ground beef.

mon—"man", but gender-and age-neutral. "Ya, mon, de jerk pork soon com."

N

nah—no, or don't. "Nah, mon. Me nah wan go a dungtung."

NGO—Non-Government Organization. A private, non-profit organization that does things that governments in developing countries can't afford to do.

nine nights—a traditional wake that lasts nine nights and often involves elements of kumina.

no prohblem—a reassurance, used as ubiquitously as "mon"and "irie."

nyam—to eat, in deep patois.

O

obeah—the Jamaican analogue of Haitian voodoo.

P

parish—one of the island's fourteen "states" or "counties."

pattie—a folded-over meat or vegetable pie.

pepperpot soup—a one-pot meal, made with calaloo, meat, dumplings, and starchy vegetables.

pickni—children, in deep patois.

PNP—Peoples' National Party.

pocomania—syncretistic cult practices with African and Christian elements, using singing and rhythmic movement to induce the experience of spirit-possession.

posse—a criminal gang, often involved in the trafficking of guns and drugs.

puri—an East Indian pan-fried pocket bread.

R

ragamuffin—a poor person or beggar in tattered clothes.

ras—arse. Often used as an exclamation of displeasure.

Rastafarian—an Afrocentric religion that claims Emperor Haile Salassie is of the lineage of the House of David and is identical with Jah–and therefore never died. Serious Rastas wear dreadlocks and memorize Christian scripture, but there is no church and no organizational hierarchy. Many Rastas smoke ganja ceremonially.

reggae—Jamaica's musical gift to the world, popularized by such artists as Bob Marley and Jimmy Cliff. An outgrowth of Jamaican musical styles known as ska and rocksteady, "roots" reggae is characterized by a distinctive rhythmic backbeat and generally upbeat and pro-social lyrics (although some reggae songs are laments). Although "dancehall" is also considered a form of reggae by many Jamaicans, others denounce it because of its emphasis on explicit sexual lyrics and its glorification of the "gangsta" ethic.

"Respect!"—a common affirmation of accord or mutual tolerance. Also, "Respect due!"

roots—having to do with Jamaica's African heritage.

roti—an East Indian flatbread-wrapped sandwich, filled with curried goat or vegetables.

rude boy—a tough gang member or yout'. "Rude" is a compliment in some circles.

rum—(rohm)made from sugar cane, it is Jamaica's most popular liquor. There is standard-proof red rum and white "overproof" rum.Some Jamaicans annoint their foreheads with rum, in the belief that it has medicinal value, and it is used ceremonially in cult and healing rituals.

S

Sister—a head nurse or a nurse tutor/instructor.

s'mahdy—somebody.

small-up—crowd together, pack it in. A frequent admonition of ductors on crowded buses.

soon com—meant to reassure that something promised is just about to be delivered, this actually means, "it will come when it comes."

spliff—a ganja joint, often rolled in a fat cone.

stoshuss—patois for snooty, putting on airs.

sympathetic magic—magic embodying the principle, "as above, so below." That is, doing something to a symbol affects the thing symbolized, as with voodoo dolls. Most spells, charms, and hexes involve sympathetic magic.

T

t'ank God for Jesus!—a popular exclamation of relief used by Jamaican Christians.

teef—a thief. Also, to steal. "Im teef de goat-dem."

tek—take.

U

unu—you, plural, in deep patois.

V

vex—(alt. "bex")to be or to make angry. "Im vex fi im nah wan' go a church wid me."

W

walk good—be safe, take care.

wanedda—another.

wisdom weed—ganja. Some Rastas apparently believe that ganja was the burning bush Moses came upon prior to receiving Jah's commandments.

Y

yah-so—here, right here.

yam—collective term for a variety of edible, starchy tubers. Not to be confused with the sweet potato.

yout'—(yoot) a youth.

****

0-595-21449-5